VIOLENT CRIME, VIOLENT CRIMINALS

Edited by
NEIL ALAN WEINER
MARVIN E. WOLFGANG

SAGE PUBLICATIONS
The Publishers of Professional Social Science
Newbury Park   London   New Delhi

For information address:

SAGE Publications, Inc.
2111 West Hillcrest Drive
Newbury Park, California 91320

SAGE Publications Ltd.
28 Banner Street
London EC1Y 8QE
England

SAGE Publications India Pvt. Ltd.
M-32 Market
Greater Kailash I
New Delhi 110 048 India

Printed in the United States of America

Library of Congress Cataloging-in-Publication Data

Main entry under title:

Violent crime, violent criminals / edited by Neil Alan Weiner and
    Marvin E. Wolfgang.
       p.   cm.
    Bibliography: p.
    ISBN 0-8039-3341-X   ISBN 0-8039-3342-8 (pbk.)
    1. Violent crimes—United States. 2. Criminal behavior—United
States. I. Weiner, Neil Alan. II. Wolfgang, Marvin E., 1924 -
HV6791.V565 1988
364.1′0973—dc19   88-18547
                                    CIP

FIRST PRINTING 1989

SB 40349 /14.50 5.89

VIOLENT
CRIME,
VIOLENT
CRIMINALS

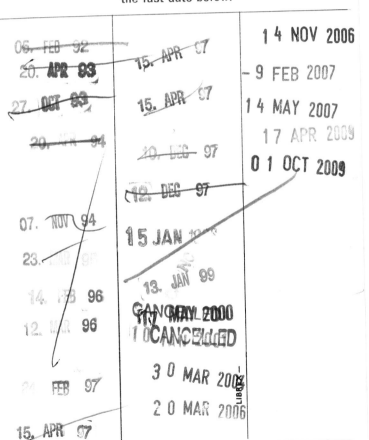

SOME OTHER VOLUMES IN THE
SAGE FOCUS EDITIONS

8. **Controversy (Second Edition)**
   Dorothy Nelkin
21. **The Black Woman**
   La Frances Rodgers-Rose
31. **Black Men**
   Lawrence E. Gary
32. **Major Criminal Justice Systems
   (Second Edition)**
   George F. Cole, Stanislaw J. Frankowski,
   and Marc G. Gertz
41. **Black Families (Second Edition)**
   Harriette Pipes McAdoo
51. **Social Control**
   Jack P. Gibbs
54. **Job Stress and Burnout**
   Whiton Stewart Paine
57. **Social Structure and Network Analysis**
   Peter V. Marsden and Nan Lin
58. **Socialist States in the World-System**
   Christopher K. Chase-Dunn
60. **The Costs of Evaluation**
   Marvin C. Alkin and Lewis C. Solmon
63. **Organizational Theory and Public Policy**
   Richard H. Hall and Robert E. Quinn
64. **Family Relationships in Later Life**
   Timothy H. Brubaker
65. **Communication and Organizations**
   Linda L. Putnam and
   Michael E. Pacanowsky
66. **Competence in Communication**
   Robert N. Bostrom
67. **Avoiding Communication**
   John A. Daly and James C. McCroskey
68. **Ethnography in Educational Evaluation**
   David M. Fetterman
70. **Children and Microcomputers**
   Milton Chen and William Paisley
71. **The Language of Risk**
   Dorothy Nelkin
72. **Black Children**
   Harriette Pipes McAdoo and
   John Lewis McAdoo
73. **Industrial Democracy**
   Warner Woodworth, Christopher Meek,
   and William Foote Whyte
74. **Grandparenthood**
   Vern L. Bengtson and Joan F. Robertson
75. **Organizational Theory and Inquiry**
   Yvonna S. Lincoln
76. **Men in Families**
   Robert A. Lewis and Robert E. Salt
77. **Communication and Group
   Decision-Making**
   Randy Y. Hirokawa and
   Marshall Scott Poole
78. **The Organization of Mental
   Health Services**
   W. Richard Scott and Bruce L. Black
79. **Community Power**
   Robert J. Waste

80. **Intimate Relationships**
   Daniel Perlman and Steve Duck
81. **Children's Ethnic Socialization**
   Jean S. Phinney and Mary Jane Rotheram
82. **Power Elites and Organizations**
   G. William Domhoff and Thomas R. Dye
83. **Responsible Journalism**
   Deni Elliott
84. **Ethnic Conflict**
   Jerry Boucher, Dan Landis, and
   Karen Arnold Clark
85. **Aging, Health, and Family**
   Timothy H. Brubaker
86. **Critical Issues in Aging Policy**
   Edgar F. Borgatta and
   Rhonda J.V. Montgomery
87. **The Homeless in Contemporary Society**
   Richard D. Bingham, Roy E. Green, and
   Sammis B. White
88. **Changing Men**
   Michael S. Kimmel
89. **Popular Music and Communication**
   James Lull
90. **Life Events and Psychological
   Functioning**
   Lawrence H. Cohen
91. **The Social Psychology of Time**
   Joseph E. McGrath
92. **Measurement of Intergenerational
   Relations**
   David J. Mangen, Vern L. Bengtson,
   and Pierre H. Landry, Jr.
93. **Feminist Perspectives on Wife Abuse**
   Kersti Yllö and Michele Bograd
94. **Common Problems/Proper Solutions**
   J. Scott Long
95. **Falling from the Faith**
   David G. Bromley
96. **Biosocial Perspectives on the Family**
   Erik E. Filsinger
97. **Measuring the Information Society**
   Frederick Williams
98. **Behavior Therapy and Religion**
   William R. Miller and John E. Martin
99. **Daily Life in Later Life**
   Karen Altergott
100. **Lasting Effects of Child
   Sexual Abuse**
   Gail Elizabeth Wyatt and
   Gloria Johnson Powell
101. **Violent Crime, Violent Criminals**
   Neil Alan Weiner and
   Marvin E. Wolfgang
102. **Pathways to Criminal Violence**
   Neil Alan Weiner and
   Marvin E. Wolfgang
103. **Older Adult Friendship**
   Rebecca G. Adams and
   Rosemary Blieszner
104. **Aging and Health**
   Kyriakos S. Markides

Contents

Acknowledgments   6

Introduction   7

1. Measuring Violent Behavior: Effects of
   Study Design on Reported Correlates of Violence
   George S. Bridges and Joseph G. Weis   14

2. Violent Criminal Careers and
   "Violent Career Criminals":
   An Overview of the Research Literature
   Neil Alan Weiner   35

3. Race and Violent Crime: Toward a New Policy
   Lynn A. Curtis   139

4. Gender and Violent Crime
   Rita J. Simon and Sandra Baxter   171

5. Street Gang Violence
   Malcolm W. Klein and Cheryl L. Maxson   198

About the Contributors   235

Acknowledgments

This volume was prepared under grant #81-IJ-CX-0086, S-2 from the Center for the Study of Crime Correlates and Criminal Behavior of the National Institute of Justice of the U.S. Department of Justice. The editors would like to thank Richard Linster, Helen Erskine, and Winifred Reed for their encouragement and counsel throughout this project.

Our deepest appreciation is extended to Selma Pastor, former librarian for the Sellin Center for Studies in Criminology and Criminal Law, who flawlessly executed the editorial work required for the completion of this volume. Her efforts in this project were inspired. We also thank Dotte Courtwright for typing the manuscript.

Introduction

In 1982, the volume *Criminal Violence* was published as part of the ongoing research program of the Center for the Interdisciplinary Study of Criminal Violence, established as one of five multiyear Research Agreements Programs (RAPS) launched in the nation by the National Institute of Justice. In the introduction of that volume, we emphasized that one of the chief concerns of the Center for the Interdisciplinary Study of Criminal Violence was "to integrate the state of our knowledge about criminal violence as a way to provide an informed departure point for future research in the area. Realizing this objective involves selecting for comprehensive review important substantive areas and major perspectives that incorporate an interdisciplinary orientation into theoretical formulations."

That objective remains as compelling today as it was then. Our continuing work at the Violence Center has persuaded us that we have only scratched the surface of significant and widely useful topics on criminal violence and related matters. This conclusion has been reinforced by substantial feedback from our colleagues both about the utility of *Criminal Violence* in research, academic, and public policy settings and about other topics whose coverage would also be beneficial in these same diverse settings.

Since the historic, comprehensive report on violence presented to the American people in 1969 by the National Commission on the Causes and Prevention of Violence (hereinafter, the Violence Commission), there have been few parallel efforts, even on more modest scales, to examine anew and systematize the burgeoning and often fragmented literature in the many areas covered by the Violence Commission and others that have developed since the dissolution of the commission. This impoverishment, especially when considering the gravity of the legally infractious behaviors of concern—ranging from lethal confrontations to less aggravated but nonetheless serious assaults—has also motivated the preparation of this and a companion volume.

The two volumes evolved from our collaborative exchanges: As editors we initially proposed a single volume as a continuation of our earlier publication, *Criminal Violence*. The size of the manuscripts we requested exceeded our expectations, and the substance of these presentations merited their inclusion in full. We and the publisher agreed that the selections could be divided meaningfully between those that were empirically descriptive of violence and those that were more etiologically oriented.

The result was to offer two separate volumes. Hence, *Violent Crime, Violent Criminals* is offered as an updated set of essays of the current research on the measurement and correlates of criminal violence. Measuring violent behavior, race, gender, street gang violence, and violent criminal careers is part of this ensemble.

But in the process of assembling significant research on violence, we recognized another theme, namely, causative claims that gave explanatory meaning to the empirical descriptions: drugs, alcohol, sexual violence, mental disorder, violence breeding violence, and the effects of criminal violence on victims. The dichotomy between descriptions of violent crime and criminals, on the one hand, and the paths that led to such behavior and to such offenders, on the other, became clearer and more compelling as a principle by which to partition the cogent literature. *Pathways to Criminal Violence* became the theme of the roots to *Violent Crime, Violent Criminals*. Each volume has its own intellectual integrity; each contributes to the other.

The impetus to review, assess, and press beyond the research and theoretical accomplishments of the last two decades is not unique to the study of criminal violence. Criminology more generally appears to be experiencing theoretical and research *angst*—manifesting as a disquiet over the pace and overall payoff in these two enterprises. There is a growing sense that the intensity of and the insights yielded by theory-building and research have diminished and require fresh thinking to ignite new productive activity. This volume is intended in part as a vehicle for reviewing prior advancements and accumulations in criminal violence research and theory in order to stimulate renewed dialogue about how we might most beneficially continue or redirect our research, theoretical, and policy efforts. We expect that one important byproduct of this reflective process will involve reconciling and interweaving often disparate conceptual and research strands. As a consequence of this close scrutiny, perhaps the least supported of these strands will be diminished and those that are most solidly established will be elevated and pursued more vigorously.

To stimulate insightful work in the study of criminal violence, we need to know critically the state of the art in key topical areas. These areas include, among others, the social settings in which criminal violence occurs and the many personal and interpersonal pathways by which these settings are entered and violent behaviors are initiated. To explore these important concerns, street gang violence, offender race and gender characteristics, substance abuse, sexual behavior, mental illness, and intergenerational dynamics are examined in both this volume and a companion volume, *Pathways to Criminal Violence*, that will follow. Methodological issues and proposals for the systematic investigation of criminal violence over life spans are also explored in chapters on measuring violent behavior and on individual violent criminal careers. The impact of violence on victims is reviewed in a selection focusing on the relationship between victims and the criminal justice system, and the manifold consequences that interpersonal violence has for those who are so victimized.

The range of methodological and substantive topics that make up this volume provides wide coverage from many theoretical and research perspectives of the interior and exterior topography of criminal violence and of related prevention and control strategies and their implementation. We do not presume, however, to have covered the full sweep and compass of pertinent material. The exploration of further territory must await future volumes. With these volumes and those that are planned, we can construct more clearly and definitively an integral latticework of up-to-date knowledge and, based on that structure, identify those central interstices that remain to be filled.

For these many reasons, then, the present volume has been assembled. Colleagues who have worked at the forefront in their respective areas of criminal violence research have graciously and enthusiastically agreed to share their comprehensive knowledge.

In "Measuring Violent Behavior: Effects of Study Design on Reported Correlates of Violence," George S. Bridges and Joseph G. Weis examine in critical detail the degree to which discrepant study findings reported between 1945 and 1983 on selected correlates of criminal violence—gender, social class, and race—are, in part, artifacts of methodological differences in study design characteristics. These study characteristics include the definition of criminal violence that is used, the sampling population that is targeted and its composition, the source of information on violence that is employed (e.g., official; self-reports; victim surveys), the study period under examination, and the statistical techniques used for data analysis. Isolating the effects of substantive relationships on criminal violence from various biasing influences of the research design are crucial to being able to confirm empirical generalizations and, based on these validated research facts, to establish firmly grounded theories of criminal violence and equally well-grounded public policies to control and halt this violence.

To explore the effects of the study design on the study findings, Bridges and Weis treated both the study design and study findings as data enmeshed in a multivariate relationship: Study findings (correlational measures) relating to race, gender, and social class constituted the dependent measures; study design characteristics constituted the independent measures. The research supports the presence of several study design features that must be taken into account when assessing the effects of social and other correlates of criminal violence. The authors conclude their chapter with recommendations about research strategies that can offset the effects of the research design on study findings.

"Violent Criminal Careers and 'Violent Career Criminals': An Overview of the Research Literature," by Neil Alan Weiner, examines the criminal life spans of violent offenders from the perspective of "individual criminal career analysis." This perspective, which has developed at an accelerating pace over the last decade, involves the construction of dynamic statistical profiles of individual violent criminal careers, of their stochastic behavioral pathways and outcomes. Research on individual violent criminal careers begins by distinguishing two related, basic components of the "violent crime rate": (1) the proportion of the population that commits violent crimes and (2) the character and extent of the violent infractions by those people who are actively involved in these crimes. This elemental analytical distinction unfolds into related ones pertaining to several structural and dynamic features of the individual violent criminal career, including the individual violent crime rate, specialization and escalation of violence, the age at initiation of the individual violent criminal career, violent recidivism and desistence probabilities, the total and residual individual violent criminal career length, the age variation in the occurrence of violent crimes, and chronic violent criminal careers. Weiner reviews study findings pertaining to each of these aspects of the individual violent criminal career.

The individual violent criminal career approach has the analytical benefit of facilitating the systematic study of violent criminal behavior as an integrated, dynamic probabilistic structure of sequential unlawful acts that advances within a wider context of causal and correlative influences. Factors that influence, for example, the initiation of the individual violent criminal career may be quite different from those factors that influence the frequency of violent offending once the violent criminal career has begun. These latter factors, in turn, may be quite different from those factors that facilitate the termination of the violent criminal career. Weiner investigates the ways in which the individual violent criminal career approach can be used to focus theory and public policy on discrete components of the individual violent criminal career, how such information can be used in formulating more systematic public policies, the potential pitfalls of such an approach, and operational and ethical issues relating to public policies that might be based on the individual violent criminal career approach. Recommendations for future research in this area are also detailed.

Lynn A. Curtis focuses, in "Race and Violent Crime: Toward a New Policy," on the role of race in producing violent criminal activity and, based on this relationship, on the most feasible and effective policy strategies that can be mounted to intervene in and reshape the complex influences of race on violent crime. Curtis agrees with the conclusions concerning the connection between race and violent crime drawn in the 1960s by two prominent commissions, the National Commission on the Causes and Prevention of Violence and the National Advisory Commission on Civil Disorders: The racial disadvantage that produces disproportionately high rates of violent crimes is, in the main, a social and economic disadvantage, most currently represented by the "underclass." Evidence of the social, economic, and political origins of the race-based underclass are marshaled in critique of flawed biological and constitutional explanations of race and violent crime, explanations that confuse substantive correlations with substantive causes and that, apparently, rely upon the selective use of research findings.

Curtis assesses traditional approaches to the reduction of criminal violence—the triad of deterrence, rehabilitation, and incapacitation. The litigations of these approaches—their huge costs and expected and actual modest benefits—lead Curtis to advocate a tripartite approach to violent-crime reduction that involves overcoming economic deprivation and racial discrimination: neighborhood development, education, and employment. The philosophies and concomitant organizational structures and beneficial outcomes of three exemplary community-based and supported programs ("bubble-up" as opposed to "top-down" programs, as Curtis refers to them) are detailed—the Argus Community, Centro Isolina Ferre, and the House of Umoja. These programs provide the occupational, cognitive, and emotional skills required to make the transition from nonsecure employment sectors of the labor market to secondary and then to primary employment sectors. The cost-effectiveness and political feasibility of these programs; their relationship to traditional criminal justice system structures and strategies; and the kinds of national leadership and resolve, and private-public partnerships that will be necessary to consolidate and widen this approach are discussed in depth.

In "Gender and Violent Crime," Rita J. Simon and Sandra Baxter examine within a cross-national context the often-noted substantial discrepancies between the extent of male and female participation in criminally violent acts. In general, the authors investigate whether women are becoming increasingly involved in these acts as some social scientists and theoretical frameworks predict. In particular, the authors examined four related issues: (1) whether there have been substantial increases in female participation in criminal activity generally, (2) whether these increases, if any, are concentrated in violent criminal offenses, (3) whether increased participation by women in violent crime has occurred in certain types of societies or across all societies, and (4) whether any observed changes in female participation in violent crime are associated with women's changing educational and occupational statuses.

The authors point out that, for the most part, theories of crime and delinquency are special theories of unlawful male behavior. "Liberation theory," "role convergence," and "role validation" theories, among others, have been proposed as "objectivist" (social structural) and "subjectivist" (psychological) explanations of female criminality. Dimensions of these theories are assessed with cross-national statistics on crime and arrest rates from 31 countries for a 19-year time period. Interwoven with an analysis of the magnitudes, patterns, and trends in violent female criminality is an examination of selected societal correlates of these rates, including the percentages of women in the labor force and in institutions of higher learning and measures of industrialization and economic opportunity. The authors found little evidence in support of expected increases in rates of female violent crime. Inconclusive results were reported with respect to the relationships . between societal indices and time trends and cross-national patterns in female violent crime. Suggestions are presented to improve future research along these lines.

In the final chapter, "Street Gang Violence," Malcolm W. Klein and Cheryl L. Maxson discuss at length some of the continuities and major changes that have occurred over the last two decades with respect to street gangs and street gang violence, what can be known about these social forms and their assaultive activities, and street gang programs. The authors observe a recent decline in research on street gangs at a time when street gang activity appears to have changed in shape and substance (e.g., age structure, ethnicity, geographical location). Contemporary changes in research paradigms and in the political climate appear to account for this research impoverishment. The combination of political conservatism and a burgeoning interest in controlling street gangs—specifically, the violent activities—through criminal justice interventions has resulted in the police being the major repository in most cities of gang information and research opportunities. (Police sources of information have led to difficulties in conducting cross-jurisdictional research because of varying data collection procedures and classification schemes.) Recent information on street gangs has not yet been integrated into either existing or new theoretical approaches to explaining this social phenomenon, resulting in a conceptualization that has been unable to explain diverse street gang activity over the last 20 years. The authors stress that what is known in this area has yet to be translated successfully into programs to control and reduce street gang-related crime and violence.

Klein and Maxson emphasize the relevance of street gang research in understanding the social (group or companionate) and cultural origins of violent activity. Definitional issues are prominently explored in this chapter: For example, one needs to know what constitutes a "gang" and, by virtue of this, how to designate "gang-related activities" in order to set the foundation for a theoretically and empirically grounded explanation of street gang violence. The authors review some recent, emergent patterns of street gang composition and the kinds of violent criminal activities engaged in by these gangs. Some new theoretical formulations are also discussed as are some current public policies, which are mostly social control and deterrent in their focus. The promise and pitfalls of these policies are also investigated, as is the ineffectiveness of policies that fail to exploit the wide store of accumulating information about street gangs and their violent activities.

—Neil Alan Weiner
—Marvin E. Wolfgang

1

Measuring Violent Behavior

Effects of Study Design on
Reported Correlates of Violence

GEORGE S. BRIDGES
JOSEPH G. WEIS

The Study of Violence

Of increasing importance in the study of crime and criminality are the correlates of violent behavior. Over the past three decades, a voluminous literature on violence and its correlates has developed, with researchers publishing over a thousand articles and books on criminal violence between 1945 and 1972 (Wolfgang et al., 1978) and another thousand articles and books on domestic violence between 1972 and 1980 (Wolfgang et al., 1981). But despite the burgeoning size of this literature, empirical studies disagree about the precise correlates of violent behavior. Whereas some studies suggest that the highest rates of violence are found among black males (see, for example, Gil, 1970; Hamparian et al., 1978; Hindelang, 1978; Thornberry and Farnworth, 1982; Wolfgang et al., 1972), other studies suggest that discrepancies in violent offense rates between blacks and whites are relatively low (Elliott and Ageton, 1980; Hindelang et al., 1981). Similarly, some studies suggest that social class is one of the factors most closely related to violence (Monahan, 1981), while others find very weak relationships between criminal and domestic violence and measures of social class

AUTHORS' NOTE: Preparation of this chapter was supported, in part, by a grant from the National Institute of Mental Health, "Improving the Measurement of Violent Behavior" (1 RO 1 MH38194-02).

(Hindelang et al., 1981; Smith and Visher, 1979; Straus et al., 1980; Tittle et al., 1979).

Contributing to this uncertainty are differences among studies in research design and measurement (Bridges and Weis, 1985; Weis and Bridges, 1983).[1] Studies using different designs and measures—for example, different sources of information on violent behavior or different definitions of violence—may often reach discrepant conclusions about the amount and correlates of violence (Bridges and Weis, 1985; Hindelang et al., 1979, 1981). The concern of this chapter is whether the apparent discrepancies among studies are related to differences in design and measurement. It is possible that methodological differences between studies "create the illusion of discrepancy when, in general, no such discrepancy has been demonstrated" (Hindelang et al., 1979: 996). If methodological differences are strongly related to study findings, then the discrepancies may be attributable to major differences in methods and methodological distortion. However, if divergent methods observe the same correlates of violence, we can be more confident that the correlations are free of distortion. This chapter explores the relationship between methodological characteristics of studies and study findings using information on the measurement and correlates of violence reported in research published between 1945 and 1983.

Differences in Studies of Violence

Owing perhaps to the multidisciplinary character of crime and violence research, empirical studies of violent behavior vary dramatically in methodology and design. They focus on different types of violent behavior and use different sources of information on violence, different sampling units, and different analytic techniques. For example, studies of crime and criminal violence published between 1945 and 1972 varied in many aspects of design—whether they tested formal hypotheses about the causes of crime and violence, whether they conducted multivariate analyses, and whether they used "hard" empirical data (Wolfgang et al., 1978).

Studies using different designs and measures of violent behavior appear to yield different findings. These discrepancies undermine efforts to generalize about the correlates of violent behavior. For example, studies using official records or victim surveys for information about violent behavior consistently find higher rates of violence among blacks than do studies using self-report surveys (see Hindelang et al., 1978, 1979; Thornberry and Farnworth, 1982). Similarly, studies on official samples of violent families suggest that violence occurs disproportionately among families that live in poverty or near-poverty circumstances (Gil, 1970; Levinger, 1966; Pelton, 1978). But self-reports of domestic and criminal violence typically find a weak relationship between social class and involvement in interpersonal violence. The most recent self-report surveys have indicated that social class may be important only in explaining violent acts among adults and blacks (Hindelang et al., 1981; Thornberry and Farnworth, 1982).

The differences between studies may be partly attributable to shortcomings in the self-report method. Reporting accuracy in self-reports of violence has been shown to vary by race, with blacks underreporting their involvement and whites overreporting theirs (Bridges, 1987; Hindelang et al., 1981). Also, smaller race differences between blacks and whites may occur in self-report surveys because these surveys typically employ scales that are unable to discriminate frequent, chronic offenders from all others. If blacks are more likely than whites to be high-frequency offenders, then self-report surveys may be unable to detect black/white differences in frequent violent behavior.

Two elements of design are thought to foster dramatic differences in research findings. The first is *measures of violent behavior.* Over the past decade, research on the prevalence and correlates of violence has used the self-report method of measurement, owing primarily to concerns about the inaccuracy of other sources of information (Gelles, 1980; Weis and Bridges, 1983). A dominant view among violence researchers is that information from other sources, particularly officially defined populations of violent persons or victims of violence, is the product of selective practices of law enforcement and the administration of social services (Gelles, 1980; Schur, 1973). As a result, the findings of studies using samples of officially defined populations are thought to be seriously biased.

An example illustrates this perspective. Many studies using official measures of domestic violence find a stronger relationship between social class and violent behavior than do studies using self-report surveys. Critics of official measures interpret this discrepancy as the direct result of class biases in official data. Stronger class/violence correlations occur because violent acts among poor families are more likely to be recorded in law enforcement statistics or data maintained by social service agencies than are the violent acts occurring among families in higher social classes. The critics point to the difficulty of separating such selection biases in official measures from factors related to actual class differences in violent behavior (Gelles, 1980).

Equally troublesome is the fact that information in official records on chronic violent offenders may be particularly poor (Weis, 1986). The offense history attributes of these offenders are subject to the most serious recording errors simply as a function of their more frequent contact with the justice system, more time being covered by the records, more jurisdictions and agencies being involved, more information recorded, more varied and complex cases, more mobility, and more discontinuity in records over time and place. Thus long-term, complicated offense histories are probably less valid and reliable than recent, simple ones. And the likelihood of more errors in the records of chronic violent offenders opens to question the accuracy of analyses of violent crime based solely on official records.

The alternative view is that self-report methods are subject to serious measurement problems. In discussing several weaknesses of self-reports of delinquency, Reiss (1975) asserted that

> the methodological and technical foundation of these [self-report] studies do not invite confidence in the conclusions. . . . Surveys of self-reported delinquency pay little attention to the formulation of indicators and indexes, problems of validity and reliability, and general inattention to the standardization of instruments [p. 215].

More recent studies on self-reports of violent behavior support this conclusion. Weis and Bridges (1983) and Weis (1985) have suggested that the validity of measures of domestic violence is doubtful and that few researchers have carefully explored whether those measures accurately describe the incidence or prevalence of violence occurring between family members. Because of difficulties in establishing the precise validity of self-reports, many researchers believe there is no compelling reason to reject the results of studies based on official measures (Nettler, 1974; Pelton, 1978; Reiss, 1975; Wolfgang et al., 1972).

Recent research has focused on differences between studies using official records and those using self-reports (Bridges, 1978, 1981; Elliott and Ageton, 1980; Hindelang, 1978; Hindelang et al., 1981). Of concern are the apparent discrepancies in correlates of violence reported in studies using the different measures. Studies using official measures of violence—such as police arrest records, court dockets, or hospital records—find a stronger relationship between social class and violent behavior than do studies using self-report surveys (see Hindelang, 1978; Hindelang et al., 1979; Pelton, 1978). Some researchers suggest that the differences in the findings are attributable in part to problems of response error in self-reports of crime and violence—that is, the respondents inaccurately report their involvement in crime and violence.

Of particular importance is the variation in accuracy of reporting across entire categories of respondents. This differential reporting accuracy is pronounced in reports of serious and violent crime. One of the few studies known to the authors in which official records and self-reports of violence were compared as part of the study design found a significant race difference in reporting accuracy (Hindelang et al., 1981). Black males underreported official contacts at a significantly higher rate than did whites. The difference between whites and blacks was particularly high for serious and violent offenses: Whereas black males failed to report 62% of their police contacts for weapons offenses, white males failed to report only 22%. Other studies have reported similar discrepancies. Bridges (1983) reported that among the follow-up interview sample of the Philadelphia cohort study, significant race differences in reporting accuracy occurred across many aspects of offense histories—the number of offenses resulting in arrest, ages at the time of the offenses, the types of offenses, and the number of others arrested.

Other researchers suggest that the differences may be attributable to the structure of self-report instruments and, particularly, their insensitivity to the total frequency of serious and violent acts. Elliott and Ageton (1980) asserted that important class differences in crime and violent behavior occur *only* among those persons who are frequent offenders. It is argued that discrepancies between self-reports and official records occur because most self-report instruments do not measure the total frequency of criminal acts and are thus incapable of distinguishing between frequent and occasional offenders.

A related and equally important element of design is the *operational definition of violence*. Some researchers define violence in terms of the consequences of action, such as the severity of resulting injury or the destruction of property. For example, Gil defined violence against children as "physical attack or nonaccidental physical injury ranging from minimal to fatal injury inflicted upon a child by a person or persons having de facto caretaking responsibilities for him" (1979: 177). Yet others may define it in broader, more inconclusive terms: for example, "acts characterized by the application or overt threat of force which is likely to result in injury to people" (Megargee, 1976: 7). Obviously, studies using different definitions may reach substantially different conclusions about the amount and correlates of violence, regardless of other aspects of their study design. Studies that include threats and less serious forms of assault within their definitions of violence report substantially larger amounts of violence and weaker correlations between violence and important explanatory factors such as race, gender, and social class compared with studies of only the most serious assaultive acts (Bridges and Weis, 1985; Hindelang et al., 1979; Weis, 1985).

Discrepancies in measures of domestic violence have fueled controversy over the results of family violence studies. In their national survey of domestic violence, Straus, Steinmetz, and Gelles (1980) included the following items in their scale of violence:

Threatened to hit or throw something at the other one.
Threw or smashed or hit or kicked something.
Threw something at the other one.
Punched, grabbed or shoved the other one.
Slapped or spanked the other one.
Kicked, bit, or hit with a fist.
Hit, or tried to hit, with something.
Beat up the other one.
Threatened with knife or gun.
Used a knife or gun [Appendix].

Critics of previous self-report studies assert that some of the items overstate the seriousness of domestic violence. For example, Pelton (1978) argued:

For all we know, the same person who answered affirmatively [in self-report studies] to the "used a knife or gun" question might have meant that she once brandished the knife or gun, hit the child on the rear with the butt of an unloaded pistol, rapped the child's knuckles with a butter knife, or indeed shot at or stabbed the child. And what does "beat up" mean? To one parent, it might signify the repeated severe hitting of a child in a manner that leaves injuries. To another, it might mean spanking the child a few times on the rear [p. 194].

Because many of these less serious offenses typically are not recorded in police statistics, their inclusion in self-report instruments is thought to create discrepancies between the findings of violence studies using self-reports and studies using official measures.

In sum, aspects of study design may produce substantial discrepancies in research findings on violent behavior. Previous studies of crime and violence suggest that the sources of information on violent behavior and operational definitions of violence may contribute the largest share of differences among studies. No previous research has explored the combined effects of these and other aspects of study design on an empirical analysis of the actual findings of studies on violence. The next section examines the relationship between characteristics of study design and study findings using information on the designs and findings of a sample of previously published studies. To illustrate the effects of study design and measurement on correlates of violence and, at the same time, allow for comparisons with previous studies of the measurement of crime (Hindelang et al., 1979; Tittle et al., 1979), the analysis is limited to findings on the association between violence and gender, social class, and race.

The Study

The research was designed to cross-classify study designs and findings. Narrative reviews of large literatures, particularly those examining complex differences in research designs and findings, are often poorly organized because of difficulties in evaluating and integrating research results. Reviewers using traditional literature methods tend to reject all but a few studies as deficient in analysis or design and thus dispose of valuable information about research results. To overcome this problem, the present study examines study designs and findings as empirical data about previous violence research.

The study used data collected on the findings and design characteristics of empirical studies of violence published between 1945 and 1983. Data collection and coding proceeded in separate steps. In the first step, the study identified and collected all empirical research publications on violent behavior during the study period.

To ensure the most comprehensive literature search possible, three independent search strategies were employed. First, all publication titles and abstracts maintained in eight major computerized abstracting services and five printed abstract indices were searched with keywords pertaining to research on violent behavior. Because many of the abstracting services include research published only after the mid-1960s, the second search strategy entailed manual identification of studies published prior to the creation of the indices. Following the search of the automated and printed indices, a list of 50 professional journals was constructed to include those journals that had published the majority of the articles on violence since the creation of the indices. This list was used to construct an issue-by-issue search of each journal for relevant studies published prior to 1965. The third search sought studies of violence published as books, monographs, and reports. Using an automated indexing system of all holdings in the Library of Congress, a list of keywords pertaining to research on violent behavior was developed and used to search the system for relevant publications.

Following collection of the publications, extensive information on research methods and findings was coded for a 50% sample of the studies identified in step one (Bridges and Weis, 1985). The initial search produced a pool of 21,299 articles and reports, 800 monographs, and 717 dissertations. Using screening procedures described elsewhere (Bridges et al., 1985), a master list of eligible publications was constructed and validated against bibliographic reference lists from 17 other sources, including Wolfgang et al.'s (1978) exhaustive compilation of research on crime. At the end of this process, 516 publications remained on the master list. A 50% systematic sample of publications was selected for coding information on study design, sources of information on violence, measures of violent behavior, sample composition, study period, and study findings.

Study Design

Aspects of study design were coded into five categories or groups corresponding to (1) field experimental; (2) cross-sectional; (3) longitudinal, such as panel, time series, and cohort designs; (4) cross-section of a time series; and (5) nonexperimental matched group designs. Because the categories were not mutually exclusive, the designs were coded such that a single study could incorporate multiple design types. Designs meeting either of the experimental design categories were coded according to experimental types and not as longitudinal designs because experiments are longitudinal by definition.

Sources of Information on Violence

Information on types of data was collected for each study as a whole. Because different sources of data may be used within studies, data sources were also coded for each measure of violence and correlate of violence included in the study. Types of data sources were coded as *official data* for variables maintained by government agencies such as the *Uniform Crime Reports* of the FBI. Subjects' *self-reports* of violent offenses included self-report surveys distinguished by their methods of administration, such as personal interviews and questionnaires involving paper/pencil answers to questions or psychological tests. Subjects' *victim reports* included victimization surveys. Finally, researchers' *observations* included data collected using participant or nonparticipant observational methods.

Measures of Violent Behavior

Although many factors in the measurement of violence may influence observed correlates of violent behavior, four factors seemed particularly important: the levels of aggregation, the actual type of behavior studied, the type of measure, and to whom the measure of violence refers— victim or offender. The *level of aggregation* was coded in terms of the focus of study and whether the focus was individuals or larger social groups. The *type of violent behavior studied* was coded to distinguish studies that define and measure violence in terms of serious physical assault from those that use broader operational definitions. The study findings were grouped on a finding-by-finding basis of those that pertained to (1) serious violent acts, including homicide, rape, robbery, and serious assault, and (2) other types of violent behavior, such as physical aggression and child abuse involving minor injuries.

Information was also collected on the types of measures—that is, whether measures of violence were incidence or prevalence measures. Race, gender, or class differences may be greater for measures of prevalence—that is, whether a person ever commits a violent act—than for measures of its incidence—the number of violent acts a person has committed. This may occur because there is greater statistical variation in prevalence measures of violence. These measures typically classify more people as "violent" than do incidence measures. Whereas a substantial share of the population may have committed a single violent or assaultive act, very few persons have committed many violent acts. With greater statistical variation, prevalence measures are more likely to yield strong correlations with explanatory factors such as race, gender, and class.

A final measurement issue is whether the measures of violent behavior refer to specific actors in violent episodes or to the environment associated with violent acts. All measures were coded according to whether they referred to a violent offender, a victim of a violent act, or some aspect of the environment in which violence occurs.

Sample Composition

Because the composition of the study samples—that is, the types of persons included as subjects—may influence research findings, the study collected information on the characteristics of the sample subjects. Of particular concern was whether sample designs that target institutional populations, such as incarcerated offenders, find stronger race/violence, gender/violence, or social class/violence relationships than those targeting the general public. This type of purposive sampling has the effect of selecting subjects on the dependent variable, such as conviction for a violent crime. The result may be distorted estimates of the correlates of violent behavior (see Hirschi and Selvin, 1967, for a discussion of this problem).

The Study Period

The period of a research study may also influence that study's findings. Over time, the strength of some types of relationships reported in studies may change as the result of changes in the content of the empirical data. For example, findings of studies of social class and crime using official crime data have found a stronger class/crime relationship prior to 1970. Tittle et al. (1979) suggested that changes in the class/crime relationship may be attributable to fewer class biases in official data in recent years. To ensure that the study period was included in the analysis, the year of publication was coded for each study finding.

The Study Findings

The unit of analysis in the present study was the research finding—that is, the statistical association between a measure of violence and a measure of gender, social class, or race. Data on two types of findings were collected and coded. The first type comprised all nonredundant correlations between measures of violent behavior and explanatory variables included in each study. The collection of this type of information was complicated by the fact that statistical methods used by researchers vary significantly across studies. To ensure that comparable statistical data on associations between violence and explanatory factors were obtained, all findings—including raw data and bivariate and multivariate statistics—were transformed to zero-order correlation coefficients following Glass's (1978) convention. In studies using multiple regression analyses, the standardized beta weights were coded as the measures of association. The other variables included in the regression equation were coded as statistical controls. The findings and transformations yielded 115 gender/violence associations from 34 studies, 276 social class/violence associations from 51 studies, and 337 race/violence associations from 71 studies.[2]

The associations were coded such that a positive race/violence correlation indicated greater nonwhite than white involvement in violence. Similarly, a positive gender/violence correlation was coded to indicate greater male than female involvement in violence. Finally, social class/violence findings were coded such that a negative correlation between social class and violence indicated greater involvement in violence of the poor or lower-status persons than of persons with higher status. It is expected that characteristics of design such as the type of data may be associated with stronger or weaker correlations, depending on the aspect of the study design in question. For example, stronger race/violence correlations—that is, correlations between race and violence substantially greater than zero—would be expected for findings based upon official measures of violence than for findings based upon self-reports. Similarly, weaker social class/violence correlations—that is, correlations less likely to be strongly negative—would be expected for findings based upon official measures of violence than for findings based upon self-reports of violence.

Results

Table 1.1 exhibits the features of study design included in the sample, reported by each type of finding. The majority of the findings were based on samples of the general public. Violence was measured most commonly in terms of official records of serious assaultive acts, with approximately one-third of the findings based on official data. An equal percentage of the findings was based on self-reports of violent behavior. Finally, approximately three-fourths of the social class/violence and race/violence findings and all but three of the gender/violence findings were based on individual level data.

TABLE 1.1
Design Characteristics of Studies (Reported by Findings)

Design Characteristics	Race/Violence		Gender/Violence		Social Class/Violence	
	N	%[a]	N	%[a]	N	%[a]
Prevalence measure	269	79.8	106	92.2	181	65.6
Official data	143	42.4	35	30.4	82	29.7
Self-report data	70	20.7	49	42.6	82	29.7
Institutionalized or official sample	71	21.1	37	32.2	14	5.1
Analysis of individuals	267	79.2	112	98.2	201	72.8
Analysis of offenders	187	55.5	77	66.9	136	49.3
Serious violence only[b]	179	53.1	63	54.8	156	56.5
Statistical controls	65	19.3	11	9.6	46	16.7
Totals	337		115		276	

NOTE: a. Column percentages do not sum to 100 because design characteristics do not constitute mutually exclusive categories.

b. Serious violence includes homicide, serious physical assault, robbery, rape, or attempted rape.

Studies yielded substantially different findings on the correlates of violence. The race/violence findings are useful for illustrating these differences. Many of the findings were weakly positive, indicating no strong correlational relationship between race and violence. For example, race/violence associations based upon violent acts by institutionalized or "official" samples—such as incarcerated offenders, individual delinquents, and ex-mental patients—typically ranged between .01 and .15, with some studies reporting negative race/violence findings (Cazenave and Straus, 1979; Wolfgang, 1983). In contrast, other studies have reported much stronger associations and thus substantially greater involvement of nonwhites in violent behavior. For example, Curtis's (1974) analysis of violent crimes in five U.S. cities yielded correlations averaging .27, with a maximum race/violence correlation of .67. More recent studies on violent crime rates have reported even stronger findings, with correlations between race and violence ranging between .40 and .80 (Messner, 1983; Parker and Smith, 1979).

In order to explain these discrepancies, three separate regression analyses that examined the influence of design characteristics on study findings were performed, one for each set of findings. In these analyses the dependent variables were study findings—that is, the statistical correlations between violence and race, social class, or gender. The independent variables were research design characteristics.

Before proceeding, it may be useful to note that in this type of analysis unstandardized regression coefficients correspond to the actual effect, positive or negative, of a design characteristic on the correlation between violence and the correlate of interest. For example, a positive, unstandardized regression coefficient for race/violence findings on official data would mean that the measurement of violence with official data increases—that is, influences in a positive direction—race/violence correlations. A negative coefficient would mean that the use of official data decreases—that is, influences in a negative direction—race/violence correlations.

Table 1.2 exhibits the results of the regression analyses of gender/violence, race/violence, and social class/violence correlations on study design characteristics. Contrary to expectations and previously published writing, neither the types of data—self-report or official—nor the domain of (that is, the types of crimes included in) the measures of violence used in previous studies contribute significantly to discrepancies in the studies' findings. These results are not trivial. The assertion that "domain" differences explain disparities among study findings on violence is not supported. Other factors—for example, the level of aggregation used in the analysis, whether the analysis focused on offenders, and the presence of statistical controls for other correlates—contributed to the differences across all three types of findings.

The level of aggregation was coded as a dichotomous variable—that is, as a variable with two values, in this instance "0" and "1." Findings based on analyses of individuals were assigned the value "1," whereas findings based on larger aggregations, such as households, census tracts, and SMSAs, were assigned the value "0." The unstandardized regression coefficient for this factor exhibited in Table 1.2 indicates that findings were based on higher levels of aggregation. In the case of the race/violence findings, the unstandardized regression coefficient for the level of aggregation (−.278) indicated that race/violence correlations would be .278 lower among studies of individuals than among studies using higher levels of aggregation, if other characteristics of design and measurement were equal. For class/violence findings the correlations were typically negative. Those based on social aggregates such as census tracts or SMSAs were negative and stronger than those based on individuals—.228 stronger. In contrast, studies of individuals typically found a very weak class/violence relationship—a correlation very close to zero.

A second significant factor was whether the findings were based on offenders. Race/violence and gender/violence findings based on of-

TABLE 1.2

Regressions of Study Findings on Design Characteristics
of Studies (Reported by Findings)

Design Characteristics	Race/Violence			Gender/Violence			Social Class/Violence		
	b	B	SE	b	B	SE	b	B	SE
Prevalence measure	-.028	-.052	.028	.085	.111	.069	.007	.016	.029
Official data	.006	.013	.013	.094	.211	.059	-.102	.207	.053
Self-report data	-.044	-.082	.034	.051	.123	.059	-.039	-.079	.038
Institutionalized or official sample	.016	.029	.031	-.073	-.166	.047	-.081	-.078	.054
Analysis of individuals	-.278[b]	-.519	.044	-.307[a]	-.195	.155	.229[b]	.454	.056
Analysis of offenders	.059[a]	.136	.028	.192[a]	.440	.049	.036	.080	.032
Serious violence only[c]	.037	.085	.023	-.052	-.126	.041	-.024	-.052	.026
Year	-.001	-.010	.002	-.079	-.003	.004	.005[a]	.126	.002
Statistical controls	-.069[a]	-.126	.034	.022	.031	.077	.129[b]	.215	.037
Constant	.364			.442			-.607		
R^2	.284			.297			.304		
R^2 (adjusted)	.264			.236			.280		
N	337			115			276		

NOTE: a. $p \leq .05$

     b. $p \leq .001$

     c. Serious violence includes homicide, serious physical assault, robbery, rape, or attempted rape.

fenders were stronger (.059 and .192, respectively) than those based on victims. An example may assist in interpreting these findings. The gender/violence correlation was significantly stronger among offenders than among victims, indicating that men were more likely to be offenders in violent acts and that women were more likely to be victims. This finding is consistent with the widely held belief that women are more frequently assaulted by males than vice versa across most forms of interpersonal violence. As a result, the gender/violence relationship— defined in the present context as disproportionate male involvement in violent behavior—was weaker than in studies of offenders. Thus the strong influence of the orientation of analysis, that is, whether the focus is victims or offenders, indicates that greater evidence of disproportionate minority and male involvement in violence is found among studies of offenders than among studies of victims.

Third, the statistical controls used in previous studies diminish significantly the correlations between race, social class, and violence. In the instance of *race,* findings adjusted for the effects of other factors were .069 *lower* than findings with no adjustments. Factors used as controls in these cases included measures of social status, family structure, and characteristics of the surrounding community, such as urban/rural differences between communities and the density of resident populations. For *social class,* findings adjusted for the effects of controls were .129 greater than findings with no controls, meaning that studies using controls observed substantially *weaker* social class/ violence correlations than did studies using no controls. In these instances, controls typically included demographic characteristics such as population density and the availability of health care facilities.

The effects of differences in types of data approached statistical significance only in the gender/violence and social class/violence findings and only for data from official sources. Gender/violence findings based on official measures of violence typically find greater male/female differences in violent behavior than findings based on other measures (b = .094), once other aspects of the research design are taken into account. Social class/violence findings based on official measures are more likely to be negative (b = –.102) than findings based on other measures. Differences in the domain of violence measures, reflected in the seriousness of violent acts, approach significance only for race/violence findings. Studies that define violence solely in terms of serious assaultive acts causing injury or physical harm to victims find stronger race/violence relationships—.037 stronger on the average— than studies adopting definitions that include less serious behaviors.

Discussion and Conclusions

An important issue in the study of criminal violence is whether aspects of study design, particularly the measurement of violence, produce substantial discrepancies in research findings on the amount and correlates of violent behavior. The issue lies at the center of controversy over the causes and control of violence. Among scientists concerned with the causes of violence, the issue is whether different methods of research yield significantly different findings. Differences in methods—and the liabilities and benefits associated with the differences—may yield different correlates of violent behavior. Among those concerned with the prevention and control of violence, the issue is whether the correlates of violent behavior identified in empirical research are artifacts of study design and, as a result, are actually poor predictors of violent acts.

The present research observes that aspects of study design explain substantial discrepancies between studies on the correlates of violent behavior. Findings based on *individuals* yield substantially weaker race/violence, gender/violence, and social class/violence correlations than do findings based on *higher levels of aggregation.* Findings based on *offender characteristics* are significantly stronger than are those based on *victim characteristics* or *the situation of the offense.* Also, *statistical controls* for other correlates of violence significantly reduce the strength of race/violence and social class/violence correlations.

Equally important, differences in the sources of data used in violence studies, once other aspects of study design are taken into account, yield no significant differences in correlations between race, gender, social class, and violence. Similarly, differences in the domain of measures of violence yield no significant differences in correlations. Thus the sources and domain of violence measures *do not* create major discrepancies in violence research. Contrary to expectations, differences in the type and domain of data explain few of the differences among findings.

At least two explanations for these findings are plausible. The first is that most studies find relatively little violence recorded in different sources of data. Empirical studies typically use as subjects individuals drawn from the general population who have no significant history of violence. In this instance, different sources of data contribute little to differences in findings because there is actually little variation in findings between sources. The strength of any empirical association depends, in large part, upon variability in the independent and dependent variables—in the present case, variability in sources of data and in study findings. But in the case of race, gender, and social class, there is little variation across study findings. Most of the studies yielded quite similar correlations with violence, particularly when studies using different sources of data were compared. As a result, the relationship between sources of data and study findings is extremely weak. And sources of data may be of little value in explaining variation among study findings.

The second explanation is that measures of violence, regardless of source, may be more accurate than measures of other types of crime and social deviance. These measures may be less subject to recording or reporting biases in official records on crime and response biases in self-report surveys of crime and violence. As a result, these measures may be more likely to yield similar estimates of the prevalence and incidence of violent acts and less likely to yield discrepant findings on the correlates of violent behavior than would measures of other types of crime. If different sources may portray the incidence, prevalence, and types of violent acts with equal accuracy, particularly for the most serious forms of violent behavior, then correlations between measures of violence and other factors are less likely to be attenuated by differences in error. Empirical research supports this reasoning. Studies find little evidence of bias in official measures of assault and other more serious violent acts (Bridges, Weis, and Day, 1985; Elliott and Ageton, 1980; Hindelang, 1978; Hindelang et al., 1981). Further, self-reports of violent offenses are more likely to equal official levels than are self-reports of other types of crime (Hindelang et al., 1981; Tracy and Fox, 1981). Thus the consistency of findings between studies using different sources of data may occur because the sources are subject to less error, in terms of the types and amounts of behavior they measure, than are data on other forms of crime and deviance.

Thus discrepancies in the findings of violence research—at least with respect to race, social class, and gender—are attributable to aspects of design related to, but not solely within, the domain of measurement. It is beyond the scope of the present study to explain fully the differential influence of study design on research findings. Nevertheless, the factor with uniformly strong influence on study findings is the level of aggregation, with correlations based on analyses of social aggregates being much stronger—either positive or negative—than those based on analyses of individuals.

That ecological correlations are stronger than those based on individuals is necessarily not surprising. Stronger correlations are expected for aggregated data than for individual data because, for the same data aggregated at different levels, the magnitude of the correlation between two variables will increase with the level of aggregation. This occurs, in part, because the effects of random measurement errors are reduced in ecological data by the process of aggregation across individuals. As these effects are reduced, correlations become stronger. Although it is not possible with the present data to determine with certainty whether the differences between ecological and individual findings are attributable to this type of statistical artifact, preliminary analyses suggest they are not.[3]

If, however, ecological correlations are stronger than those based on individuals because the actual relationships between measures such as race or class and violence are ecological and not individual, then a clearer distinction may be needed between the social contexts in which violence occurs and the social characteristics of individuals committing violent acts. In 1950, Robinson described the fallacy of comparing ecological correlations—that is, correlations based on *aggregates* of individuals—with individual-level correlations. The former may offer

little useful information about the characteristics of individuals that are important to understanding their behavior (Hirschi and Selvin, 1967). Thus ecological correlates of violence such as social class, gender, and race may shed substantial light on the formal social settings in which violent behavior occurs but little light on precisely who is committing violent acts within those settings.[4]

The finding that levels of analysis are important also has implications for clinical predictions of violent behavior. It is impossible to construct a valid profile of the violent offender from aggregate data describing the social context in which violence occurs. In the absence of strong individual-level correlations between sociodemographic factors and violence, clinical predictions based on those factors may be grossly inaccurate.

An important first step in future research on violence is separating design effects from the effects of explanatory factors. Research endeavors like the present study are useful for estimating empirically the influence of each major aspect of study design on the correlates and causes of violent behavior. The study shows that this influence varies significantly by each major correlate of violence, with different aspects of design affecting the strength of correlations. Other analyses of these data indicate that the influence of design also varies by type of violent crime (Bridges and Weis, 1985), with some aspects of design having a greater impact on the correlates of violence among intimates than violence among strangers or acquaintances. Additional analyses of design effects in previous research would assist in identifying those aspects of design that have the most serious distorting effects. It would also assist in developing strategies for controlling their effects in subsequent studies.

Future studies must explore measurement, study design, and correlates of violent crime. And in order to identify the causes of violence and to make more accurate predictions of violent behavior, subsequent studies must attempt to neutralize the effects of measurement and design on research findings. This task is complicated by the differential influence of design characteristics on the correlates of violent behavior. Nevertheless, studies must take into account the effects of design. The most viable approach to developing valid causal or predictive models of violence, while neutralizing the effects of design on study findings, would be to incorporate multiple types of design—different levels of aggregation, different types of statistical control, a focus on offenders and victims—into a single design. Without such features, it would seem impossible to separate design effects and the effects of important explanatory and predictive factors.

NOTES

1. Particularly important to understanding differences in findings among studies are the mechanisms by which characteristics of study design influence estimates of the amount and correlates of violence. In the context of this chapter the term *measurement* refers to those procedures by which researchers obtain symbols that can then be used to represent the concepts under study (Ackoff, 1962). This is a broad conception of measurement, not limited solely to issues such as the derivation and validation of measures of particular concepts. Rather, measurement in the present context involves the principal aspects of study design, such as sampling, data collection, and analysis.

2. Complete bibliographic listings of the studies can be obtained from the authors upon request. The search procedure used to identify the studies is described in Bridges et al. (1985).

3. To ascertain whether the stronger ecological correlations are a statistical artifact, two additional analyses were performed. The *first* examined the variances of the measures used in study findings. Typically, the larger the variance in a measure of violence owing to random measurement error, the lower the level of variance in the dependent variable—in this instance, violent behavior—explained by the independent variable. To compensate for the effects of measurement error on variances in the dependent and independent variables, regressions were performed like those presented in Table 1.2 that included two additional variables: the variances of the dependent and independent variables used to create the study findings. The regression analyses examined whether the effects of design characteristics, such as level of aggregation, diminish once the variances of measures were controlled. The *second* examined whether differences in the number of findings across studies influence the effects of design characteristics on studies. To compensate for differences in findings, regressions were also performed in which the samples were weighted by the reciprocal of the number of findings yielded in each study. Although the effects of many design characteristics do diminish once differences in variances and the number of findings in each study are controlled, effects of the level of aggregation persist. This suggests that the ecological relationships reported between race, gender, class, and violence may not necessarily be statistical artifacts and may actually be stronger than the corresponding relationships for individuals.

4. Ecological analyses are useful for pointing to intermediate-level variables that influence violence. These middle-range variables explain or provide the links between ecological and individual factors.

REFERENCES

Ackoff, R. (1962) Scientific Method. New York: John Wiley.

Bridges, G. S. (1978) "Errors in the measurement of crime: an application of Jöreskog's method for the analysis of general covariance structures," pp. 9-29 in C. F. Wellford (ed.) Quantitative Studies in Criminology. Beverly Hills, CA: Sage.

Bridges, G. S. (1981) "Estimating the effects of response error in self-reports of crime," pp. 59-76 in J. A. Fox (ed.) Quantitative Methods in Criminology. New York: Academic Press.

Bridges, G. S. (1987) "An empirical study of error in reports of crime and delinquency," in M. E. Wolfgang, T. Thornberry, and R. M. Figlio (eds.) From Boy to Man, From Delinquency to Crime. Chicago: University of Chicago Press.

Bridges, G. S. and J. G. Weis (1985) Study Design and Its Effects on Correlates of Violent Behavior. Report to the National Institute of Mental Health. Seattle: Center for Law and Justice.

Bridges, G. S., J. G. Weis, and L. E. Day (1985) Race, Social Class, and Differential Validity in the Measurement of Criminal Violence. Report to the National Institute of Mental Health. Seattle: Center for Law and Justice.

Bridges, G. S., J. G. Weis, L. E. Day, and J. A. Stone (1985) On the Acquisition of Publications for Meta-Analysis. Report to the National Institute of Mental Health. Seattle: Center for Law and Justice.

Cazenave, N. A. and M. A. Straus (1979) "Race, class, network embeddedness, and family violence: a search for potent support systems." Journal of Comparative Family Studies 10: 281-300.

Chaiken, J. and M. Chaiken (1982) Varieties of Criminal Behavior. Santa Monica: Rand Corporation.

Cloward, R. and L. Ohlin (1961) Delinquency and Opportunity. New York: Free Press.

Costner, H. L. (1969) "Theory, reduction, and rules of correspondence." American Journal of Sociology 75: 254-263.

Curtis, L. A. (1974) Criminal Violence. Lexington, MA: D.C. Heath.

Elliott, D. S. and S. S. Ageton (1980) "Reconciling race and class differences in self-reported and official estimates of delinquency." American Sociological Review 45: 95-110.

Gelles, R. J. (1980) "Violence in the family: a review of research in the seventies." Journal of Marriage and the Family 42: 873-885.

Gil, D. (1968) "Incidence of child abuse and demographic characteristics of persons involved," pp. 19-40 in R. E. Helfer and C. H. Kempe (eds.) The Battered Child. Chicago: University of Chicago Press.

Gil, D. (1970) Violence Against Children. Cambridge, MA: Harvard University Press.

Gil, D. (1979) "Violence against children," pp. 1973-1999 in D. Gil (ed.) Child Abuse and Violence. New York: AMS Press.

Glass, G. (1978) "Integrating findings: the meta-analysis of research." Review of Research in Education 5: 351-379.

Gold, M. (1970) Delinquent Behavior in an American City. Monterey, CA: Brooks/Cole.

Hamparian, D. M., R. Schuster, S. Dinitz, and J. P. Conrad (1978) The Violent Few. Lexington, MA: Lexington.

Hindelang, M. J. (1978) "Race and involvement in common law personal crimes." American Sociolgoical Review 43: 93-109.

Hindelang, M. J., T. Hirschi, and J. G. Weis (1979) "Correlates of delinquency: the illusion and discrepancy between self-report and official measures." American Sociological Review 44: 995-1014.

Hindelang, M. J., T. Hirschi, and J. G. Weis (1981) Measuring Delinquency. Beverly Hills, CA: Sage.

Hirschi, T. and H. Selvin (1967) Delinquency Research: An Appraisal of Analytic Methods. New York: Free Press.

Levinger, G. (1966) "Sources of marital dissatisfaction among applicants for divorce." American Journal of Orthopsychiatry 26: 803-807.

Megargee, E. (1976) "The prediction of dangerous behavior." Criminal Justice and Behavior 3: 3-21.

Messner, S. F. (1983) "Regional and racial effects on the urban homicide rate: the subculture of violence revisited." American Journal of Sociology 88: 997-1007.

Monahan, J. (1981) Predicting Violent Behavior: An Assessment of Clinical Techniques. Beverly Hills, CA: Sage.

Nettler, G. (1974) Explaining Crime. New York: McGraw-Hill.

Parker, R. N. and M. D. Smith (1979) "Deterrence, poverty, and type of homicide." American Journal of Sociology 85: 615-624.

Pelton, L. H. (1978) "Child abuse and neglect: the myth of classlessness." American Journal of Orthopsychiatry 48: 192-196.

Reiss, A. J. (1975) "Inappropriate theories and inadequate methods as policy plagues: self-reported delinquency and the law," pp. 211-222 in N. J. Demerath, III, O. Larsen, and K. F. Schuessler (eds.) Social Policy and Sociology. New York: Academic Press.

Robinson, W. S. (1958) "Ecological correlations and the behavior of individuals." American Sociological Review 15: 351-356.

Schur, E. M. (1973) Radical Nonintervention: Rethinking the Delinquency Problem. Englewood Cliffs, NJ: Prentice-Hall.

Smith, D. A. and C. Visher (1979) "Gender and crime: an empirical assessment of research findings." American Sociological Review 48: 509-514.

Straus, M. A., S. Steinmetz, and R. Gelles (1980) Behind Closed Doors: Violence in the American Family. New York: Anchor.

Thornberry, T. P. and M. Farnworth (1982) "Social correlates of criminal involvement: further evidence on the relationship between social status and criminal behavior." American Sociological Review 47: 505-518.

Tittle, C. R., W. J. Villemez, and D. A. Smith (1979) "The myths of social class and criminality: an empirical assessment of the empirical evidence." American Sociological Review 43: 643-656.

Tracy, P. E. and J. A. Fox (1981) "Validation of randomized response." American Sociological Review 43: 643-656.

Weis, J. G. (1985) "The incidence of various forms of family violence." Background paper for the Workshop on Family Violence as a Crime and Criminal Justice Problem, National Institute of Justice.

Weis, J. G. and G. S. Bridges (1983) Improving the Measurement of Violent Behavior: Research Program. Proposal to the National Institute of Mental Health. Seattle: Center for Law and Justice.

Wolfgang, M. E. (1983) "Delinquency in two birth cohorts." American Behavioral Scientist 27: 75-86.

Wolfgang, M. E. and F. Ferracuti (1982) The Subculture of Violence. Beverly Hills, CA: Sage.

Wolfgang, M. E., R. M. Figlio, and T. Sellin (1972) Delinquency in a Birth Cohort. Chicago: University of Chicago Press.

Wolfgang, M. E., R. M. Figlio, and T. Thornberry (1978) Evaluating Criminology. New York: Elsevier.

Wolfgang, M. E., N. A. Weiner, and W. D. Pointer (1981) Domestic Violence: A Selected Bibliography. Washington, DC: Government Printing Office.

2

Violent Criminal Careers and "Violent Career Criminals"

An Overview of the Research Literature

NEIL ALAN WEINER

One common and productive way to investigate the social lifespan has been to identify significant behavioral benchmarks in the social progression and to map onto these benchmarks concepts that cast them as part of an integral, dynamic framework. An approach consistent with this perspective now current in criminology is that of individual criminal career analysis. Criminal biography has been redefined from its traditional focus on the criminal career of an individual—for example, the professional thief or fence, largely a compound of ethnography, biographical journalism, and clinical case history (see Booth, 1929; Klockars, 1974; Martin, 1952; Shaw, 1930, 1931; Sutherland, 1937)—to a new focus on aggregate biography involving the construction of dynamic statistical profiles of individual criminal careers. These profiles involve probabilistic descriptions of the structural and dynamic behavioral features of criminal careers and their stochastic behavioral pathways and outcomes. This chapter employs the criminal career approach to depict statistically some salient milestones in the individual violent criminal career.

AUTHOR'S NOTE: My appreciation to Jaqueline Cohen for her careful reading of this chapter. Her critical comments greatly improved the content. I am grateful also to Selma Pastor for her fine editing and for the preparation of tabular material.

Definitional Issues: Violent Crime, Violent Criminal Careers, and "Violent Career Criminals"

Violence and Violent Crime

The main behavioral nodes of those criminal careers that are of present concern—legally proscribed violence—are commonly specified by reference to criminal statutes stipulating those types of conduct that are impermissibly assaultive and injurious in their potential or actual outcomes. Appealing to criminal statutes to specify these acts will likely result, with some variation, owing to different jurisdictional enactments and terminology, in the inclusion of the following infractions as violent: homicide (murder and nonnegligent manslaughter), forcible and attempted rape, robbery, aggravated and simple assault, involuntary deviate sexual intercourse, and kidnapping. Leaving definitional matters in the form of this statutory-based listing meets the practical consideration of designating for purely descriptive purposes the main unlawful points of interest in an individual violent criminal career. Although useful for purposes of bounding the domain of *criminally* violent behavior, proceeding in this way does not provide sufficient definitional balance and focus because it fails to raise some pertinent conceptual issues concerning the behavioral and interactional dimensions of *violence*.[1] As the following discussion suggests, however, both the statutory and conceptual pathways to greater definitional specification recommend that the same array of behaviors be studied with respect to individual violent criminal careers.

Criminal violence may be defined generally as the actual or threatened, knowing, or intentional application of statutorily impermissible physical force by one person directly against one or more other persons for the purpose of securing some end against the will or without the consent of the other person or persons.[2] The threatened or actual application of physical force may serve one or a combination of ends or functions: (1) a purely *hostile* injurious purpose, also called "angry" violence (for example, the direct and personally rewarding goal of harming the victim, perhaps to save face in response to an insult or to avenge some deceit) or the function of discharging an *expressive* or emotional arousal or excitation (for example, impulsive behavior initiated in the "heat of the moment" wherein physical injury, though not directly intended, results from an attack that is nonetheless knowingly pursued), and (2) an *instrumental* nonviolent or noninjurious purpose (for example, forcibly taking money or property in order to acquire some other valued goods or services). Criminal homicide, forcible and attempted rape, other sexual offenses, and the nonlethal gradations of physical assault have usually been treated in the research context as exemplary of *hostile* or *expressive* violent crimes (the latter term is more commonly used generically), and robbery and kidnapping as exemplary of *instrumental* violent crimes.[3]

The foregoing definition of criminal violence is quite general and encompasses a wider set of phenomena than the statutory proscriptions listed earlier. Behaviors as disparate as individual involvement in collective violence (for example, race and ethnic riots and union-management conflicts) and in state-sponsored ("reign of terror") or state-opposed ("state of siege") violence (for example, terrorism, torture, or genocide) could fall within the orbit of the definition as it presently stands. Some restriction is needed to delimit the definition of criminal violence so that more conceptually contiguous phenomena are investigated within the present discussion of the individual violent criminal career.

Toward the end of greater specificity, we propose to focus on *interpersonal* criminal violence: Interpersonal violent crimes entail dynamic interactions among directly counterpoised individuals whose assaultive exchanges and injurious inflictions are influenced by both their personal characteristics and the social dimensions of the immediate context (or "situation," as it is increasingly being called)—for example, the demographic characteristics of the participants; the numbers of victims, offenders, and bystanders; the presence and types of weapons and controlled substances; the social relationship among the participants; and the sequence of verbal and gestural actions and reactions of the participants. Quite different precedents and precipitants and interactional dynamics distinguish interpersonal violence from kindred forms such as collective and politically inspired violence: It is important to note that interpersonal criminal violence is not generally or primarily characterized by the organizational and institutional underpinnings, ideological influences, or mass behavioral dynamics that shape and propel collective violence or the polarities of state-related violence.[4]

Statutory and conceptual considerations converge, then, to recommend delimiting the discussion of individual violent criminal careers. Consistent with these considerations, the general definition of violence presented here can be modified to yield a specific definition: As used in this chapter, criminal violence refers to the actual or threatened, knowing or intentional application of statutorily impermissible physical force by one person directly against one or more other persons outside the contexts both of formal institutional or organizational structures and of civil or otherwise collective disorders and movements for the purpose of securing some end against the will or without the consent of the other person or persons. As noted earlier, this definition encompasses the same kinds of expressive and instrumental violent conduct identified previously based on criminal statutes.

The Violent Criminal Career and the "Violent Career Criminal"

Research on individual violent criminal careers begins by distinguishing two related aspects of the aggregate violent crime problem, generally referred to as the "violent crime rate": (1) the proportion of the population that commits violent crimes and (2) the character and extent of the violent infractions by those people who are actively involved in violent crimes. This distinction for individual violent criminal careers relies on the main structural features of individual criminal careers generally, as identified in the recent comprehensive report by the National Research Council Panel on Research on Criminal Careers (hereinafter the NRC Panel), *Criminal Careers and "Career Criminals"* (Blumstein et al., 1986). As the NRC Panel underscored:

> This partitioning is important because the two components can be influenced by very different factors and call for quite different policy responses: the first—participation—is associated with efforts to prevent individuals from ever becoming involved in crime; the second—frequency, seriousness, and career length—is central to the decisions of the criminal justice system. Together, these four key dimensions characterize criminal careers:
>
> (1) *Participation*—the distinction between those who engage in crime and those who do not;
> (2) *Frequency*—the rate of criminal activity of those who are active;
> (3) *Seriousness* of offenses committed;
> (4) *Career length*—the length of time an offender is active [Blumstein et al., 1986: 1].

Partitioning the violent criminal career—the sequence of offenses by violent offenders, particularly the subset of violent incidents and related criminal justice responses to these incidents—into the foregoing components has several potential analytical and policy payoffs. Most basic and important, this approach facilitates the *systematic* study of violent criminal behavior as an integrated, dynamic structure of sequential unlawful acts that advances within a wider context of causal and correlative influences, including, among others, those of biological, psychological, and informal social and formal criminal justice origins.

The participation component specifically prompts questions about which factors and processes promote and retard entry into violent delinquent or criminal careers. Within the framework of public health and epidemiology, which has recently begun to focus in-depth on violence as a public health issue, knowledge of these factors and processes might assist in formulating "primary intervention"—that is, prevention—strategies. Factors that influence participation in violent crime may differ in type or strength from those that maintain a violent criminal career, once initiated, and that govern the frequency with which constituent offenses are committed and the types and seriousness of those offenses.

Information about the frequency, seriousness, and duration of the violent criminal career might be useful (again borrowing from the lexicon of public health and epidemiology) for developing "secondary or tertiary interventions"—that is, strategies to control and reduce violent crime over the course of an active criminal career or to promote the termination of a continuing violent criminal career through behavioral change or confinement. These interventions are likely to take different forms with respect to different types or "varieties" of violent criminal careers—for instance, those careers that are "expressive," those that are "instrumental," and those that involve a mixture of the two.

The individual violent criminal career perspective, like other criminological and criminal justice orientations, considers the promise and pitfalls of three main intervention strategies: prevention, behavioral alteration through rehabilitation or deterrence, and collective and selective incapacitation. Which option proves to be the most effective will depend, in part, on the type of violent criminal career at issue and the point or process that is targeted in the violent criminal career. Blumstein et al. (1986: 109-154) and Chaiken and Chaiken (1984) have discussed the utilities, limitations, and potential successes of these policy options within the general framework of the individual criminal career.

Analysis of the individual violent criminal career promotes greater sensitivity to additional behavioral foci that can enhance the formulation of criminal justice policy. For example, examination of short violent criminal careers can help to identify factors that curtail or halt the violent progression. Conversely, analysis of long violent criminal careers can help to identify factors that accelerate and prolong such careers and, in turn, might be used to identify individuals early in their violent criminal career sequences for purposes of selectively marshaling and allocating criminal justice and social service resources to retard and shorten the violence progression.

Information on the individual violent criminal career can be used by decision makers at successive points in the criminal justice system—for example, with respect to decisions about which suspected violent offenders the police should focus prearrest and postarrest resources on, which violent offenders a prosecutor should proceed against and with what resource allocations, which violent offenders a magistrate should detain or release prior to trial, what disposition and duration a sentencing judge should impose, and which inmates who are confined for acts of violence a parole board should select for release and under what restrictions. These decisions involve differentiating individuals according to either legal (for example, blameworthiness) or behavioral (for example, dangerousness) criteria or both. Centrally, but not exclusively, these decision makers employ predictive inference, based sometimes on personal judgment and past experience and sometimes on more formal classification rules about key components of the individual violent criminal career—for example, prior violence record and convictions, the type of immediate violent offense, recent rate of violent offending, patterns in escalation in seriousness of violence, and the amount of time an offender is expected to remain violently criminally active.

The violent criminal career has been depicted diagrammatically by the NRC Panel. Figure 2.1 reproduces the panel's diagram of the general criminal career sequence, which can be applied to the subset of violent criminal careers of interest here. According to the panel,

> The top of the figure represents a sequence of events during the criminal career of an active offender. On the line, the symbol X denotes the times at which the offender committed crimes. Symbols of crimes for which the offender was arrested are circled, and the crimes for which the arrest led to conviction are enclosed in a square. The shaded area indicates a period when the offender was incarcerated following conviction. . . .
>
> A person initiates criminal activity at some time. . . . Once the offender has begun his criminal involvement, it continues for some period of time, perhaps increasing or decreasing in frequency. Finally, the person terminates his criminal career.
>
> The minimum representation, which clearly omits many of the complexities of a real career, is represented in the lower portion of Figure

[2.1]. The offender is assumed to begin criminal activity at some "age of onset," a_O, but his official record does not reflect onset until some later time, at the point of his first arrest. Once begun, the offender continues to commit crimes at a constant rate λ during any time that he is not incarcerated. The career ends when the last crime is committed, represented at age a_T in Figure [2.1].

The representation in Figure [2.1] invokes three primary elements of information: the frequency or mean individual crime rate, λ, the age at career initiation, and the duration of the criminal career, T. Each of these three dimensions of career varies across offenders. The variation may be influenced by personal events associated with the individual or by broader forces such as sanction levels or other community characteristics. . . .

This simple representation can be extended to more richly describe a criminal career. Possibilities include a "start-up" time during which an offender's frequency increases, a decrease in frequency toward the end of a career, and sporadic spurts or intermittent recesses from criminal activity. . . . Distinctions among different offense types can also be made, permitting attention to single offenses (e.g., "robbery careers") or to patterns of switching among offense types during a career. In this context, it is important to know whether offenders are more likely to be "specialists" (who engage in only one or a small group of offenses) or "generalists" (who switch more widely among a range of offenses). Last, extensions of the basic model can address whether offending patterns typically "escalate" in the seriousness of successive events so that crimes later in the career are more serious, or whether they peak in seriousness in mid-career and then begin to decline in seriousness as a career nears its end [Blumstein et al., 1986: 21-22].

Consistent with the foregoing, an individual criminal career is considered violent and designated a "violent criminal career" if the crime sequence is punctuated by at least one violent infraction, indicated by either official records or self-report interviews, depending on the data-gathering method used. Research can focus either on the entire criminal career of the violent offender or on just the violent segment of that career.[5] "Violent career criminals" are individuals who participate in serious violent offenses with *high frequency* over an *extended period*. Researchers have referred to these individuals as "dangerous," "chronic," "persistent," or "habitual" violent offenders.

The remaining sections of this chapter will review studies on the behavioral structure and dynamics of the individual violent criminal career. Overall, there have been few studies focusing directly on this topic; and their findings have rarely been assembled for systematic presentation. Formal responses to the individual violent criminal career

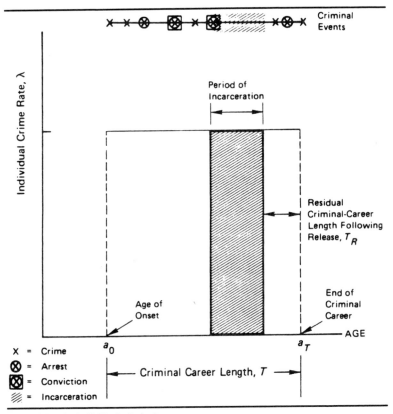

Figure 2.1. An individual criminal career.
Source: Blumstein et al. (1984: 21)

by the criminal justice system that affect several important criminal career stages, such as the risks of arrest, conviction, incarceration, and length of incarceration, are beyond the purview of this chapter. One should consult Blumstein et al. (1986) and Greenwood and Abrahams (1982) for discussions of these issues.

The studies selected for review have been drawn mainly from research that followed subjects either prospectively or retrospectively (in the latter case, through "catch-up" data collection) over time, for the purpose of documenting official or self-reported participation in delinquent and criminal behavior, including the violent subset of these involvements. The great majority of these studies have focused on American subjects, although several British and Scandinavian studies are also reported. A few studies have selected violent criminal careers and their violent offenses for separate or exclusive treatment.

For convenience of reference and to avoid burdening the forthcoming discussion with repeated descriptions of repeatedly cited studies, Table 2.1 presents a synopsis of each study reported, including information on the study site, the number of subjects, the gender and age composition of the subjects, whether the delinquency or crime data were from official records or self-reports and, when applicable, special subject selection or sampling requirements.

Dimensions of Violent Criminal Careers

Violent Criminal Career Participation

The extent of participation in violent criminal careers is measured in several related ways: the *age-specific violent initiation rate* refers to that proportion of a population that participates in a first violent offense—and, by so doing, initiates violent criminal careers—at a specified age. (See the section on "Age at Initiation of Violent Criminal Careers" for a review of the pertinent research). The *cumulative violent participation rate* is the sum of the age-specific violent initiation rates over an age interval of interest—for example, the delinquent years, the adult years, or a lifetime. The *current violent participation rate* refers to that proportion of a population that participates in at least one violent offense during a designated age interval or time period, irrespective of whether the violent offense is the initial offense or a subsequent offense in the violent criminal career.

Tables 2.2 to 2.7 present cumulative and current juvenile and adult violent participation rates. These rates are presented separately for males and females and for official and self-report data sources. Cumulative juvenile violent participation rates have been reported for several birth cohorts and other study groups. These findings are presented in Tables 2.2 and 2.3. Table 2.2 arrays violent participation rates based on police contacts for several Philadelphia birth cohorts; Table 2.3 presents findings based on self-report data on other samples. In both tables, columns indicate the type of violent infraction, and rows identify the research study, the birth cohort, or other study sample under review, whether the violent participation rate is based on the total cohort (that is, all subjects) or on only the delinquent members, and the age range under consideration.

TABLE 2.1

Summaries of Major Research on Aspects of
Individual Violent Criminal Careers

Researchers	Samples
Bachman et al. (1978)	self-reports collected from 2,213 tenth-grade boys in a national sample selected in 1966 and followed until 1974
Barnett et al. (1987)	official conviction records through age 25 of 411 boys enrolled in six schools in a working-class area of London (see Farrington, 1983)
Blumstein and Cohen (1979); Blumstein et al. (1982)	all arrests through 1975 accumulated by 5,338 adult males and females arrested in 1973 in Washington, D.C., for homicide, rape, robbery, aggravated assault, burglary, or motor vehicle theft
Blumstein and Greene (1976)	juvenile and adult arrest records of approximately 9,600 males and females who had been arrested in Pittsburgh between January 1, 1967, and December 31, 1969, and had at least two arrests
Blumstein and Moitra (1980)	all juvenile Philadelphia police contacts of the 9,945 boys born in 1945 who resided in Philadelphia from their tenth through their eighteenth birthdays (see Wolfgang et al., 1972)
Blumstein et al. (1985)	official records from four birth cohorts: (1) all juvenile police contacts of the 9,945 boys born in 1945 who resided in Philadelphia from their tenth through their eighteenth birthdays (see Wolfgang et al., 1972); (2) official conviction records through age 25 of 396 boys enrolled in six schools in a working-class area of London (see Farrington, 1983); (3) juvenile arrests through age 18 for nontraffic offenses of 356 boys born in 1942 who resided in Racine, Wisconsin, from their tenth through their eighteenth birthdays (see Shannon, 1982); and (4) all police contacts of 714 boys residing in Marion County, Oregon, who were selected in 1964 when they were high school sophomores and who were followed through age 30 (see Polk et al., 1981)
Buikhuisen and Jongman (1970)	all 21-year-old males, totaling 948 individuals, residing in the Netherlands who were convicted in 1964 or 1965 and had accumulated at least three convictions
Bursik (1980)	all juvenile police contacts of a sample of 469 male and female youths adjudicated delinquent in Cook County, Illinois, who had accumulated at least five police contacts and had reached their seventeenth birthday by the time of the study

(continued)

TABLE 2.1 Continued

Researchers	Samples
Cernkovich and Giordano (1979)	self-reports collected in 1977 from a sample of 822 male and female students enrolled in two urban high schools in a large midwestern state
Chaiken and Chaiken (1982)	self-reports and arrest records of a sample drawn from an incoming jail and prison cohort of adult males in California, Michigan, and Texas. The 810 jail inmates and 1,380 prison inmates who were selected were interviewed between October 1978 and January 1979
Clarke (1975)	all Philadelphia police contacts for incidents involving personal injury to a victim or property theft or damage of the 381 boys born in 1945 who resided in Philadelphia from their tenth through their eighteenth birthdays and had been confined at least once in a correctional facility prior to their eighteenth birthdays
Denno (1982)	all Philadelphia contacts through age 18 of a sample of 987 males and females born in Philadelphia between 1959 and 1962 who resided in the city from their tenth through eighteenth birthdays
Elliott et al. (1983); Elliott et al. (1986)	self-reports collected from a national probability sample of 1,725 males and females selected in 1976 when they were between ages 11 and 17; the subjects were interviewed annually through 1980
Facella (1983)	all juvenile Philadelphia police contacts of the 14,453 girls born in 1958 who resided in Philadelphia from their tenth through eighteenth birthdays
Farrington (1983)	self-reports and official conviction records collected for all 411 boys enrolled in six schools in a working-class area of London and followed prospectively through interviews every two or three years from 1961 to 1962, when the boys were ages 8 and 9, until their twenty-fifth birthdays.
Figueria-McDonough et al. (1981)	self-reports collected in 1980 from 1,735 tenth-grade boys and girls, approximately age 15, enrolled in six public and three parochial schools in four communities in one midwestern county
Guttridge et al. (1983)	all police contacts of 31,436 males born between January 1, 1944, and December 31, 1947, to mothers who were residents of Copenhagen, Denmark; records were tracked retrospectively until ages 27 to 30 for the three respective cohorts

(continued)

TABLE 2.1 Continued

Researchers	Samples
Hamparian et al. (1978)	police arrest records through age 18 of all 811 boys and girls arrested in Columbus, Ohio, between 1956 and 1958 for at least one violent offense
Hindelang et al. (1981)	self-reports collected from a Seattle, Washington, sample of 2,174 males and 889 females ages 15 to 18 during the 1978-79 academic year; the subjects fell into one of the following three groups: nondelinquent students, delinquents having only a police record, and delinquents having at least one court record
Høgh and Wolf (1983)	police records of a Danish cohort of all 11,540 males born in 1953 within the city municipalities of Copenhagen, Frederiksberg, and Gentofte and the adjacent counties of Copenhagen, Roskilde, and Frederiksberg; the subjects were followed through 1975-76, when they were age 23
Kratcoski and Kratcoski (1975)	self-reports collected in the mid-1970s from a sample of 104 male and 144 female female eleventh and twelfth graders, ages 16 to 18, enrolled in three public high schools
Lab (1984)	all juvenile police contacts, through age 18, of all boys and girls in three Racine, Wisconsin, cohorts born in 1942, 1949, and 1955 (comprising 1,352, 2,099, and 2,676 subjects, respectively) who had resided in Racine from their sixth through eighteenth birthdays, with absences of no more than three years (see also Shannon, 1982)
McCord (1980)	conviction records of 201 boys residing in congested urban neighborhoods in Cambridge-Somerville, Massachusetts, who were enrolled, between ages 5 and 13, in a treatment program designed to prevent delinquency; the subjects were followed through 1976 when they were in their early to mid-40s
Miller et al. (1982)	arrest records of a sample of 1,591 adult males arrested in Columbus, Ohio, between 1950 and 1976 for murder, rape, assault, or robbery
Mitchell and Rosa (1981)	criminal convictions of a sample of 642 male subjects who were between ages 5 and 15 in 1961 when they attended local schools in Buckinghamshire, England; the subjects were followed until 1976, when they were age 20 or older
Petersilia et al. (1977)	self-reports and arrest records for 49 adult male inmates of a medium-security prison in California in 1975; the subjects were serving time for a current armed robbery and had at least one prior prison term

(continued)

TABLE 2.1 Continued

Researchers	Samples
Peterson et al. (1980)	self-reports and arrest records for a sample of 624 adult male felons incarcerated in five California state prisons; the subjects were interviewed in the summer of 1976
Piper (1983)	all juvenile Philadelphia police contacts of the 27,160 boys and girls born in 1958 who resided in Philadelphia from their tenth through their eighteenth birthdays
Piper (1985)	all juvenile Philadelphia police contacts of the 13,160 boys born in 1958 who resided in Philadelphia from their tenth through their eighteenth birthdays
Polk et al. (1981)	self-reports and police contacts for a sample of 714 males residing in Marion County, Oregon, who were selected in 1964, when they were high school sophomores, and who were followed through age 30
Porterfield (1946)	self-reports collected between 1940 and 1942 from 337 male and female students enrolled in three colleges in northern Texas
Robins (1966)	juvenile and adult arrest records of (1) a sample of 524 white male and female patients enrolled between 1924 and 1929 in a St. Louis, Missouri, child guidance clinic, who were between ages 6 and 17, and (2) 100 nonclinic controls who were enrolled in St. Louis schools; the subjects were followed for approximately three years
Rojek and Erickson (1982)	juvenile arrest records of a sample of 1,619 males and females who had been processed by the Pima County, Arizona, juvenile court between their eighth and eighteenth birthdays, had at least one prior arrest, and had resided in the county for at least two years
Shannon (1982)	all juvenile police contacts and adult arrests of three male and female Racine, Wisconsin, cohorts born in 1942, 1949, and 1955 (comprising 1,352, 2,099, and 2,676 subjects, respectively) who had resided in Racine from their sixth through eighteenth birthdays, with absences of no more than three years; the cohorts were followed until ages 32, 25, and 21, respectively
Short and Nye (1958)	self-reports collected in 1955 from a sample of 2,350 males and females from three high schools in a far western state and 596 males and females from three high schools in a rural, rural-urban fringe district and from a suburban town in a midwestern state

(continued)

TABLE 2.1 Continued

Researchers	Samples
Smith and Smith (1984)	arrest records of all 767 males ages 13 to 18 who were confined in New Jersey correctional facilities between October 1977 and December 1978; arrest records were tracked between ages 8 and 18
Tittle (1980)	self-reports collected in 1972 from area probability samples of 1,993 males and females ages 15 or older in New Jersey, Iowa, and Oregon
Tracy et al. (1984)	all juvenile Philadelphia police contacts of the 13,160 boys in 1958 who resided in Philadelphia from their tenth through eighteenth birthdays
Walker et al. (1967)	two samples: (1) conviction records of 264 Glaswegian males who had accumulated at least one violent conviction—the subjects had been convicted for the first time for any crime in 1947 and had their subsequent eleven-year records tracked; (2) conviction records of 500 London males who had accumulated at least one violent conviction—the subjects had been convicted for any offense in March or April of 1957 and had their entire earlier records and their subsequent five-year records tracked
Weiner (1985)	all violent and injurious juvenile Philadelphia police contacts of the 13,160 boys born in 1958 who resided in Philadelphia from their tenth through eighteenth birthdays
Weis (1976)	self-reports collected in the early 1970s from 301 male and female eleventh graders from a middle-class community
Wikström (1985)	police records for all 15,117 males and females born in 1953 who resided in the greater Stockholm area of Sweden in 1963; records were followed through ages 25-26 (July 1979)
Wolfgang et al. (1972)	all juvenile Philadelphia police contacts of the 9,945 boys born in 1945 who resided in Philadelphia from their tenth through eighteenth birthdays
Wolfgang et al. (1987)	all juvenile Philadelphia police contacts and adult arrests through age 30 of a 10% sample of 975 males born in 1945 who resided in Philadelphia from their tenth through eighteenth birthdays

Table 2.2 reports violent delinquent and, to set a comparative baseline, overall delinquent participation rates for the Philadelphia birth cohorts. Cumulative juvenile participation for the male cohort

members for all police contacts tightly cluster between approximately 31.0% and 35.0%. The corresponding rate for the cohort females is about half the male rate. As expected, cumulative violent juvenile participation rates for both males and females are well below their corresponding juvenile participation rates based on all police contacts. For example, among the boys in the 1945 and 1958 Philadelphia birth cohorts, the cumulative participation rates for serious personal assaults (the combination of homicide, forcible rape, and aggravated assault) for the total cohort was 2.3% and 4.3%, respectively: about one-fifteenth and nearly one-eighth their overall cumulative juvenile participation rates, respectively. Among the female subjects studied by Denno (1982), the cumulative juvenile participation rate in serious personal assaults, as measured by police contacts, was 1.2%, or nearly one-twelfth the overall juvenile participation rate for all cohorts. As expected, these same patterns are preserved when only the cohort delinquents are considered: About 1 in 15 and nearly 1 in 8 delinquent boys in the 1945 and 1958 birth cohorts, and almost 1 in 12 delinquent girls in the four cohorts studied by Denno participated in a serious personal assault.

By definition, cumulative juvenile participation rates for the component serious personal assaults are lower than (or, at most, can be equal to) the global rate: For both males and females, homicide exhibits the lowest cumulative juvenile participation rate, followed in increasing order by forcible rape (for males only, given the negligible female rate) and aggravated assault (Table 2.2). Among the males in the 1945 birth cohort, attempted and completed robbery exhibits a cumulative juvenile participation rate that is lower than that observed for the composite serious personal assault group. However, this relationship is reversed in the 1958 birth cohort. Regardless of the type of violent offense, the boys in the more recent cohort registered higher cumulative juvenile participation rates than did their counterparts in the older cohort, suggesting the possibility of greater violent participation in more recent cohorts.

Cumulative violent juvenile participation of females is well below that of males, irrespective of the type of violent crime. For example, Denno (1982) found that the cumulative juvenile participation rates for females for serious personal assaults were 1.2% and 8.7%, based on all four cohorts and on only the delinquent subjects in all four cohorts, respectively, which are one-fourth and one-half the corresponding male participation rates (Table 2.2). Similarly, Facella's (1983) data indicated that the female members of the 1958 Philadelphia birth cohort registered an initial participation in each type of violent delinquency

TABLE 2.2

Cumulative Juvenile (age ≤ 17) Participation in Violent Crimes (Official Records)

	All Police Contacts %	Personal Crimes[a] %	Serious Personal Assault[b] %	Homicide %	Forcible Rape %	Aggravated Assault %	Robbery, Attempted and Completed %	Robbery Completed[c] %	Injury[d] %
U.S. Studies									
Males									
Tracy et al. (1984)									
of total cohort									
1945 cohort	34.9	g	2.3	.1	.4	1.9	1.6	g	7.5
1958 cohort	32.8	g	4.3	.4	.7	3.5	6.0	g	8.7
of delinquents									
1945 cohort	e	g	6.7	.4	1.2	5.4	4.5	g	21.5
1958 cohort	e	g	13.1	1.3	2.0	10.5	18.3	g	26.5
Denno (1982)									
of all cohorts	31.0	g	5.0	f	.4	5.0	g	6.8	g
of delinquents in all cohorts	e	g	16.6	f	1.3	14.6	g	21.9	g
Facella (1983)									
of total 1958 cohort	g	g	g	g	g	g	g	g	g
of 1958 cohort delinquents	g	g	g	g	g	g	g	g	g

Females

Tracy et al. (1984)									
of total cohort									
1945 cohort	g	g	g	g	g	g	g	g	g
1958 cohort	g	g	g	g	g	g	g	g	g
of delinquents									
1945 cohort	g	g	g	g	g	g	g	g	g
1958 cohort	g	g	g	g	g	g	g	g	g
Denno (1982)									
of all cohorts	14.0	g	1.2	f	1.0	g	g	g	g
of delinquents in all cohorts	e	g	8.7	f	7.3	g	f	g	g
Facella (1983)									
of total 1958 cohort	13.1	2.2	g	f	.7	g	g	g	1.7
of 1958 cohort delinquents	e	16.5	g	.3	.1	5.3	2.1	g	12.7

SOURCES: Denno (1982: Table 3.14); Facella (1983: Tables 2, 13-15); Tracy et al. (1984: Tables 16a-b, 35a-b). Homicide, forcible rape, and aggravated assault were calculated expressly for this chapter.

NOTE:
a. Includes homicide, forcible rape, robbery, and aggravated and other assault.
b. Includes homicide, forcible rape, and aggravated assault.
c. Designated "successful" robbery by Denno (1982).
d. Any incident in which at least one victim sustained bodily injury, ranging from minor harm, medical treatment or discharge, and hospitalization to death.
e. Not applicable.
f. Negligible: < .05%.
g. This crime category was not designated by the study or for this demographic group.

51

much less often than did their male counterparts studied by Tracy et al. (1984).

Assessing the relative magnitudes of the "actual" (or "hidden," as it is often called) and "manifest" ("observed") cumulative participation rates based on self-report and official data, respectively, for specific violent offenses for the same population is difficult because, surprisingly, cumulative participation rates based on these two sources of data have not customarily been presented in tandem, even by studies that have collected both kinds of data. Certainly, studies have repeatedly observed disparities between the proportional magnitudes of officially recorded and self-reported offenders and in the comparative numbers of offenses uncovered by these two methods (for just a few of these studies see Baker et al., 1975; Chambliss and Nagasawa, 1969; Gold, 1966; Williams and Gold, 1972); but these findings—of much higher self-reported participation and offense frequencies relative to the corresponding rates based on officially recorded data—have been, for the most part, for either global offense or global violent offense categories rather than for specified violent offenses. Despite this limitation, those studies presenting self-reported, cumulative violent juvenile participation rates lend credence to the expectation that violent participation rates are higher than would be inferred from official records.

Table 2.3 presents cumulative juvenile participation rates based on the self-report responses of total study samples. We focus first on aggravated assault to illustrate some comparative interpretative problems and corollary lines of response and resolution that arise when different samples are used to generate official-based and self-report-based estimates of juvenile participation. Cumulative juvenile male participation rates based on the total 1945 and 1958 birth cohorts studied by Tracy et al. (1984) are 1.9% and 3.5%, respectively: The corresponding cumulative participation rate for all cohorts studied by Denno (1982) is 5.0% (Table 2.2). In comparison, the self-reported cumulative male participation rates in aggravated assault appearing in Table 2.3 range from a low of 8.7% to a high of 11.7%. Based on this evidence, we may conclude that at least twice as many boys reported at least one juvenile involvement in an aggravated assault in comparison to official data.

In reaching ths conclusion, we should first bear in mind that the socially and economically disadvantaged and minorities are over-represented in Denno's (1982) birth cohorts. (Data were collected from a sample comprising individuals receiving free continuing medical care at

TABLE 2.3
Cumulative Juvenile Participation in Violent Crimes, Based on Total Sample (Self-Reports)

	Aggravated Assault %	Assault %	Weapon Use %	Rape %	Attempted Rape %	Sexual Assault %	Robbery %	Intentional Injury %
U.S. Studies								
Males								
Cernkovich and Giordano (1979) through ages 16-18	11.6[a]	c	c	c	c	c	5.0	c
Elliott et al. (1983) ages 11-17	8.7	c	c	c	c	c	3.9[b]	c
Figueira-McDonough et al. (1981) through age 15	11.6	c	6.0	c	c	c	c	c
Hindelang et al. (1981) through ages 16-18	11.7[d]	c	c	.6[e]	c	4.8	c	c
Kratcoski and Kratcoski (1975) through ages 16-18	c	c	c	c	c	c	5.2[f]	c
Porterfield (1946)	c	29.0[g]	c	c	c	c	17.0[h]	c
precollege	c	3.0[i]	c	c	5.5	c	c	c
college	c	1.0[j]	c	c	3.0	c	c	c
Short and Nye (1958) through high school								
midwest school	c	15.7[g]	c	c	c	c	6.3[k]	22.7[l]
western school	c	13.9[g]	c	c	c	c	c	15.8[i]
U.S. Studies								
Females								
Cernkovich and Giordano (1979) through ages 16-18	6.6[a]	c	c	c	c	c	.9	c

(continued)

TABLE 2.3 Continued

	Aggravated Assault %	Assault %	Weapon Use %	Rape %	Attempted Rape %	Sexual Assault %	Robbery %	Intentional Injury %
Elliott et al. (1983) ages 11-17	3.1	c	c	c	c	c	2.0[b]	c
Figueira-McDonough et al. (1981) through age 15	3.9	c	1.8	c	c	3.3	c	c
Hindelang et al. (1981) through ages 16-18	4.6[d]	c	c	.7[e]	c	c	1.9[f]	c
Kratcoski and Kratcoski (1975) through ages 16-18	c	8.0[d]	c	c	c	c	5.0[h]	c
Porterfield (1946) precollege	c	1.0[i]	c	0.0	c	c	c	c
college	c	c	c	c	c	c	c	c
Short and Nye (1958) through high school midwest school	c	5.7[k]	c	c	c	c	1.3[k]	10.4[j]
western school	c	3.1[g]	c	c	c	c	c	9.3[j]

SOURCES: Cernkovich and Giordano (1979: Table 1); Elliott et al. (1983: Tables 3.1, 3.5); Figueira-McDonough et al. (1981: Table 2.1); Hindelang et al. (1981: derived from Table 2.2 and Appendix B); Kratcoski and Kratcoski (1975: Table 1); Porterfield (1946: Table 3); Short and Nye (1958: Tables 1-2).

NOTE:
a. "Use weapon to attack someone."
b. Includes strong-arm methods to obtain something of value from persons other than teachers and students.
c. This crime category was not designated by this study or for this demographic group.
d. "Beat someone up so badly they probably needed a doctor."
e. "Forced another person to have sex relations with you when they did not want to."
f. "Used physical force . . . to get money from another person."
g. "'Beat up' on kids who hadn't done anything to you."
h. "Used force to get money from another person."

a major urban hospital in compensation for study participation. Participation in the study was generally more attractive to the disadvantaged and minorities.) To the extent that the socially and economically disadvantaged and minorities have a higher cumulative participation rate than the socially and economically advantaged and majorities (in the main, research seems to support this position), one can infer that the 5.1 juvenile participation figure cited by Denno is inflated upward relative to what might have obtained had more representative cohorts been assembled. Should this cumulative participation rate be adjusted downward to offset this potential source of upward bias by, let us say, just 1.0%, which is probably a conservative reduction, the participation rates of the cohort boys in aggravated assault are uniformly at least half their corresponding self-reported estimates.

This disparity in cumulative juvenile participation is probably still an underestimate because the self-report items used to measure aggravated assault are more restrictive than the analogous official measures. For example, the cumulative participation rates reported by Cernkovich and Giordano (1979) and Hindelang et al. (1981) were based on the following items, respectively: "use weapon to attack someone" and "beat someone up so badly they probably needed a doctor." These items are more restrictive than the spectrum of behaviors statutorily qualifying as aggravated assaults. Were the self-report items more equivalent to the statutory-based definitions, the self-report cumulative juvenile participation rates would almost certainly have been higher.

A similar argument can be made with respect to comparisons between official and self-reported cumulative juvenile participation in robbery. Cumulative "robbery" (attempted and completed) participation rates based on police contacts of the total group of 1945 and 1958 Philadelphia birth cohort boys were 1.6% and 6.0%, respectively (Table 2.2). The corresponding self-reported, male cumulative participation rates for "robbery" are bracketed by a low of 3.9% (Elliott et al., 1983) and a high of 17.0% (Kratcoski and Kratcoski, 1975; Table 2.3). Except for the cumulative participation rate reported by Kratcoski and Kratcoski at the upper end of the range, the other rates cluster around 5.0%. These robbery participation rates are based mainly on items focusing on strong-arm or physical-force tactics. Had armed robbery been included, the participation rates in the neighborhood of 5.0% would surely have surged higher, resulting in what we would expect to be higher robbery participation rates based on self-reports. These cumulative juvenile participation rates would likely have exceeded, for example, the 6.0% police-contact figure cited by Tracy et al. (1984).

Self-reported cumulative participation in violent or injurious offenses by females are uniformly below the male rates, which parallels the pattern based on official records. Also, self-reported, cumulative juvenile participation, as expected, appears greatest in the broad "assault" and "intentional injury" categories, ranging between about 15.0% and 29.0% (Table 2.3).

Table 2.4 presents current juvenile participation rates. Annualized participation rates appear in the top portion of the table; nonannualized rates in the bottom portion. When an annualized participation rate is cited for an age interval, the rate applies to each age in that interval. Nonannualized current participation rates refer to the proportion of the sample that participated in at least one of the indicated violent offenses during that age interval and is interpreted simply as the current participation rate.

Bachman, O'Malley, and Johnston reported on national data later used by the NRC Panel (Blumstein et al., 1986) to estimate annualized current assault and robbery participation rates for two contiguous age intervals, 13 to 15 and 16 to 17. Results indicate an incline in male participation in both assault and robbery across these age intervals (from 9.0% to 12.7% and from 2.0% to 2.7%, respectively), although the incline was clearly marginal for robbery (Table 2.4). Annualized current participation in assault in each age interval was about four times greater than the corresponding annualized current robbery participation.

Weis (1976) reported age-trend results for current juvenile assault participation that are apparently at odds with those just discussed. Annualized current participation declined by half from 2.6% to 1.3% from ages 12 to 14 to ages 15 to 17 (Table 2.4). Moreover, these rates are much lower than those reported by Bachman et al. (1978). However, the youths studied by Weis resided in a middle-class neighborhood, which may account in part for their lower current assaultive participation. (As noted, some research has observed that socially and economically advantaged youths exhibit more modest levels of delinquent involvement.)

Elliott et al. (1986) presented national self-report data on age-specific male participation in "serious violence," a composite category comprising involvements in three or more aggravated assaults, sexual assaults, gang fights, or strong-arm robberies of students or others, except teachers. Participation rates hovered between 7.0% and 8.0% from ages 12 to 17 (Table 2.4). Because qualification for participation in "serious violence" was contingent on at least three involvements in any

TABLE 2.4
Current Juvenile Participation in Violent Crimes,
Based on Total Sample

	Robbery %	Felony Assault[a] %	Males Assault %	Serious Violence[c] %	Fighting %
Annualized[b] Self-Reports					
U.S. Studies					
Bachman et al. (1978)[d]					
13-15	2.0	e	9.0	e	e
16-17	2.7	e	12.7	e	e
Elliott et al. (1983)					
12-16	e	e	e	e	e
Elliott et al. (1986)					
12	e	e	e	6.8	e
13	e	e	e	7.3	e
14	e	e	e	7.0	e
15	e	e	e	7.5	e
16	e	e	e	7.8	e
17	e	e	e	7.6	e
Weis (1976)[d]					
12-14	e	e	2.6	e	e
15-17	e	e	1.3	e	e
Nonannualized Self-Reports					
Foreign Studies					
Farrington (1983)					
10-14	e	e	e	e	23.8
15-18	e	e	e	e	62.3
Nonannualized Official Records					
Foreign Studies					
Farrington (1983)					
10-13	e	e	.5[g]	e	e
14-16	e	e	.5[g]	e	e

(continued)

combination of the foregoing violent offenses, the participation rates would certainly incline if the more customary selection rule of at least one involvement had been stipulated. What the magnitudes of participation rates of the component crimes would look like is a matter of conjecture. However, results in Table 2.3 and by Bachman et al. (1978)

TABLE 2.4 continued

	Robbery %	Females Felony Assault[a] %	Assault %	Serious Violence[c] %	Fighting %
Annualized[b] Self-Reports					
U.S. Studies					
Bachman et al. (1978)[d]					
13-15	e	e	e	e	e
16-17	e	e	e	e	e
Elliott et al. (1983)					
12-16	e	e	e	e	e
Elliott et al. (1986)					
12	e	e	e	2.9	e
13	e	e	e	2.8	e
14	e	e	e	2.8	e
15	e	e	e	2.5	e
16	e	e	e	2.2	e
17	e	e	e	1.5	e
Weis (1976)[d]					
12-14	e	e	.9	e	e
15-17	e	e	.2	e	e
Nonannualized Self-Reports					
Foreign Studies					
Farrington (1983)					
10-14	e	e	e	e	e
15-18	e	e	e	e	e
Nonannualized Official Records					
Foreign Studies					
Farrington (1983)					
10-13	e	e	e	e	e
14-16	e	e	e	e	e

(continued)

in Table 2.4 suggest the general pattern that current juvenile participation in aggravated assault would outpace that of participation in robbery.

Current participation in "assault" (involving injury), based on conviction, and in "fighting," based on self-reports, has been calculated by Farrington (1983) for a London cohort. Substantial disparity appears between the two measures: Approximately half a percent

TABLE 2.4 continued

	Robbery %	Felony Assault[a] %	Total Assault %	Serious Violence[c] %	Fighting %
Annualized[b] Self-Reports					
U.S. Studies:					
Bachman et al. (1978)[d]					
13-15	e	e	e	e	e
16-17	e	e	e	e	e
Elliott et al. (1983)					
12-16	4.0[f]	13.5[f]	e	e	e
Elliott et al. (1986)					
12	e	e	e	4.8	e
13	e	e	e	5.0	e
14	e	e	e	5.0	e
15	e	e	e	5.1	e
16	e	e	e	5.1	e
17	e	e	e	4.8	e
Weis (1976)[d]					
12-14	e	e	e	e	e
15-17	e	e	e	e	e
Nonannualized Self-Reports					
Foreign Studies					
Farrington (1983)					
10-14	e	e	e	e	e
15-18	e	e	e	e	e
Nonannualized Official Records					
Foreign Studies					
Farrington (1983)					
10-13	e	e	e	e	e
14-16	e	e	e	e	e

SOURCES: Bachman et al. (1978, cited in Visher and Roth, 1986: Table A-4); Elliott et al. (1983: Figure 2.12; see note f below); Elliott et al. (1986: Table 1); Farrington (1983: Tables C4-C5); Weis (1976; cited in Visher and Roth, 1986: Table A-4).

NOTE: a. Includes aggravated assault, sexual assault, and gang fights.

b. Participation rates were, in some cases, annualized, thereby representing the participation rate that was applicable to each age in the age interval. (The same participation rate applies, then, to each age in the interval.)

c. Comprises involvement, at the designated age, in three or more aggravated assaults, sexual assaults, gang fights, or strong-arm robberies of students or others, except teachers.

d. As cited by Visher and Roth (1986: Table A-4).

e. This crime category was not designated by this study or for this demographic group.

f. This annual participation rate is approximate because it was visually extrapolated from Elliott et al. (1983: Figure 2.12).

g. Involves injury to a victim.

participated in an assault during both age intervals 10 to 13 and 14 to 16, whereas almost 24.0% and more than 62.0% were involved in fighting during the age intervals 10 to 14 and 15 to 18, respectively (Table 2.4). Restrictively defining assault to involve injury to a victim and, furthermore, using conviction status for qualification as an assaulter, requiring as it does deep penetration into the juvenile justice system, are surely responsible in part for one end of this disparity—the very low assault participation rate. In addition, that the general category of "fighting" was used as the self-report item rather than the more restrictive category of physical assault involving injury explains in part the other end of the disparity—the high current participation rates.

Consistent with earlier observed patterns, females exhibited much lower self-reported current juvenile participation in violent incidents— at least half the male rates in all instances (Table 2.4).

Current violent participation rates of males for the young adult years, through age 24, are presented in Table 2.5. Examining the arrests of the 1945 and 1958 Philadelphia birth cohort subjects, the magnitude ordering of the offense-specific participation rates, based on the total cohorts, mirrors almost uniformly the ordering of the corresponding cumulative juvenile participation rates (Table 2.2): Participation is least in homicide, followed, in increasing order, by forcible rape, aggravated assault, and robbery. Furthermore, the adult rates are almost invariantly greater than their respective juvenile counterparts. (Only robbery participation based on the total 1958 birth cohort violates this pattern.) Except for forcible rape, the 1958 birth cohort registers the higher current participation rates, although only marginally so with respect to homicide.

Adult assault conviction data analyzed by Farrington (1983) yielded patterns consistent with the aggravated assault arrest data for the two Philadelphia birth cohorts, despite the quite different definitions of these two offenses. For example, current assault participation rates for ages 17 to 20 and 21 to 24 were 3.7% and 2.5%, respectively, not far distant from the current aggravated assault participation rates of 2.7% and 4.4% from ages 18 to 24 exhibited by the 1945 and 1958 Philadelphia birth cohorts, respectively (Table 2.5). Also consistent with the Philadelphia data, the current assault participation rates calculated by Farrington are greater in the young adult periods than in the juvenile periods: the juvenile rates are stable at .5% for ages 10 to 13 and 14 to 16 but then increase more than sevenfold for ages 17 to 20 and fivefold for ages 21 to 24 (3.7% and 2.5%, respectively; Tables 2.4 and 2.5).

TABLE 2.5
Current Adult (age ≥ 18) Participation in Violent Crimes: Males

	Homicide %	Forcible Rape %	Aggravated Assault %	Robbery %	Assault[a] %	Fighting %
Official Records						
U.S. Studies						
Weiner (ages 18-24)[b]						
of total cohort						
1945 cohort	.6	1.5	2.7	3.3	d	d
1958 cohort	.7	1.0	4.4	4.7	d	d
of offenders						
1945 cohort	2.3	5.8	10.0	12.3	d	d
1958 cohort	3.4	4.9	21.1	22.3	d	d

(continued)

TABLE 2.5 continued

	Homicide %	Forcible Rape %	Aggravated Assault %	Robbery %	Assault[a] %	Fighting %
Foreign Studies						
Farrington (1983) of total cohort						
17-20	d	d	d	d	3.7	d
21-24	d	d	d	d	2.5	d
Self-Reports						
Foreign Studies						
Farrington (1983) of total cohort						
19-21	d	d	d	d	d	39.5
22-24	d	d	d	d	d	30.3

SOURCE: Farrington (1983: Tables C4-C5).

NOTE: a. Involves injury to a victim.

b. Computed expressly for this chapter using the 1945 Philadelphia birth cohort follow-up sample and the entire 1958 Philadelphia birth cohort.

c. Negligible: < .05%.

d. This crime category was not designated for this study or for this demographic group.

The juvenile-to-adult age pattern in current fighting participation generated by Farrington's (1983) survey data differs from the age pattern generated by the corresponding assault convictions. Rather than observing the lowest fighting participation rates during the juvenile years followed by an increase during the adult years, as exhibited by the assault conviction data (Tables 2.4 and 2.5), the self-reports indicate a substantial downward spiral from a high of 62.3% exhibited from ages 15 to 18 (Table 2.4) to 39.5% and 30.3% from ages 19 to 21 and 22 to 24, respectively (Table 2.5). Unsurprisingly, these fighting rates are well above their respective conviction rates.

Several studies have presented self-report data on age-specific violent participation rates for the young adult years or have had these data converted by other researchers into annualized participation rates. Also, although it is rarely calculated, some annualized violent participation rates have been generated for the older adult years. The annualized rates appear in the upper portion of Table 2.6. Bachman et al. (1978) have reported age-specific figures for males for assault and robbery. Consistent with the finding for the juvenile ages (Table 2.4), adult assault participation rates substantially exceed their respective robbery rates, ranging between nearly 3 and 11 times those rates. At its zenith, at age 19, fully one in five male subjects participated in assault, followed by age 18 (slightly more than one in six) and age 23 (one in nine). Robbery followed a parallel age-specific adult pattern.

Current and age-specific participation rates exhibit a pattern of initial incline over the juvenile years followed by a decline after either the more advanced juvenile or the young adult years for both official and self-report data. For instance, Farrington (1983) reported assault conviction participation rates for males that increase from .5% of the total cohort at each adjacent age interval 10 to 13 and 14 to 16 to 3.7% at the young adult ages 17 to 20, but that then decline to 2.5% at ages 21 to 24 (Tables 2.4 and 2.5). A similar pattern for males is traced by the self-reported assault data gathered by Bachman et al. (1978): Current participation inclines from a low of 9.0% at ages 13 to 15 to a high of 20.0% in young adulthood at age 19, followed by a decline to 11.0% at age 23 (Tables 2.4 and 2.6). The robbery data reported by these researchers follow this same path (Tables 2.4 and 2.6). The composite, self-reported category of "serious violence" created by Elliott et al. (1986) exhibits, also for males, a parallel course of initial age-specific upturn, albeit modest, over the delinquent years, followed by an adult downturn (Tables 2.4 and 2.6). However, unlike the results reported by

TABLE 2.6
Current Juvenile and Adult or Only Adult Participation
in Violent Crimes (Self-Reports; U.S. Studies)

	Robbery %	Aggravated Assault %	Assault %	Serious Violence[d] %	Fighting %
			Males		
U.S. Studies					
Annualized[a]					
Bachman et al. (1978)[b]					
18	4.0	c	16.0	c	c
19	7.0	c	20.0	c	c
23	1.0	c	11.0	c	c
Elliott et al. (1986)					
18	c	c	c	6.9	c
19	c	c	c	5.3	c
20	c	c	c	4.1	c
21	c	c	c	3.1	c
Tittle (1980)[b]					
15-24	c	c	c	c	c
25-44	c	c	c	c	c
45-64	c	c	c	c	c
65+	c	c	c	c	c
Nonannualized					
Elliott et al. (1983)					
15-21	1.8[e]	6.4	c	c	c

(continued)

Bachman et al. (1978), the upward trajectory occurs exclusively during the juvenile years, followed by a continuous decline over each of the young adult years. (Unfortunately, the shape of the age-specific participation trajectory cannot be ascertained at this time for each component serious violent offense.) In contrast to the male pattern, serious violence among the females, which was uniformly below the male rate, declined from the early juvenile years through young adulthood.

Annualized assault participation rates for males and females combined were presented by Tittle (1980) for a much wider age band than were presented by the other studies: Consistent with the pattern established by the other research, the rates decline across successive age intervals, from 5.2% (ages 15 to 24) to 2.0% (ages 25 to 44) to .8% (ages

TABLE 2.6 continued

	Robbery %	Females Aggravated Assault %	Assault %	Serious Violence[d] %	Fighting %
U.S. Studies					
Annualized[a]					
Bachman et al. (1978)[b]					
18	c	c	c	c	c
19	c	c	c	c	c
23	c	c	c	c	c
Elliott et al. (1986)					
18	c	c	c	1.0	c
19	c	c	c	.5	c
20	c	c	c	.5	c
21	c	c	c	.3	c
Tittle (1980)[b]					
15-24	c	c	c	c	c
25-44	c	c	c	c	c
45-64	c	c	c	c	c
65+	c	c	c	c	c
Nonannualized					
Elliott et al. (1983)					
15-21	.1[e]	2.5	c	c	c

(continued)

45 to 64) and, finally, to .2% (ages 65 and older, Table 2.6). The peaking in the participation rate during the later juvenile years or during young adulthood observed in the other studies might have been reproduced had the youngest age interval been split more finely into juvenile and young adult segments.

Several studies, presented in Table 2.7, have calculated cumulative participation rates based on official records bridging the juvenile and adult years, some spanning as far as the mid-40s. Cumulative male participation rates through young adulthood, between ages 22 and 30, have been calculated for several samples based on all offenses. These results indicate a broad range, from a low of 31.0% to a high of 47.0%. All three studies at the lower end of the range are foreign, conducted in either Denmark or Sweden, whereas the highest figure is recorded by the 1945 Philadelphia birth cohort, suggesting the possibility of cross-national divergence in overall criminal participation.

TABLE 2.6 continued

	Robbery %	Aggravated Assault %	Total Assault %	Serious Violence[d] %	Fighting %
U.S. Studies					
Annualized[a]					
Bachman et al. (1978)[b]					
18	c	c	c	c	c
19	c	c	c	c	c
23	c	c	c	c	c
Elliott et al. (1986)					
18	c	c	c	4.2	c
19	c	c	c	3.1	c
20	c	c	c	2.3	c
21	c	c	c	1.6	c
Tittle (1980)[b]					
15-24	c	c	5.2	c	c
25-44	c	c	2.0	c	c
45-64	c	c	.8	c	c
65+	c	c	.2	c	c
Nonannualized					
Elliott et al. (1983)					
15-21	1.0[e]	4.6	c	c	c

SOURCES: Bachman et al. (1978, cited in Visher and Roth, 1986: Table A-4); Elliott et al. (1983: Tables 3.1, 3.5); Elliott et al. (1986: Table 1); Farrington (1983: Table C5); Tittle (1980, cited in Visher and Roth, 1986: Table A-4).

NOTE: a. Participation rates were, in some cases, annualized, thereby representing the participation rate that was applicable to each age in the age interval. (The same participation rate applies, then, to each age in the interval.)
b. As cited by Visher and Roth (1986: Table A-4).
c. This crime category was not designated by this study or for this demographic group.
d. Comprises involvement, at the designated age, in three or more aggravated assaults, sexual assaults, gang fights, or strong-arm robberies of students or others, except teachers.
e. Strong-arm methods to obtain something of value from persons other than teachers or students.

Participation rates based on the entire sample for convictions for serious personal crimes range from nearly 17.0% (McCord, 1980) to approximately 2.0% (Guttridge et al., 1983; Høgh and Wolf, 1983; Table 2.7). The highest figure is certainly in part a function of the much longer cumulative period, falling about 15 years above the upper age bound of the next longest period. However, it is unlikely that this alone explains the entire disparity: Definitional dissimilarities and cross-national differences in violence participation are also probably at play. For example, Høgh and Wolf (1983) defined serious personal crimes less inclusively than did McCord (1980; as the tabular notes indicate), which accounts for some additional portion of the discrepancy. However, Guttridge et al. (1983) reported a low participation rate in serious personal crimes despite a broad definition. Unless civilian reporting and police recording practices are extremely different in Copenhagen and Philadelphia, actual differences in violence participation are likely to explain some portion of the rate disparity.

Only the study by Guttridge et al. (1983) presents cumulative cohort participation rates for specific violent offenses (Table 2.7). Participation rates were uniformly low and concordant in their respective rankings to results reported earlier for only the juvenile and only the adult years: Both homicide and rape were negligible, followed, in increasing but very modest order of magnitude, by aggravated assault (.1%) and robbery (.5%). Robins (1966) presented cumulative participation rates for selected violent crimes for two sets of cases: (1) youngsters referred to a child guidance clinic for behavioral, psychological, and learning problems, and (2) matched nonreferred controls (Table 2.7). Clinical cases exhibited rates that were higher than both those of the controls and those of the cohorts studied by Guttridge et al. (1983). The combination of the longer time period and the criterion of clinical referral resulting from behavioral or other problems partly account for the invariantly higher cumulative participation rates observed by Robins. Except for Robins, who reported much lower cumulative female participation rates than rates for males in homicide, rape, and robbery, no other results have been reported for females.

Overall then, cumulative and current juvenile and adult participation rates in serious violent offenses are modest for males and more so for females. Regardless of the type of serious violent offense, participation rates based on the whole sample do not exceed 6% when based on official records, except in the extreme case of subjects characterized by behavioral problems and other personal deficits who are observed over extended time periods. Self-reported violent participation is, as expected, higher than the corresponding participation rates based on official tallies, although the precise magnitudes of these differences are still uncertain. Violent participation appears to increase over the juvenile and young adult periods and then, upon peaking, to decrease.

TABLE 2.7

Cumulative Juvenile and Adult Participation in Violent Crimes, Based on Total Sample (Official Records)

	All Offenses %	Serious Personal or Serious Property %	Serious Personal %	Homicide %	Rape %	Robbery %	Aggravated Assault %	Assault %
Males								
U.S. Studies								
McCord (1980)								
≤ mid–40s	a	35.3[b]	16.9[c]	a	a	a	a	a
Robins (1966)								
≤ 43								
clinic cases	61.0	a	a	.7	1.5	11.0	a	a
controls	22.0	a	a	d	d	d	a	a

Wolfgang et al. (1987)								
≤ 30	47.1	a	a	a	a	a	a	a
Foreign Studies								
Guttridge et al. (1983)								
≤ 25-30								
of all cohorts	33.0	a	2.5[g]	d	d	.5	.1	2.1
of all cohort offenders	e	a	6.7[g]	d	.2	1.3	.3	5.4
Høgh and Wolf (1983)								
≤ 22								
of cohort	34.5	a	2.0[f]	a	a	a	a	a
of offenders	e	a	6.0[f]	a	a	a	a	a
Wikström (1985)								
≤ 26								
of cohort	31.0	a	a	a	a	a	a	a
of offenders	e	a	a	a	a	a	a	a

(continued)

TABLE 2.7 continued

	All Offenses %	Serious Personal or Serious Property %	Serious Personal %	Homicide %	Rape %	Robbery %	Aggravated Assault %	Assault %
Females								
U.S. Studies								
McCord (1980)								
≤ mid-40s		a	a	a	a	a	a	a
Robins (1966)								
≤ 43								
clinic cases	30.0	a	a	d	d	d	a	a
controls	d	a	a	d	d	d	a	a
Wolfgang et al. (1987)								
≤ 30	a	a	a	a	a	a	a	a

Foreign Studies

Guttridge et al. (1983)								
≤ 25-30								
of all cohorts	a	a	a	a	a	a	a	a
of all cohort offenders	a	a	a	a	a	a	a	a
Høgh and Wolf (1983)								
≤ 22								
of cohort	a	a	a	a	a	a	a	a
of offenders	a	a	a	a	a	a	a	a
Wikström (1985)								
≤ 26								
of cohort	a	a	a	a	a	a	a	a
of offenders	a	a	a	a	a	a	a	a

SOURCES: Guttridge et al. (1983, derived from Table 11-4 and population figures: 213); Høgh and Wolf (1983: 252); McCord (1980: 124); Robins (1966: Table 3.2); Wikström (1985: 117, 119); Wolfgang et al. (1987: Table 3.1).

NOTE:
a. This crime category was not designated for this study or for this demographic group.
b. Serious personal offenses include murder, attempted murder, assault, attempted or completed rape, and kidnapping. Serious property offenses include larceny, arson, motor vehicle theft, and breaking and entering.
c. See note b for serious personal offenses.
d. Negligible: < .05%.
e. Not applicable.
f. Includes homicide, minor and major assault (excludes rape and robbery).
g. Includes murder, rape, violence against authority, bodily injury, violence—threat concerning violence, and robbery with violence or threat of violence.
h. Includes murder, manslaughter, assault, robbery, molestation, and threats.

71

The Individual Violent Crime Rate

The *individual violent crime rate* is the average frequency, or velocity, of violent offending by those individuals who are *actively* participating in violent crime, and is commonly calculated on the basis of a year's time at-risk in the community.[6] To calculate the rate, the number of violent criminal acts in a year is divided by the number of offenders responsible for those acts. This calculation provides specificity to one aspect of the popular notion of an individual's active violent criminal involvement: the numerical intensity with which violent criminal activity is pursued while the individual is at liberty to engage in this activity. Those offenders who inhabit the uppermost percentiles of violent intensity and who engage in enduring violent activity represent the "violent career criminals" discussed earlier.

The individual violent crime rate is distinguished from the more commonly known (although not always in this terminology) *aggregate violent incidence rate,* which is the average frequency of violent offending by both those individuals who are actively participating in violent crime *and* those who are not actively participating. This rate is popularly termed the aggregate violent crime rate or just the violent crime rate. The distinction is important because, for example, the central policy goal of designing targeted, or selective, incapacitation strategies depends on information about the individual violent crime rate, not the aggregate violent incidence rate.

Few official or self-report studies have looked at the frequency with which active violent offenders commit their violent offenses. Much of the work along these lines, particularly the earlier studies from the mid-1970s, has yielded limited insight into the rates at which violent crimes are committed. Most limiting in this research has been the inclusive crime categories used for analysis. For example, Clarke (1975) and Greene (1977) estimated from official records that offenders accumulate very few *UCR* index crimes. Clarke calculated nearly one per year per incarcerated delinquent active in index offenses (1975: 531-532); Greene calculated between 1.4 and 2.8 for persons arrested. If these figures are accurate, by implication, the *UCR* violent index crime rate must be less, but by how much is unclear. Furthermore, the computations of these rates were not fully documented by the authors, raising concerns about possible estimation biases (see, for example, Cohen, 1986). Similar problems appear in the study by Shinnar and Shinnar (1974: 597) who, in using data on offenders arrested on federal charges in 1969 who had multiple career arrests, concluded that the average involvement in "safety crimes" (the combination of homicide, robbery, felonious assault, and burglary) was between 6 and 14 crimes yearly. Estimates for the specific offense types were not presented.

Some of the most systematic estimates of individual violent crime rates have been derived from official records by Blumstein and Cohen (1979) and more recently by Cohen (1983). These findings, reported in Table 2.8, used arrest histories compiled for two groups: (1) all adults apprehended in Washington, D.C., for a *UCR* index offense (except larceny) in 1973 and (2) all adults apprehended in the Detroit Standard Metropolitan Statistical Area (SMSA) for a *UCR* index offense (except larceny) between 1974 and 1977. These two sets of *arrest* histories were converted into criminal *offense* histories through a series of sampling restrictions applied to those arrested (to create cohorts for the analysis of crime sequences) and substantively derived adjustments involving arrest probabilities. These histories yielded estimates, after adjusting for confinement time, of individual violent arrest and offense rates for the young adult years, after age 21, of active offenders. As Table 2.8 indicates, individual violent arrest rates were, on the average, modest: Robbers and aggravated assaulters in Washington, D.C., were *arrested* .23 and .19 times per year for each crime, respectively, indicating that, on the average, adults accumulated police records for robbery and aggravated assault once every four years and once every five years, respectively. The corresponding annual robbery and aggravated assault *offense* rates were substantially higher, nearly 15 times (3.41) and slightly more than nine times (1.72), respectively. The Detroit SMSA data produced concordant offense estimates of 4.7 for robbery and 2.9 for aggravated assault.

Cohen reported the adjusted average annual individual robbery and violent arrest (the combination of homicide, forcible rape, and aggravated assault) rates for the juvenile years of the 1945 Philadelphia birth cohort to be .23 and .13, respectively (Table 2.8). The juvenile violent arrest rate and, more so, the juvenile robbery arrest rate fall very close to the adult robbery and adult aggravated assault rates calculated by Blumstein and Cohen (1979; also in Table 2.8. That aggravated assault dominates the juvenile violent crime group makes its comparison with adult aggravated assault reasonable.).

The NRC Panel (Blumstein et al., 1986) also estimated the age-specific juvenile police contact rates for robbery and violent crimes for the 1945 Philadelphia birth cohort boys. These figures, subjected to

TABLE 2.8
Individual Violent Arrest and Crime Rate (Official Records)

					Age						Males and Females (Annualized)
						Males					
	10	11	12	13	14	15	16	17	18-20	21-24	>21
U.S. Studies											
Blumstein and Cohen (1979): Washington, DC											
robbers											
arrests	a	a	a	a	a	a	a	a	a	a	.23
offenses[b]	a	a	a	a	a	a	a	a	a	a	3.41
aggravated assaulters											
arrests	a	a	a	a	a	a	a	a	a	a	.19
offenses[b]	a	a	a	a	a	a	a	a	a	a	1.72
Cohen (1986): Detroit SMSA											
robbery											
arrests	a	a	a	a	a	a	a	a	a	a	4.70
aggravated assault											
arrests	a	a	a	a	a	a	a	a	a	a	2.90
Cohen (1986): 1945 Philadelphia birth cohort											
robbery[h]	⌐				.23			⌐	a	a	a
violent crime[c, h]	⌐				.13			⌐	a	a	a
Weiner (1987) homicide											
1945 cohort[h]	a	a	a	a	a	a	a	a		.14	a

74

1958 cohort[h]	a	a	a	a	a	a	a	[.27]	a
forcible rape[h]									
1945 cohort[h]	a	a	a	a	a	a	a	[.15]	a
1958 cohort[h]	a	a	a	a	a	a	a	[.26]	a
robbery									
1945 cohort[h]	a	a	a	a	a	a	a	[.20]	a
1958 cohort[h]	a	a	a	a	a	a	a	[.36]	a
aggravated assault									
1945 cohort[h]	a	a	a	a	a	a	a	[.18]	a
1958 cohort[h]	a	a	a	a	a	a	a	[.26]	a
Wolfgang et al. (1972)[c, d]									
robbery	a	a	.12	.12	.39	.36	.16	[a]	a
violent crime[e]	a	f	.08	.08	.12	.19	.08	[a]	a
Foreign Studies									
Farrington (1983)									
assault[g, h]	[.3]		[.3]		.3		.3		a

SOURCES: Blumstein and Cohen (1979: Tables 17, 19); Cohen (1986: Tables B-22, B-26); Farrington (1983: Table C4); Weiner (1987, computed expressly for this chapter using the 1945 Philadelphia birth cohort follow-up sample and the entire 1958 Philadelphia birth cohort); Wolfgang et al. (1972, cited in Cohen, 1986: Tables B-26, B-28).

NOTE:

a. This age was not applicable to this study.

b. "Offenses" refer to estimates of the total crimes committed annually of the indicated type. For the robbers and aggravated assaulters, the individual offense rate is the average number of robberies by robbers and aggravated assaults by aggravated assaulters, respectively. Arrests are, of course, those offenses resulting in official processing by law enforcement agencies.

c. Cited in Cohen (1986: Table B-26, column 3, and Table B-28).

d. The age-specific individual arrest rates refer to the average number of robberies per year and violent crimes per year for robbers and violent offenders, respectively, who were actively engaged in those offenses during that year.

e. Violent crimes include murder, rape, and aggravated assault.

f. Too few cases were available for the estimates to be statistically reliable.

g. Involves victim injury.

h. Rates are annualized to apply to each age in the age interval designated by the brackets.

technical adjustments outlined by Cohen (1986: 337-353), are presented in Table 2.8. Both robbery and violent crime incline over the younger juvenile years, peaking at ages 15 and 16, respectively, and then receding. (These rates, which never exceed .39, are somewhat low, however, because they are based on computations that failed to exclude confinement time, although this bias is mitigated somewhat by the fact that the computations did exclude that portion of time at the designated age until the qualifying arrest occurred.) The robbery rates are invariantly higher than the composite violence category, more than three times at age 15.

Weiner calculated the average annual individual police contact rates for each of the *UCR* violent index crimes for the young adult years, extending from ages 18 to 24, for the males in the 1945 and 1958 Philadelphia birth cohorts (Table 2.8). Estimates were calculated by dividing the number of violent crimes during the at-risk period by the number of offenders accumulating these crimes, producing raw frequency rates. (To annualize the rate, this result was divided by 7.) Because confinement-time data are presently unavailable, no adjustment for this source of bias could be made, which, as noted, depresses the resulting estimate. Nor were the rates adjusted for the violent arrest that qualified the offender for inclusion in the age interval, producing an upward bias. (See Cohen, 1986: 337-353 for a discussion of these two sources of bias. It is important to note, with respect to the latter bias, as the raw individual violent crime rate increases, the qualification bias decreases.) Despite these biases, the unadjusted frequency rates are still quite modest, perhaps owing to, among other possibilities, moderate actual behavioral involvement and a strongly countering confinement influence.

The raw frequency rates registered by the 1945 birth cohort are consistently lower than the corresponding rates of the more contemporary 1958 cohort, ranging between about one-half and two-thirds of those rates (Table 2.8). Homicide and forcible rape exhibited the lowest and nearly equal rates, followed in increasing order by aggravated assault and robbery.

It is important to note that, for purposes of establishing research concordance and thereby generality, the adult robbery and aggravated assault arrest rates computed by Weiner for the two cohorts (robbery: 1945 cohort, .20; 1958 cohort, .36; aggravated assault: 1945 cohort, .18; 1958 cohort, .26) fall within the neighborhoods of the respective adult arrest rates calculated by Blumstein and Cohen (1979; robbery .23;

aggravated assault .19) and the overall adjusted juvenile rates of the 1945 cohort calculated by Cohen (1986; robbery .23; violent crime .13). These results show consistently modest arrest frequencies. Furthermore, because of the close proximity in magnitude across studies and age ranges, there is little evidence as yet that overall individual violent arrest rates rise with increasing age. Whether self-report data or dis-aggregations of the arrest data (for example, by gender and race) yield similar results remains to be answered.

Farrington (1983) reported a stable annual average individual assault conviction (involved victim injury) rate per active convicted assaulter of .3 across four sequential juvenile and young adult age intervals (Table 2.8). Unlike the estimates by Blumstein and Cohen (1979), these rates were adjusted neither for the conviction that qualified the individual to be included in the age interval (by deleting it), which functions to inflate the rate, nor for time served in jail or prison (by excluding it), which produced an opposite effect. What the magnitudes might be of these countervailing influences is uncertain. However, the net effect of these influences (and, certainly, other unspecified and therefore unaccounted-for influences) produces rates that nevertheless still exceed the ag-gravated assault rate derived by Blumstein and Cohen, perhaps because the Farrington computations pertain exclusively to younger ages that may be the more intensely active assault years. Despite the disparity, the rates are not far in excess of those prepared by Blumstein and Cohen, adding to the accumulating research convergence just pointed out.

Several studies have computed individual violent offense rates based on self-report data. In addition, the NRC Panel (Blumstein et al., 1986) estimated annual individual violent offense rates from several other well-known self-report studies. These two sets of findings are presented in Table 2.9. In examining the national youth survey data collected by Elliott et al. (1983), the panel found that the annual individual robbery offense rate and the annual felony assault (the combination of aggravated assault, sexual assault, and involvements in gang fights) offense rate for males and females combined were 7.5 and 3.9, respectively. The overall juvenile rate for males was greater than for females, more than two and a half times so for robbery and more than one and two-thirds so for felony assault. Age-specific offending frequencies for males and females combined from ages 13 to 19 remained relatively stable for both violent offense types, hovering between about 5.5 and 6.5 for robbery and, at a lower range, between 3.5 and 5.5 for felony assault.

TABLE 2.9
Individual Violent Offense Rates of Selected Violent Offenses (Self-Reports)

		Juveniles							Gender		
		Age									
	13	14	15	16	17	18	Juvenile	Male	Female	Total
U.S. Studies											
Chaiken and Chaiken (1982) [average annual rate; median annual rate]											
robbery	c	c	c	c	c	c	c	c	c	c
business establishment	c	c	c	c	c	c	c	c	c	c
personal	c	c	c	c	c	c	c	c	c	c
assault	c	c	c	c	c	c	c	c	c	c
Elliott et al. (1983)[a] [average annual rate]											
robbery	6.3	5.4	15.3[d]	6.7	6.5	5.6	c	8.4	3.3	7.5
felony assault[b]	4.0	3.4	5.5	3.3	3.4	3.7	c	4.4	2.6	3.9
Elliott et al. (1986) [average annual rate] serious violent[e]	[	8.4	][g]	[7.6]		c	c	9.3	5.3	8.3
Petersilia et al. (1977) [average annual rate] violent offenders[f]	c	c	c	c	c	c	1.2	c	c	.1

	Age						Adults		Gender		Total
	19	20	21	22	23	24	Young Adult	Adult	Male	Female	
Peterson et al. (1980) [average annual rate; median rate]											
robbery, armed	c	c	c	c	c	c		c	c	c	c
aggravated assault (beating)	c	c	c	c	c	c		c	c	c	c
assault with a deadly weapon (shot/cut)	c	c	c	c	c	c		c	c	c	c
attempted murder	c	c	c	c	c	c		c	c	c	c
rape	c	c	c	c	c	c		c	c	c	c
Foreign Studies											
Farrington (1983) [average annual rate] fighting	c	c		4.4				c	c	c	c
U.S. Studies											
Chaiken and Chaiken (1982) [average annual rate; median annual rate] robbery	c	c	c	c	c	c	c	c	41-61[h] [5.0][i]	c	c

(continued)

TABLE 2.9 continued

	Age						Adults		Gender		
	19	20	21	22	23	24	Young Adult	Adult	Male	Female	Total
business establishment	c	c	c	c	c	c	c	c	21-36 [4.6]	c	c
personal	c	c	c	c	c	c	c	c	40-56 [4.3]	c	c
assault	c	c	c	c	c	c	c	c	5.2-5.8 [2.4]	c	c
Elliott et al. (1983)[a] [average annual rate]											
robbery	5.2	c	c	c	c	c	c	c	c	c	c
felony assault[b]	6.6	c	c	c	c	c	c	c	c	c	c
Elliott et al. (1986) [average annual rate] serious violent[c]	c	c	c	c	c	c	c	c	c	c	c
Petersilia et al. (1977) [average annual rate] violent offenders[f]	c	c	c	c	c	c	1.9	2.4	c	c	c
Peterson et al. (1980) [average annual rate; median rate] robbery, armed	c	c	c	c	c	c	c	c	5.2 [1.5]	c	.2

aggravated assault (beating)	c	c	c	c	c	c	c	c	c	c	2.8 [.8]	c	c
assault with a deadly weapon (shot/cut)	c	c	c	c	c	c	c	c	c	c	2.0 [.9]	c	c
attempted murder	c	c	c	c	c	c	c	c	c	c	1.6 [.9]	c	c
rape	c	c	c	c	c	c	c	c	c	c	2.9 [.7]	c	c

Foreign Studies

Farrington (1983)
[average annual rate]

fighting	[1.8]		[1.4]			c					c		c

SOURCES: Chaiken and Chaiken (1982: Tables 2.C.a, A.4-7); Elliott et al. (1983, cited in Cohen, 1986: Table B-31); Elliott et al. (1986: Table 3); Farrington (1983: Table C5); Petersilia et al. (1977, derived from Table 13); Peterson et al. (1980: Table 10a).

NOTE: a. Cited in Cohen (1986: Table B-31).

b. Includes aggravated assault, sexual assault, and gang fights.

c. The rate was not calculated for this study.

d. This rate is due to an extreme value. When that value is excluded, the rate is reduced to 5.8.

e. Serious violent offending involves three or more aggravated assaults, sexual assaults, gang fights, or strong-arm robberies of students or others, except teachers. The minimum rate for these offenders is, by definition, three serious violent offenses.

f. Includes rape, aggravated assault, robbery, and purse snatching. The computation includes offenders not active in that crime.

g. The rate enclosed within the brackets refers to each age within the age interval.

h. The two figures represent the low and high estimates of the mean number of offenses per year of street time among all offenders. See Chaiken and Chaiken (1982: Appendix A).

i. Median annual rate.

Farrington's (1983) self-report data exhibited a decline in the annual average individual fighting rate of the males in the London cohort over three age intervals stretching from adolescence to young adulthood: from 4.4 per year per subject aged 15 to 18 to 1.8 per subject aged 19 to 21, and finally, to 1.4 per subject aged 22 to 24 (Table 2.9). (Apparently, no adjustments were made for either confinement time or the age-qualifying incident.) The fighting rate of 4.4 over ages 15 to 18 dovetails with the average juvenile, male felony assault rate reported by the NRC Panel (Blumstein et al., 1986) for the Elliott et al. (1983) data, which is also 4.4.

Elliott et al. (1986: Table 3) calculated individual offending rates for the "serious violent" youngsters (involvement in at least three of the designated violent offenses; see the tabular footnote) in order to focus on the most repetitively gravely violent youths in the study. Overall, these offenders accumulated, on the average, 8.3 such offenses per year (Table 2.9). Neither race nor age differences were observed. However, males outstripped females in this respect (9.3 per year versus 5.3 per year; Table 2.9). Disaggregating serious violence into its component crime types and, furthermore, calculating individual offense rates without imposing an intensity floor of three offenses, as was done to define serious violence, will provide significant future insights into violent criminal careers.

In the first of several related studies by the Rand Corporation, Petersilia et al. (1977) interviewed a small sample of 49 incarcerated adult California inmates (apparently males, although this was not stated explicitly) whose current offense was armed robbery and who had been imprisoned previously at least once (the "habitual felons"). Violent offense (rape, assault, robbery, and purse snatching) rates for these inmates were not stable, shifting over both individuals and age. (Rates were calculated based on all inmates rather than only on those active in the designated offense type.) The subjects reported increasing involvements in violent crime across the juvenile, young adult, and adult years of 1.2 (per year of street time), 1.9 and 2.4 respectively, for an overall violent crime rate of 1.8 across the three periods (Table 2.9). This upward slope, however, might have reflected the inmate status of the sample: Their current incarceration might have followed on the heels of a recent flurry of criminal activity, which produced the upward pattern. Whether the observed incline represents more general career trajectories is presently uncertain.

Petersilia et al. (1977: Table 16) identified two contrasting offender groups based in part on the inmates' differential personal and professional commitments to their criminal careers: "intensives" and "intermittents." The former group reported an average annual violent offense rate over the interview period more than five times higher than that of the latter group (4.5 per year versus .8 per year). The velocity of this group's violent crime production increased steadily from 1.5 to 5.2 to 7.4 over the course of their juvenile, young adult, and adult periods, respectively. (The caveat just noted about inmate status also applies here.) The intermittent offenders logged rates of .9, .5, and 1.2, respectively.

Subsequent studies by the Rand Corporation, based on interviews with prison and jail inmates, resulted in the confirmation and extension of the earlier findings. Analyzing interview data for male California inmates, Peterson et al. (1981) computed individual annual offense rates for armed robbery (median 1.5; mean 5.2), aggravated assault (median .8; mean 2.8), attempted murder (median .9; mean 1.6), and rape (median .7; mean 2.9; Table 2.9). Low- and high-rate offender groups were distinguished for each type of violent crime considered, using as the dividing line the median offense rate of offenders involved in that offense type. High-rate armed robbers participated in armed robbery almost 13 times more frequently than their low-rate counterparts (9.42 versus .73; Peterson et al., 1981: Table 10b). Similarly striking differences were found for aggravated assaults involving beatings (4.91 versus .59), assaults with a deadly weapon involving shooting or cutting (3.56 versus .64), attempting murder (2.52 versus .61), and rape (3.02 versus .57). This polarity conforms to the one revealed by Petersilia et al. (1977).

When considering inmate studies like the Rand surveys, it is important to note that confined offenders are not likely to reflect accurately the population of active offenders who are on the street at any particular time because, in general, inmates typically have committed more serious offenses at a more rapid rate than the wider offender population from which they are drawn. Using their inmate interviews, Peterson et al. (1981) estimated individual crime rates for selected violent offenses for a *hypothetical* group of "street-offenders"—that is, a group of individuals who experience some risk of imprisonment for an offense. The annual violent offense rates estimated for these hypothetical offenders were .16 for homicide, .97 for rape, 1.97 for armed robbery, and 2.38 for assault (Peterson et al., 1981: Table 11). As expected, the rates for rapists and armed robbers notch considerably downward after the adjustment, relative to the corresponding mean rates presented in Table 2.9.

Another Rand Corporation study, conducted by Chaiken and Chaiken (1982), examined self-report data obtained from interviews with adult male prison and jail inmates in California, Michigan, and Texas. The majority of these inmates reported very low annual violent offense rates: Their median annual rates of business robbery, personal robbery, and assault were 4.6, 4.3, and 2.4, respectively (Table 2.9). Unsurprisingly, the lower and upper bounds of the corresponding mean rates are substantially higher in each instance. (As pointed out, both the mean and median centrality estimates are somewhat inflated owing to a sampling bias introduced by the subjects' inmate status.) Comparisons of annual robbery and assault rates between jail inmates and prison inmates and across inmates in the three states yielded no consistent patterns (Table 2.C.4).

One noteworthy segment isolated by Chaiken and Chaiken (1982) comprised very high rate offenders: the "violent predators." This group, distinguished from the other criminal varieties, engaged in robberies, assaults, and drug offenses at an exceedingly rapid pace. Their median rate and mean rate of business robbery were 7.0 and 21.0, respectively, and of personal robbery, 6.0 and 40.0, respectively (Chaiken and Chaiken, 1982: Tables A.18-19). These robbery rates were higher than those observed for "robber-assaulters," "robber [drug] dealers," and "robbers ('income')." Also, their rates of burglary, theft, and other property crimes usually exceeded the rates of the other offender types who also committed these crimes (Chaiken and Chaiken, 1982: Tables A.17-28). Consistent with the earlier, related Rand research, a high-rate serious offender group had been isolated.

Table 2.10 reproduces analyses of individual violent offense rates that were prepared by the NRC Panel (Blumstein et al., 1986) using self-report data obtained from several studies of drug addicts. One study, by Sechrest (1979, cited in Cohen, 1986: Table B-32), examined the offense behavior of addicts enrolled in drug treatment programs in Santa Clara, California, and Brooklyn, New York. These addicts were interviewed over a four-year span—two years before and two years after entry into the programs. The individual annual robbery offending rates were 8.4 in Santa Clara and 6.1 in Brooklyn; assault rates were much lower, about 3.0 in both locations. Robbery and assault arrest rates, on the other hand, exhibited no differences in either city. Johnson et al. (1983, cited

TABLE 2.10
Individual Violent Offense Rates of Selected Types of Violent Offenses:
Drug Abusers

Johnson et al. (1983)[a] heroin users active in that offense	irregular use (0-2 days per week)	regular use (3-5 days per week)	daily use (6-7 days per week)	Total
robbery[b]	8.9	16.7	26.5	20.4

| Sechrest (1979)[a] drug addicts in a treatment program active in that offense | arrests | | offenses | |
	Santa Clara	Brooklyn	Santa Clara	Brooklyn
robbery	.8	.4	8.4	6.1
assault	.7	.4	3.3	3.1

Inciardi (1979)[a] heroin users active in that offense	Males	Females
robbery[b]	29.7	28.7
assault[b]	3.3	2.7[c]

NOTE: a. Cited in Cohen (1986: Tables B-32-B-34).
        b. Refers to offenses, not arrests.
        c. Based on too few cases to be reliable.

in Cohen, 1986: Table B-33) collected offense data from weekly interviews with active heroin addicts in New York City over a 57-day period. The annual robbery offense rates inclined steadily across groups reporting more frequent drug use, each time by a factor of more than one and a half: from 8.9 for "irregular" users to 16.7 for "regular" users and, finally, to 26.5 for "daily" users, underscoring the potent influence of drug use on instrumental violent crime. The Inciardi (1979, cited in Cohen, 1986: Table B-34) data on active heroin users in Miami yielded overall annual robbery offending rates for both males (29.7) and females (28.7) that were consistent with the total robbery rate of the subjects studied by Johnson et al. (20.4). Inciardi's study also yielded annual assault offense rates of about 3.0 for both males and females, which are in line with the assault rates derived from Sechrest's study.

Many of the above studies have shown that the distribution of individual violent offense rates across offenders is highly skewed: The great majority of offenders commit violent offenses at a low ambient annual rate, while a few offenders commit these offenses at a very high rate. Indicative of this pattern are median annual rates that are much lower than their corresponding mean rates. Peterson et al.'s (1981) interview study found, for example, that the median annual armed robbery rate of the California inmate sample was 1.5, compared with a mean rate of 5.2 (Table 2.9). Similar disparities between these two centrality measures appeared for aggravated assault (beating and shot/cut), attempted murder, and rape. This repeated observation resulted in the distinction between "high-rate" and "low-rate" subgroups. Petersilia et al. (1977) and Chaiken and Chaiken (1982) unearthed similar skews.

That a small group of violent offenders propel through their careers at a rapid pace is an important finding. Should this pace be sustained over a substantial time period, identification of this group of violent career criminals at an early juncture in their career progression can enable the allocation of scarce justice system resources in a way that can have an optimum payoff in crime control. Focused incapacitation policies depend on identifying precisely this group in order to avert, in a cost-effective way, the greatest number of serious violent crimes. Rehabilitation and special deterrence strategies will also be maximally effective to the extent that these high-rate offenders are identified.

Overall, the relatively few studies that have focused on individual violent arrest or offense rates indicate modest annual violent arrest rates and, as expected, higher corresponding annual violent offense rates. Individual violent offense rates commonly exhibit a pronounced skew: The great majority of individuals engage in violent offenses at low annual rates; few individuals engage in these activities at high rates. Age-specific violent juvenile arrest rates appear to rise and then decline over the adolescent range. In contrast, age-specific violent offense rates exhibit greater stability. Overall violent juvenile arrest rates and overall violent adult arrest rates do not appear to be markedly different. However, findings suggest that overall individual violent offense rates may decline across the juvenile and adult periods, placing these findings at some odds with estimates issuing from official records. Age-specific official and self-report data for the full age range will be needed to resolve this inconsistency. Magnitude estimates across studies of various individual violent arrest and offense rates appear to be convergent, adding credibility to their joint observations. Drug addiction seems to be an important facilitator of instrumental violent activity.

The Violent Criminal Career Sequence

Specialization. A main focus of violent criminal career research involves the extent to which violent offenders repeat—or "specialize" in—the same violent offense type as their careers unfold. (The contrasting pattern is one of generalization, or diversification.) Two types of specialization can be distinguished: (1) *strict violent specialization,* which is involvement in only one violent offense type (for example, participation in only robberies, in only rapes, and so forth), and (2) *violent offense clustering,* which comprises the dual tendencies of (a) a greater chance of involvement in those offenses comprising a group of related violent offenses (for example, participation in "expressive" violence) and (b) a lesser chance of involvement in offenses not comprising the designated violent offense group (for example, participation in "instrumental" violence or in property crimes). Studies have examined, for example, whether specialization is restricted to certain types of violent offenses and whether it becomes more accentuated as offenders age and offenses accumulate. However, few studies have concentrated on the overall mixture of the criminal involvements of just violent offenders or, more specifically, on the mix of just their violent offenses.

In general, the studies reviewed next combine related types of offenses to create a global category of "violent offenses" or "personal injury crimes." As a result of this strategy, strict violence specialization generally has not been investigated except with respect to robbery: Specialization in a violent offense cluster has been examined more routinely. Because self-report surveys engender memory-recall and distortion problems that make it difficult to map accurately the sequence of career offenses, all specialization studies to date have relied on official records of police contacts, arrests, or convictions.

The most widely used procedure to study specialization in violent offenses involves the analysis of offense "transition matrices" that describe the progression from an array of offense types at one point in the criminal career sequence (for example, the first offense) to the next point in that sequence (for example, the second offense).[7] Two statistical techniques, both involving contingency table methods, have been employed to examine the violent offense transition process: (1) analysis of violent offense transition probabilities and (2) contingency table analysis of "adjusted standardized residuals" (ASR) that focuses on differences between expected and observed tabular frequencies at each transition level (see Cohen, 1986, for a review of these techniques). These methods permit the exploration of several issues relating to specialization in violent criminal careers: (1) whether the probability of movement from one type of violent offense to another is stable ("stationary") across transitions, (2) whether study subgroups differ in their violent transition dynamics, (3) whether violent offense specialization or escalation exists, and (4) related issues (for example, the Markov or "memoryless" property of transition matrices).

Cluster specialization was examined among all the boys in the 1945 Philadelphia birth cohort (Wolfgang et al., 1972), as was a comparative analysis of specialization in this cohort and in the companion 1958 Philadelphia birth cohort (Tracy et al., 1984). Police contacts were classified according to their behavioral characteristics—whether they involved just physical injury to a victim, just property theft or just property damage, some combination of these three elements, or none of them. With respect to the comparative cohort analysis, the summary transition matrices of the entire offense sequence of offenders indicated a modest degree of specialization, including the injury-to-injury progression across successive incidents (Tracy et al., 1984: Tables 58a-58b). The degree of specialization remained fairly stable over increasingly higher transitions in the offense chain, indicating stability in transition dynamics. The probability at any point in the transition string of committing a contiguous pair of injury offenses was .09 and .11 in the 1945 and 1958 cohorts, respectively.

In addition to the transition probability approach, Tracy et al. (1984) examined cluster specialization in the two birth cohorts using the ASR method. When all delinquent boys were included in the analysis regardless of the number of police contacts they had accumulated, specialization in offenses resulting in injury to a victim was found in both cohorts, although this pattern was more pronounced in the more recent cohort (pp. 251-259). The tendency to specialize did not increase with additional criminal career involvements, indicating a stable offense transition progression. Further analyses were restricted to two groups of chronic delinquents—those who had accumulated five or more police contacts and, among this group, those who had accumulated nine or more such contacts. The patterns observed for the entire group of delinquents were repeated for these two chronic segments: Specialization in injury offenses appeared in both cohorts, although more strongly in the more recent cohort (pp. 259-280). The tendency to repeat injury offenses was stable across advancing offense transitions.

In looking at specialization patterns based on police contacts for the juvenile (below age 18) and adult (ages 18 to 30) criminal careers of the 1945 birth cohort follow-up sample using the transition probability approach, Wolfgang et al. (1987) found no marked general tendency toward specialization either in the juvenile or adult periods separately or in the combined age range (pp. 50, 53-55). However, they observed limited specialization in injury offenses that was exhibited more strongly in the adult period.

Piper's analyses of the transition probabilities of just those 1958 Philadelphia birth cohort boys who had registered at least one police contact for a *UCR* violent index offense failed to uncover evidence of cluster specialization in offenses in which one or more victims has sustained a physical injury (Piper, 1983: Table 6.8). This finding applied to both white and nonwhite youngsters. A similar finding emerged when the police contacts of these same youths were classified alternatively in terms of their statutory definitions: Transition probabilities failed to show specialization in personal injury offenses, regardless of the cohort boys' race (Piper, 1983: Table 6.16). Modest evidence of specialization in robbery offenses appeared (Piper, 1983: Table 6.16).

Bursik (1980), Rojek and Erickson (1982), and Smith and Smith (1984) investigated the issue of delinquent specialization in offense clusters across successive incidents for three diverse groups of youngsters: those who were adjudicated delinquent, those who were processed by the juvenile court, and those who were placed in secure facilities, respectively. Bursik (1980) observed some evidence of specialization after examining the delinquency transition ASRs of 500 male and female youths (gender composition was inferred from the text discussion) who had been adjudicated delinquent and who had sustained at least five police contacts and court appearances in Cook County (Chicago), Illinois. Youths involved in personal injury, personal property (for example, robbery), impersonal property (for example, burglary), and "other" offenses tended to repeat these offenses (Bursik, 1980: Table 2). (Personal injury specialization was observed only among nonwhites.) Specialization did not become more pronounced as criminal careers unfolded (Cohen, 1986: 385 n. 25). When defined as involvement in personal injury or personal property offenses in at least half of an offender's career, very little specialization was evident: Less than 2.0% of the youths specialized in either of these serious violent offense types (Bursik, 1980: Table 5).

Rojek and Erickson (1982) reviewed the delinquent careers of male and female youths processed by the juvenile court in Pima County,

Arizona. Arrests for personal and property crimes, runaway and other status offenses, and miscellaneous "other" crimes were included for analysis. Little evidence of delinquent specialization was found using transition matrix probabilities (p. 14). When the ASR approach was used, no specialization in personal crimes appeared, although some specialization was observed in property offenses and runaway violations (Rojek and Erickson, 1982: Table 3).

Smith and Smith (1984) analyzed the arrest histories of male youngsters who had been confined in state delinquency facilities in New Jersey between 1977 and 1978. Career transitions were examined for personal injury offenses (homicide, rape, and assault and battery), robbery, property and damage offenses, and nonindex offenses. Based on the transition probabilities for these five offense groups, the authors concluded that some limited specialization existed but that diversity in offending was the more usual fare (pp. 138-140). The transition probabilities further indicated that offenses fell into two clusters relating to offense gravity—a robbery/injury dyad and a nonindex/property/damage triad (p. 140).

Smith and Smith (1984) also used an alternative procedure, involving the first arrest, to examine specialization. Looking at the offense type of the first arrest, the mean number of subsequent arrests for each offense type was observed to be highest for that first type (Smith and Smith, 1984: 141, Table 2). Also, the offense type of the first arrest was more likely than any other type to be repeated at least one more time in the criminal career (Smith and Smith, 1984: 143, Table 3). Robbery offenders provided the greatest support for the specialization thesis: Those offenders whose first offenses were robberies were more likely than other offenders to repeat a robbery or an injury offense, to commit on the average more subsequent robberies, and to be incarcerated for another robbery or injury offense (p. 155).

Lab (1985) examined the first three police contact transitions through age 18 for the male and female youngsters in three Racine, Wisconsin, cohorts born in 1942, 1949, and 1955. Employing transition probabilities to identify specialization in personal offenses across adjacent police contacts, he found little evidence to support such specialization (Lab, 1985: Tables 1-3); diversification was the more usual pattern.

Blumstein and Greene (1976) analyzed Pittsburgh arrest data for the years 1967 to 1969 for juveniles and adults who had at least two arrests in their careers. Gender and, more prominently, age were related to the formation of offense clusters: As subjects aged, there was a greater tendency for clustering to occur, especially after age 25, and for these clusters to differ from those observed for juveniles (pp. 38-40). Robbery and property offenses exhibited strict specialization and cluster specialization, respectively, although neither to an extreme degree. Personal violent crimes failed to exhibit a discernible cluster pattern.

Analyses of ASRs performed by the NRC Panel, using previously published data for the three juvenile samples reviewed separately here (the 1945 Philadelphia birth cohort; Cook County, Chicago; and Pima County, Arizona) and for the three adult samples (the Detroit SMSA; the southern Michigan counties; and Washington, D.C.), indicated important differences in specialization patterns between juveniles and adults (Cohen, 1986: Table B-48). The juvenile subjects exhibited sporadic and weak specialization in personal injury offenses across successive incidents. The adult subjects exhibited a consistent and strong pattern of accumulating at successive arrests personal injury (murder, rape, and aggravated assault) and personal property (robbery) offenses.

Further analyses performed by the NRC Panel of adults who had been arrested (the Detroit SMSA; the southern Michigan counties; and Washington, D.C.) and of juveniles confined in secure institutions in New Jersey (Smith and Smith, 1984) indicated the presence of clusters comprising violent offenses (murder, rape, aggravated assault, and weapons violations) and property offenses (burglary, larceny, auto theft, and fraud; Cohen, 1986: 395-397, Tables B-49-B-50). Clustering was similarly observed for the youngsters processed by the juvenile court in Pima County, Arizona, but mainly between traditional common law crimes and status offenses and secondarily between violent and property offenses.

Based on the association between the presence of a police record of violence and of selected other offense types, Wikström (1985) concluded that the males and females in the 1953 Stockholm birth cohort showed a weak tendency to specialize in violent activity and a limited tendency to cluster their violent infractions with property-damage offenses (pp. 126-127). Focusing on the proportion of all violent offenses in the careers of those violent offenders who had accumulated three or more offenses of all types, Wikström reported that only 7.0% of the offenders exhibited careers in which 50.0% or more of their offenses were violent (Wikström, 1985: Table 51).

The three Rand Corporation self-report surveys of habitual felons and jail and prison inmates reported some clustering of offenses amid considerable diversification (Chaiken and Chaiken, 1982; Petersilia et al., 1977; Peterson et al., 1981). For example, the criminal careers of habitual felons were marked by impressive offense versatility: Over the span of their careers, the overwhelming majority (98.0%) reported committing two or more offense types; and nearly three-quarters, four or more offense types (Petersilia et al., 1977: Table 6). In the survey of California inmates over their entire criminal careers, more than four in five inmates reported involvements in two or more crime types, and one in two reported involvements in at least four crime types (Peterson et al., 1981: Table 17). As the inmates aged, however, the range of different types of criminal involvements constricted (Peterson et al., 1981: Table 28). Analysis of the inmates' criminal involvements indicated two offense dimensions: the "violent offense" factor and the "property offense" factor (Peterson et al., 1981: Table 18). The former represented the tendency of armed robbery, aggravated assault, weapons use, threats with a weapon, and attempts to kill to appear together as part of a career cluster.

When defined narrowly as involvement in just a single crime type, Chaiken and Chaiken (1982) also found little evidence of specialization, especially among the high-rate offenders. However, they identified several predominant varieties of offenders (Chaiken and Chaiken, 1982: Tables 2.B.2-2.B.3). Of these, the "violent predators" were most noteworthy, for they typically engaged in the serious offenses of robbery, assault, and drug dealing and, moreover, as mentioned earlier, did so at higher rates than those other offender groups that were also involved in these offenses (Chaiken and Chaiken, 1982: Table III.1).

Elliott et al. (1986) found that the seriously violent (three or more designated violent offenses within a year's time) male and female youngsters in the National Youth Survey reported involvements in a wide range of infractions. For example, in 1976 the youths averaged per year, among their other offenses, 8.3 serious violent incidents, 65.2 minor assaults, 51.0 public disorders, 6.5 felony thefts, and 49.7 drug sales (Elliott et al., 1986: Table 5). Diversification appeared to be the rule.

One study examined specialization by considering whether selected patterns in violent offending exceeded a purely random distribution. Buikhuisen and Jongman (1970) reviewed the conviction records of all male 21-year-olds convicted in the Netherlands in 1964 and 1965 who had accumulated until that time at least three convictions. Those offenders who began their criminal careers with a personal aggressive (excluding sex offenses) crime tended subsequently to commit more of these same crimes than would be expected by chance (Buikhuisen and Jongman, 1970: Table 4). The researchers also found that there were more aggressive offenders with multiple involvements exclusively in personal aggressive offenses than would be expected by chance (Buikhuisen and Jongman, 1970: Table 6).

Guttridge et al. (1983) examined whether the men in their three Copenhagen cohorts accumulated, through ages 27 to 30, more recorded police contacts for violent offenses than would be expected by chance given the total number of offenses in their official record. Results indicated that the number of offenders with more than one violent offense in their criminal careers was greater than expected at all ranks of total career offenses (Guttridge et al., 1983: Table 11-3), pointing to some violence specialization. This finding appeared across the combined juvenile to adult age range and for juveniles separately.

In general, the various studies of violence specialization indicate some violence focus amid extensive diversification. What specialization exists is limited mainly to a violence cluster (personal injury offenses) or robbery. Some research has shown that mixtures of violent and property crimes occur, manifesting themselves as distinct criminal varieties. Specialization appears to increase with age, emerging most clearly in adulthood.

Escalation. There is evidence of some violence specialization embedded within considerable diversification. But what of the closely related question of escalation: Do offenders progress from nonviolent offenses to violent offenses as their criminal careers advance? Or, viewed more restrictively, is there a tendency to commit progressively graver violent offenses as violent offending continues? Research on this question is sparse.

Violence escalation can be understood both restrictedly and generally. Its restricted form focuses on whether violent offenders commit progressively more serious violent offenses within a specific offense type—for instance, within robbery, graduating from nonassaultive robbery to nonlethal assaultive robbery and, finally, to lethal robbery. This pattern represents *intraoffense* escalation. The more general form, which includes the restricted form as a special case, focuses on whether violent offenders graduate from less serious to more serious violent offenses across the range of violent offenses or, most generally, from less serious to more serious offenses across the range of all possible offenses—for instance, from petty larceny to grand larceny to nonassaultive robbery to nonlethal assaultive robbery and, finally, to lethal robbery. This pattern represents *interoffense* escalation. Both formulations of violent career escalation will be examined.

Hamparian et al. (1978) examined the delinquent records of males and females with at least one notation for a violent offense to compare the risks of progressing from an initial violent offense to a more serious violent offense at each of the first three violent-to-violent offense transitions. Seriousness was calibrated in terms of the statutory sentencing severity assigned to the offense. Violent offenses included murder, manslaughter, rape and other sex offenses, robbery, and simple and aggravated assault. No discernible general escalation appeared: Advancements to the less serious violent offenses were as likely as advancements to the more serious ones (Hamparian et al., 1978: Table 5-6).

Using an offense seriousness scale derived from personal judgments of the quantitative gravity of various behavioral components of an offense, Tracy et al. (1984) computed average seriousness scores for five offense types separately at successive offenses for all of the 1945 and 1958 Philadelphia birth cohort boys: Offenses examined involved just injury to a victim, just property theft, just property damage, some combination of these three elements ("combination" offenses), and none of the three elements ("nonindex" offenses). Patterns in intraoffense type escalation diverged across the two cohorts. In the 1945 cohort, only injury offenses showed an incline across successive offenses, although the authors recommended a cautious interpretation of this finding owing to the strong influence exerted by the extreme seriousness scores of the last two offenses (Tracy et al., 1984: Table 52a). In the 1958 cohort, in contrast, injury offenses alone failed to show an upward pattern; rather, seriousness fluctuated irregularly (Tracy et al., 1984: Tables 52a-52b).

The NRC Panel reexamined the 1945 Philadelphia birth cohort data with respect to escalation, adopting as its criterion switching from less serious to more serious offense types as the criminal career extended. The panel observed general interoffense escalation for the cohort boys, as reflected in the greater probability of switching from both nonindex and combination offenses to personal injury offenses at the more advanced offenses (Cohen, 1986: 402).

The follow-up sample of the 1945 Philadelphia birth cohort was also examined for specific escalation, using the seriousness scaling protocol and offense types outlined earlier. The average seriousness scores for adult injury offenses were more than two and a half times those of the juvenile injury offenses (Wolfgang et al., 1987: Table 3.8). Furthermore, the average seriousness scores of successive offenses across the juvenile and adult years combined displayed increases for each offense type, particularly for the injury offenses (Wolfgang et al., 1987: Figure 3.2).

Piper's (1983) analyses of escalation, also using the seriousness scale described previously, showed that among those youths in the 1958 Philadelphia birth cohort who were involved in at least one *UCR* violent index offense, little or just modest supporting evidence of violent escalation was observed using several escalation measures: The average seriousness of violent delinquencies across violent delinquents at successive offenses failed to increase continuously or systematically (Piper, 1983: Table 6.21); the average difference in seriousness between successive pairs of violent offenses showed a general, but not invariant, pattern of increase (Piper, 1983: Table 6.22); however, when the total number of violent offenses in a youngster's career was held constant, neither the average seriousness of violent offenses at successive offenses nor the average difference in seriousness between successive pairs of violent offenses showed a systematic pattern in increasing seriousness (Piper, 1983: Tables 6.23-6.24); the average seriousness of violent offenses, with respect to their sequential positions in the overall delinquent career, failed to exhibit a clear upward pattern (Piper, 1983: Table 6.25); the average seriousness of violent offenses showed a very modest rising pattern according to the age (10 and older) at which the violent offense occurred (Piper, 1983: Table 6.26); however, there was no clear increase in the average seriousness as violent offenses were accumulated when holding constant the age of the youngster at the time of the offense (Piper, 1983: Table 6.27A).

Rojek and Erickson (1982: 16-17) concluded that there was no tendency for the Pima County, Arizona subjects to escalate in their delinquent offending based on a finding of invariance in offense-switching patterns across successive offense transitions. However, a review of these data by the NRC Panel concluded otherwise: Switches from minor runaway and status offenses to more serious personal offenses and "other" offenses became more likely as the offense transition notched higher (Cohen, 1986: 399-400).

Smith and Smith (1984) analyzed the arrest records of 767 juvenile males who were incarcerated in New Jersey correctional facilities between 1977 and 1978 and who had accumulated at least six arrests. No pattern in escalation was found (p. 151).

The three samples of arrested adults (the Detroit SMSA, the southern Michigan counties, and Washington, D.C.) studied by the

NRC Panel exhibited either downward or stable (when controlling for the length of the arrest record) trends in seriousness as their criminal careers progressed (Cohen, 1986: 402). Violent offenses, though, were not considered separately.

The limited research on violence escalation indicates that modest general, interoffense escalation may occur as the violent criminal career presses forward. This escalation seems confined to personal injury offenses.

Age at Initiation of Violent Criminal Careers

The age at which violent offenders initiate their criminal careers has commonly been defined in two ways: (1) *the age-specific violent initiation rate*, calculated as the proportion of violent offenders who commit their first violent offense at a particular age divided by the total number of violent offenders who were originally at-risk to commit such offenses, and (2) *the age-specific violent hazard rate,* calculated as the proportion of violent offenders who commit their first violent offenses at a particular age divided by the number of violent offenders who have not yet committed their first violent offenses by the start of the designated age.[8]

The first calculation yields the unconditional, or absolute, age-specific violent initiation rate: It represents the initiation rate expressed as the simple proportion of all offenders at risk to begin their violent criminal careers who, in fact, began their violent criminal careers at a specific age. The second calculation produces the conditional, or relative, age-specific violent initiation rate: It represents the initiation rate expressed as the proportion of offenders who began their violent criminal careers at a specific age conditional upon not having begun their violent criminal careers by the commencement of that age. This rate calibrates, then, the risk run by individuals who are *not* yet offenders at the start of a specified age of participating in a first violent offense at that age. The conditional violent initiation rate has the interpretative advantage over its unconditional counterpart of signaling those ages at which personal, social, or other influences create the greatest hazards of an initial violent involvement, given that one has remained violence-free up to that age.

Almost all of the limited research that has examined the age-specific commencement of the individual violent criminal career has reported the age-specific initiation rate rather than the age-specific hazard rate.

This research has been based almost exclusively upon official records.

Table 2.11 displays data from several studies on the age at initiation of violent criminal careers for males and females separately. The upper portion of the table traces the career initiation patterns of various groups of violent offenders irrespective of whether the initial offense was violent or not. The lower portion of the table flags criminal career initiation based on the age at which the first violent offense occurred.

When the full age spectrum is considered, violent criminal careers generally begin during late adolescence and early adulthood. Miller et al. (1982), for example, observed this pattern among a sample of males who had sustained at least one arrest for a murder, rape, aggravated assault, or robbery in Columbus, Ohio, between 1950 and 1976. More than two-thirds of the personal injury offenders (the combination of murderers, rapists, and aggravated assaulters) initiated their overall criminal careers between ages 15 and 24. The robbery (personal property) offenders began their overall criminal careers between these ages in even higher proportions (more than four-fifths). The greater concentration of overall career start-ups at the lower ages of the robbers indicates an earlier career initiation than that for their personal injury counterparts.

As expected, the ages at initiation of the personal injury and the personal property offenders were higher when the initiation milestone was counted as a violent offense: The bulk of first *UCR* violent index arrests of the personal injury offenders fell between ages 18 and 34 (more than three-quarters), whereas, as noted earlier, a nearly comparable segment began their overall personal injury careers between the younger and more restricted age range of 15 and 24. Similarly, the great majority—nearly nine-tenths—of initial *UCR* violent index arrests of the robbers fell between ages 18 and 34, whereas, again as pointed out earlier, almost this same proportion concentrated between the younger ages and briefer age interval of 15 and 24.

Robbers were at greater risk to begin their *UCR* violent index arrest careers earlier than the personal injury group. Nearly three-quarters of the robbers experienced their violent career onset between ages 18 and 26 in contrast to slightly more than half of the personal injury offenders. Few members of either offender group registered a first *UCR* violent index arrest before age 18—less than 1 in 20.

Piper (1983) examined for the juvenile years the age-specific violent criminal career initiation rates of the boys in the 1958 Philadelphia birth cohort. When the type of initiation police contact was either a violent or

TABLE 2.11

Age at Initiation of Criminal Career and Violent Criminal Career of Violent Offenders (Official Records)

	Males																					
	≤10 %	11 %	12 %	13 %	14 %	15 %	16 %	17 %	18 %	19 %	20 %	21 %	22 %	23 %	24 %	25 %	26 %	27 %	28 %	29 %	30-34 %	35+ %
U.S. Studies																						
first offense of any type																						
Hamparian et al. (1978)	a	a	a	a	a	a	a	a	a	a	a	a	a	a	a	a	a	a	a	a	a	a
Miller et al. (1982)																						
murderers, assaulters, and rapists			1.7			[c]	37.7						32.9					12.1			15.6	
robbers			2.1				61.9						23.6					8.2			4.3	
Piper (1983)	13.0	9.6	15.4	17.3	17.2	14.7	11.4	4.5	a	a	a	a	a	a	a	a	a	a	a	a	a	a
first violent offense																						
Hamparian et al. (1978)[b]	a	a	a	a	a	a	a	a	a	a	a	a	a	a	a	a	a	a	a	a	a	a
Miller et al. (1982)																						
murderers, assaulters, and rapists[c]					3.5					22.8					29.9					23.9		18.1
robbers[c]					4.2					38.5					34.3					13.6		4.5
Piper (1983)[c]	2.6	3.1	6.8	10.4	14.6	21.2	23.8	17.5	a	a	a	a	a	a	a	a	a	a	a	a	a	a
Foreign Studies																						
first violent offense																						
Wikström (1985)[d]	a	a	a	a	a	a	a	a	a	a	a	a	a	a	a	a	a	a	a	a	a	a

	Females																					
	≤10	11	12	13	14	15	16	17	18	19	20	21	22	23	24	25	26	27	28	29	30-34	35+
	%	%	%	%	%	%	%	%	%	%	%	%	%	%	%	%	%	%	%	%	%	%
U.S. Studies																						
first offense of any type																						
Hamparian et al. (1978)	a	a	a	a	a	a	a	a	a	a	a	a	a	a	a	a	a	a	a	a	a	a
Miller et al. (1982)																						
murderers, assaulters, and rapists	a	a	a	a	a	a	a	a	a	a	a	a	a	a	a	a	a	a	a	a	a	a
robbers	a	a	a	a	a	a	a	a	a	a	a	a	a	a	a	a	a	a	a	a	a	a
Piper (1983)	5.8	5.5	21.3	21.7	11.7	16.2	12.0	5.8	a	a	a	a	a	a	a	a	a	a	a	a	a	a
first violent offense																						
Hamparian et al. (1978)[b]	a	a	a	a	a	a	a	a	a	a	a	a	a	a	a	a	a	a	a	a	a	a
Miller et al. (1982)																						
murderers, assaulters, and rapists[c]	a	a	a	a	a	a	a	a	a	a	a	a	a	a	a	a	a	a	a	a	a	a
robbers[c]	a	a	a	a	a	a	a	a	a	a	a	a	a	a	a	a	a	a	a	a	a	a
Piper (1983)[c]	2.8	2.8	17.2	17.9	11.7	19.6	15.5	12.7	a	a	a	a	a	a	a	a	a	a	a	a	a	a
Foreign Studies																						
first violent offense																						
Wikström (1985)[d]	a	a	a	a	a	a	a	a	a	a	a	a	a	a	a	a	a	a	a	a	a	a

(continued)

99

TABLE 2.11 continued

	≤10 %	11 %	12 %	13 %	14 %	15 %	16 %	17 %	18 %	19 %	Total 20 %	21 %	22 %	23 %	24 %	25 %	26 %	27 %	28 %	29 %	30-34 %	35+ %
U.S. Studies																						
first offense of any type																						
Hamparian et al. (1978)	13.4	9.4	9.0	18.0	20.0	11.8	8.4	9.9	a	a	a	a	a	a	a	a	a	a	a	a	a	a
Miller et al. (1982)																						
murderers, assaulters, and rapists	a	a	a	a	a	a	a	a	a	a	a	a	a	a	a	a	a	a	a	a	a	a
robbers	a	a	a	a	a	a	a	a	a	a	a	a	a	a	a	a	a	a	a	a	a	a
Piper (1983)	a	a	a	a	a	a	a	a	a	a	a	a	a	a	a	a	a	a	a	a	a	a
first violent offense																						
Hamparian et al. (1978)[b]	5.1	5.7	6.4	16.4	16.5	14.4	15.9	19.6	a	a	a	a	a	a	a	a	a	a	a	a	a	a
Miller et al. (1982)																						
murderers, assaulters, and rapists[c]	a	a	a	a	a	a	a	a	a	a	a	a	a	a	a	a	a	a	a	a	a	a
robbers[c]	a	a	a	a	a	a	a	a	a	a	a	a	a	a	a	a	a	a	a	a	a	a
Piper (1983)[c]	a	a	a	a	a	a	a	a	a	a	a	a	a	a	a	a	a	a	a	a	a	a
Foreign Studies																						
first violent offense																						
Wikström (1985)[d]	a	a	1.0	2.0	6.0	10.0	15.0	10.0	14.0	11.0	7.0	7.0	5.0	3.0	a	a	a	a	a	a	a	a

SOURCES: Hamparian et al. (1978: Tables 4-5, 4-9); Miller et al. (1982: Table 5-3); Piper (1983: Tables 5.6-5.7); Wikström (1985: Table 46).

NOTE:
a. This crime category was not designated for this study or for this demographic group.
b. Violent offenses include murder, manslaughter, rape and other sexual offenses, robbery, and simple and aggravated assault.
c. Violent offenses include the *UCR* violent index offenses (homicide, rape, robbery, and aggravated assault).
d. Violent offenses include murder, manslaughter, assault, molestation, and unlawful threats and intrusions.
e. The percentage presented within the brackets pertains to those offenders who initiated their criminal careers during the designated age interval.

a nonviolent incident, the delinquent careers of the cohort youths who participated in at least one *UCR* violent index offense typically began between ages 12 and 15 (nearly two-thirds), with the greatest concentrations at ages 13 and 14. The age at initiation of *UCR* violent index offending occurred later than the age of the overall criminal career initiation for the violent youngsters: The bulk of the cohort boys' first seriously violent offenses fell between ages 14 and 17 (almost four-fifths), with the main initiation ages at 16 and, marginally less, at 15.

Males and females in the 1958 Philadelphia birth cohort initiated their overall delinquent careers at approximately the same ages: Piper (1983) reported that approximately 7 in 10 in each gender group registered ages at onset that were less than 15. However, the girls began the more serious violent component of their delinquent careers at these ages at a higher rate than did their male peers (52.4% versus 37.5%). Perhaps public reporting of serious female violence or official responses to this violence are at a lower threshold than for males at younger ages, resulting in a greater willingness by authorities to intervene earlier.

Hamparian et al.'s (1978) analysis of youthful males and females found that the mass of delinquency initiations, regardless of whether the initiation offense was violent (murder and manslaughter, rape and other sexual offenses, robbery, and simple and aggravated assault) or nonviolent, fell between ages 13 and 15, with nearly half of the career-entry incidents occurring during this period. The modal entry age was 14, accounting for one-fifth of the initial police contacts. In the main, this pair of results is consistent with those reported by Piper (1983) for males and females separately. Most first arrests for violent delinquency registered by Hamparian et al.'s sample were strung out between ages 13 and 17: Between about 15.0% and 20.0% of the first violent arrests occurred at each age in this five-year interval, with the modal age at 17. The relative uniformity observed over this interval in the start-up of the violent career segment is consistent with the female pattern observed by Piper (although some downward spikes were recorded) but inconsistent with the male pattern whose career start-ups compressed between ages 15 and 17. The age at initiation of the overall delinquent careers of the violent youths studied by Hamparian et al. arrived about one year earlier than the age at initiation of the violent segments of those careers.

Wikström (1985) investigated age at violence initiation through age 25 for a cohort of males and females born in 1953 in the greater Stockholm area. The peak violence initiation ages occurred during late adolescence and young adulthood, ages 16 to 20, when three-fifths of all offenders had their first recorded violent offenses. The two highest initiation ages were 17 and 19 (approximately 15.0% at each age).

Using the self-report data of the males and females in their national youth sample, Elliott et al. (1986) have provided the only estimates to date of age-specific violent career hazard rates, which were computed for serious violent offenders for ages 12 through 21. (Recall that these are offenders with involvements at a designated age in three or more aggravated assaults, sexual assaults, gang fights, or strong-arm robberies of students or others, except teachers.) For all youngsters, the serious violence hazard rates increased from ages 12 to 15 (from 1.1% to 2.1%), climbed to their highest levels between ages 16 and 18 (2.7%, 3.7%, and 3.1%, in increasing age order), and then declined to a low (4%) at age 21 (Elliott et al., 1986: Table 2). In general, then, youngsters who had not been involved annually in three or more serious violent offenses by age 17 experienced, in comparison to the other ages, the greatest chance of becoming so involved (3.7%). Even at its zenith, however, the hazard rate is modest, reflecting in part the very high threshold for qualification as a serious violent youngster. The overall pattern in age-specific hazard rates was mirrored by the males but not by the females, because males predominantly inhabited the serious violent category (Elliott et al., 1986: Table 3): Male hazard rates first rose, peaked at ages 16 through 18, and then declined. Female hazard rates varied less, peaked earlier (ages 13 to 15; 1.5% at age 14), and decreased considerably from ages 16 to 21 (1.1% to .4%, respectively). Serious violent age-specific hazard rates for males were typically much higher than for females. For instance, the ratio of the male-to-female peak hazard rates was 4.5:1 (males, 6.8% at age 17; females, 1.5% at age 14).

In sum, findings on the initiation of both the overall violent criminal career and the violent segment of the career indicate a preponderance of start-ups in the late adolescent and early adult years, with the onset of the violent subset appearing at slightly older ages. Violent careers of robbers usually commence earlier than do the careers of personal injury offenders. Violent female careers appear to both begin and peak earlier than do those of males.

The Violent Criminal Career Span

Violent recidivism probabilities. Violent recidivism probabilities calibrate the sequential risks that offenders undergo of advancing from one violent offense to another. The probability is computed as the number of offenders who advance to their next violent offense divided by the number of offenders who were at-risk to advance by virtue of having committed a current violent offense. Because it is computed for an aggregation of violent offenders, the recidivism probability represents the overall rate at which offenders penetrate further into their violent criminal careers.

The recidivism probability is a special case of the aggregate violent incidence rate discussed in the earlier section, "The Individual Violent Crime Rate." As such, the recidivism probability is a composite measure, as is its complement, the desistence probability, to be discussed later: Both measures reflect the combined influences of the level of continued participation by active violent offenders and the magnitudes of the individual violent crime rates of those who remain violently criminally active. Failure to recidivate violently over some period can be owing to either nonparticipation in the violent criminal career, resulting from career termination, or a low individual violent crime rate of an active participant, which may lead to a violent repetition, but after the observation period. These influences typically have not been distinguished by the research literature, although their distinction is clearly important to violent crime control policies that may focus alternatively on promoting the termination of violent criminal careers or reducing individual violent crime rates, each of which functions to depress the violent recidivism probability. (For amplification, see Cohen, 1986: fn. 4.)

The recidivism progression can be described in several ways: (1) *immediate* violent recidivism, which comprises a sequence of violent repetitions across adjacent offenses; (2) *intermittent* violent recidivism, which comprises a sequence of violent repetitions across nonadjacent offenses; and (3) *general* violent recidivism, which comprises a combination of the first two sequential patterns. Research has focused on all three recidivism pathways.

To date, few studies have calculated violent recidivism probabilities. What scant research does exist has relied exclusively on official records because of several well-known limitations of self-report instruments: respondents are sometimes reluctant to report their criminally violent involvements, often find it difficult to differentiate their criminally violent involvements from their noncriminally violent involvements, and frequently are unable to recall accurately the sequence and types of their unlawful involvements.

Strings of recidivism probabilities from several studies are reproduced in Table 2.12, with rows designating the sequence number of the recidivism transition. For example, the first row represents the proportion of all offenders with a first official record who accumulated a second official record; the second row, the proportion of all offenders with a second official record who accumulated a third record; and so forth. These proportional tabular entries are interpreted as recidivism probabilities. The columns indicate the kinds of offenses included in computing the recidivism probability (all offenses in the criminal career or only the violent subset), location of the study, gender of the subjects, and the study citation.

Tracy et al. (1984) computed recidivism probabilities based on all offenses amassed by all delinquent boys (violent and nonviolent) in the 1945 and 1958 Philadelphia birth cohorts. As seen in Table 2.12, the juvenile recidivism probabilities rise over the first-to-second transition from .54 and .58, respectively, to .65 and .72, respectively, and then fluctuate between .72 and .84 in both cohorts over the remaining transitions.

Weiner (1985) examined juvenile recidivism patterns based on only the *UCR* violent index offenses accumulated by the 1958 Philadelphia birth cohort boys. The probabilities of extending the violent career over the juvenile years by progressing from one of these violent police contacts to another, regardless of whether nonviolent offenses might have intervened, increased over the five transitions analyzed, from slightly more than one-third at the first transition to nearly three-fifths at the fifth transition. Companion analyses for the far fewer female cohort members yielded much lower violent recidivism risks of .09, .31, and .00 for the first three transitions, respectively. Data on more advanced transition levels are needed to identify reliably more extended violent recidivism configurations.

Miller et al. (1982) focused on the recidivism risks of their Columbus, Ohio, sample of violent adult male offenders, computing recidivism probabilities separately for personal injury offenders (the combination of murderers, rapists, and aggravated assaulters) and robbers (personal property offenders) based on all unlawful involvements of the groups. The transition probabilities ran parallel in both groups, although a little higher among the robbers, beginning at a substantial figure, at greater than .90, declining somewhat at the second transition, and then stabilizing between about .85 and .90 across subsequent transitions.

TABLE 2.12
Recidivism Probabilities (Official Records)

	Males								Females
	U.S. Studies						Foreign Studies		U.S. Studies Violent Offenses of Violent Offenders
	All Offenses[a]				Violent Offenses of Violent Offenders			Violent Offenses of Violent Offenders	
	Miller et al. (1982)		Tracy et al. (1984)		Miller et al. (1982)		Weiner (1985)	Walker et al. (1967)		Weiner (1985)
Recidivism Transition Number	Murderers, Assaulters, and Rapists	Robbers	1945 Cohort	1958 Cohort	Murderers, Assaulters, and Rapists[b]	Robbers[b]	1958 Cohort[b]	All Violent Reconvictions[c]	All Reconvictions at Age 21 or Older[c]	1958 Cohort[b]
1	.94	.97	.54	.58	.47	.59	.36	.14	.12	.09
2	.87	.94	.65	.72	.41	.48	.48	.40	.35	.31
3	.83	.93	.72	.72	.52	.43	.48	.44	.40	.00
4	.85	.89	.72	.75	.44	.50	.64	.55	.67	d
5	.84	.88	.74	.78	.44	.50	.57	d	d	d
6	.85	.89	.79	.75	.50	.33	d	d	d	d
7	.80	.84	.77	.80	.22	d	d	d	d	d
8	.88	.86	.80	.84	d	d	d	d	d	d
9	.84	.89	.83	.81	d	d	d	d	d	d
10	.84	.85	.79	.83	d	d	d	d	d	d

SOURCES: Miller et al. (1982: Tables 6-1, 6-5); Tracy et al. (1984: Tables 51a-b); Walker et al. (1967: Tables 2, 2a); Weiner (1985: Table A2.4).

NOTE:
a. The recidivism, or transition, probabilities pertain to "all offenses" of the designated offender group. The recidivism probabilities for the 1945 and 1958 birth cohorts pertain to all offenses of all delinquents (Tracy et al., 1984). The transition probabilities for the "murderers, assaulters, and rapists" and "robbers" pertain to all offenses of the murderers, assaulters, and rapists and the robbers, respectively (Miller et al., 1982).

b. The violent offenses considered were the *UCR* violent index offenses: homicide, rape, robbery, and aggravated assault.

c. The violent offenses considered were murder, attempt to murder, culpable homicide, assaults, threats, use of firearms, and robbery.

d. This recidivism probability was not computed for this study.

The foregoing recidivism probabilities are higher at the first five or six transitions than are those reported by Tracy et al. (1984) for the Philadelphia birth cohorts. This discrepancy is probably a function, in part, of the adult status of the Columbus, Ohio, groups: Older offenders may be more committed to criminal misconduct because of either behavioral entrenchment, which occurs with increasing age, or the changing composition of the offender pool such that the more committed offenders remain active in adulthood, whereas the less committed offenders depart from their criminal careers during the juvenile period. Also probably responsible in part for the discrepancy is the fact that the computations of recidivism probabilities for the Philadelphia cohorts included both violent and nonviolent delinquents, whereas the computations for the Columbus group included only violent offenders who, in comparison to offenders overall, may be more ensconced in their criminal careers.

Miller et al. (1982) proceeded to focus on general recidivism probabilities based on *UCR* violent index crimes for the personal injury and personal property offenders. These probabilities, all lower by about half than the corresponding probabilities based on all offenses, were fairly stable across the first six transitions for the personal injury and personal property groups, although they were somewhat higher for the latter group: Among the personal injury offenders, the recidivism probabilities ranged between .41 and .52, whereas the corresponding probabilities for the personal property offenders ranged between .43 and .59. Recidivism risks in both groups dipped at the seventh transition.

Walker et al. (1967) reported general violent recidivism probabilities, based on reconviction records, for a sample of convicted Glaswegian males. Violent convictions included murder and attempted murder, culpable homicide, assaults, threats, robbery, and firearms violations. First convictions for violent offenses were modest, about 5.0% of the study group. The risk of a subsequent conviction for a violent act increased progressively with each additional conviction: from .14 to .40, .44 and .55 for the first, second, third, and later reconviction transitions. When violent convictions occurring before age 21 were disregarded, recidivism probabilities similarly rose from .12 to .35, .40, and .67 for the corresponding reconviction transitions.

Analyses of male subjects by Walker et al. (1967) and Weiner (1985) indicate inclining violent recidivism probabilities over successive recidivism levels when based exclusively on violent offenses. This pattern is not consistent with Miller et al.'s (1982) finding of relative stability.

Despite this inconsistency, disregarding the first transition, these three studies nevertheless reported fairly similar levels of violent-to-violent recidivism probabilities, ranging between .35 and .48, .40 and .52, .44 and .67, and .44 and .57, for the second through fifth transitions, respectively. Further work will be needed to confirm the generality of this convergence.

A series of studies has examined general delinquent and criminal recidivism as a stochastic, or probabilistic, process (Barnett et al., 1987; Blumstein et al., 1985; Blumstein and Moitra, 1980). This approach investigates whether the sequence of observed recidivism probabilities exhibited by a group of offenders, such as those computed sequences discussed here, can be represented parsimoniously by an underlying statistical process, or distribution, which might have generated it. Phrased interrogatively: Is the sequence of manifest recidivism probabilities consistent with some formal, well-defined stochastic model whose parameters can be estimated from the observed data?

Blumstein and Moitra (1980) argued that the overall chain of official delinquent recidivism of the 1945 Philadelphia birth cohort boys studied by Wolfgang et al. (1972) conforms to a "shifted geometric distribution." The estimated probabilities of participating in a first offense, a second offense (given a first), and a third offense (given a second) are .35, .54, and .65, respectively. The recidivism probability then stabilizes at .72 for each subsequent repetition. (After "shifting" beyond the initial three increases in recidivism probabilities, the recidivism risk is stable across remaining offenses, which is indicative of the geometric distribution.)

Blumstein et al. (1985) modified and extended the foregoing analysis. Examination of official data for all male birth cohort subjects residing in Philadelphia; Racine, Wisconsin; Marion County, Oregon; and London revealed a general pattern across jurisdictions in rapidly increasing recidivism probabilities over the first few (three or four) offenses, followed by high, stable recidivism probabilities through about the sixth offense, followed in turn by a still higher and stable recidivism probability for all subsequent offenses. The observed recidivism pattern suggests that the "shifted geometric" model be replaced by a more parsimonious model that partitions a cohort into three groups: "innocents" who exhibit no official criminal record, "desisters" who exhibit a low recidivism probability, and "persisters" who exhibit a high recidivism probability.

The authors concluded that the observed increase in recidivism probabilities was a function of a change in composition of offenders at successive offenses in the recidivism chain: Offenders did not appear to modify their behavior to become more recidivistic, rather, there appeared to be two offense groups—desisters who terminated their offending early and persisters who kept repeating offenses. The recidivism process involved the selective filtering of individuals, resulting in a core group of persistent offenders rather than behavioral changes in individuals resulting eventually in "confirmed" criminals. This recidivism postulation asserts, then, that desisters and persisters are characterized by a priori distinguishing propensities to recidivate, which are established early in life and which might be amenable to predictive identification.

Barnett et al. (1987) augmented the foregoing model in their analysis of the recidivism and termination probabilities, through age 25, of a London cohort of youthful male offenders. Several rival recidivism models were considered: Unlike earlier statistical representations, the adopted model incorporated measures of the probabilities of conviction and termination for two offender groups—"occasionals" and "frequents"—thereby formally acknowledging that both criminal recidivism and termination are stochastic in structure.

These studies of the stochastic character of recidivism have yet to focus, however, on just violent offenders or on only their violent offenses. Whether these general results apply, then, to these most serious violent and injurious offenders and offenses remains unanswered. However, these analyses provide important guideposts for the future investigation of violent criminal recidivism.

Also important to future investigations is the acquisition of data sets that will permit the analysis of longer strings of violent recidivism probabilities than presently exist. The contours of those distributions will yield insights into the extent to which the recidivism patterns are a function of changing levels of participation or of changes in the individual violent crime rates of active participants (resulting from behavioral modification or selective filtering by the juvenile and criminal justice systems).

The need for future research in these directions notwithstanding, the present findings provide limited evidence in support of an increasing sequence of violent recidivism probabilities, with robbers experiencing somewhat more elevated violent recidivism risks than personal injury offenders. Females are at much lower risk than are males of recidivating violently.

Violent desistance probabilities, total violent criminal career length, and residual violent criminal career length. Desistance from violent criminal career activity is usually measured in two ways: (1) as the *violent desistance probability* and (2) as the *residual violent criminal career length*, which is the expected time until a final violent criminal involvement given a current violent criminal involvement.

The first of these measures, the violent desistance probability, is the complement of the recidivism probability discussed in the previous section and, as such, is computed as the number of violent offenders with a present violent offense who do *not* progress to a subsequent violent offense, divided by the total number of offenders with a present violent offense. The desistance counterparts of the violent recidivism probabilities presented in Table 2.12 appear in Table 2.13. (Subtracting one from the recidivism probability yields the related desistance probability.) Detailing patterns in the violent desistance table would be redundant inasmuch as the desistance structure, when defined as it just has been, is simply the reverse of the recidivism structure. For this reason, we elect to review briefly the conclusions of the last section only as they apply to present concerns: Current findings lend limited evidence in support of a decreasing sequence of violent desistance probabilities, with personal injury offenders experiencing somewhat more elevated violent desistance opportunities than personal property offenders. Females desist at much greater rates than do males. Stochastic modeling of the violent desistance sequence is needed, much as it is needed with respect to the violent recidivism sequence. One would expect these stochastic analyses to yield insights into whether desistance is a function of the termination of violent criminal careers or of a dampening of individual violent crime rates.

Studies of the time duration from the current offense until the final offense are recent in origin and few in number. Even fewer studies include analyses of violent offenders and their complements of violent offenses. For example, Greenberg (1975: 562) used the *UCR* index offenses together to estimate the adult total *UCR* index criminal career length (computed to be approximately five years). Greene (1977: Chapter 3) also used the combination of *UCR* index offenses (except larceny) to estimate the adult total *UCR* index criminal career length, which was, on the average, between 8 and 12 years long between ages 18 and 40. Based on *UCR* statistics used by Shinnar and Shinnar (1974: 594-595) for offenders arrested in 1970 on federal charges, estimates of adult total career lengths (from first to last arrest for all recorded arrests) were five years for all arrested offenders and between four and six years for murderers, rapists, aggravated assaulters, and robbers considered separately (that is, each offender group included those offenders who

TABLE 2.13
Desistance Probabilities (Official Records)

	Males								Females
	U.S. Studies						Foreign Studies		U.S. Studies Violent Offenses of Violent Offenders
	All Offenses[a]		Tracy et al. (1984)		Violent Offenses of Violent Offenders			Violent Offenses of Violent Offenders		
	Miller et al. (1982)				Miller et al. (1982)		Weiner (1985)	Walker et al. (1967)		Weiner (1985)
Desistance Transition Number	Murderers, Assaulters, and Rapists	Robbers	1945 Cohort	1958 Cohort	Murderers, Assaulters, and Rapists	Robbers[b]	1958 Cohort[b]	All Violent Reconvictions	All Reconvictions at Age 21 or Older[c]	1958 Cohort[b]
1	.07	.03	.46	.42	.53	.41	.64	.86	.88	.91
2	.13	.06	.35	.28	.59	.52	.52	.60	.65	.69
3	.17	.08	.28	.28	.48	.57	.52	.56	.60	1.00
4	.15	.11	.28	.25	.56	.50	.36	.45	.33	d
5	.16	.12	.26	.22	.56	.50	.43	d	d	d
6	.15	.12	.21	.25	.50	.67	d	d	d	d
7	.20	.16	.23	.20	.78	d	d	d	d	d
8	.12	.14	.20	.16	d	d	d	d	d	d
9	.16	.11	.17	.19	d	d	d	d	d	d
10	.16	.15	.21	.17	d	d	d	d	d	d

SOURCES: Miller et al. (1982: Tables 6-1, 6-5); Tracy et al. (1984: Tables 51a-b); Walker et al. (1967: Tables 2, 2a); Weiner (1985: Table A2.4).

NOTE:
a. The desistance probabilities pertain to "all offenses" of the designated offender group. The desistance probabilities for the 1945 and 1958 birth cohorts pertain to all offenses of all delinquents (Tracy et al., 1984). The desistance probabilities for the "murderers, assaulters, and rapists" and "robbers" pertain to all offenses of the murderers, assaulters, and rapists and the robbers, respectively (Miller et al., 1982).

b. The violent offenses considered were the *UCR* violent index offenses: homicide, rape, robbery, and aggravated assault.

c. The violent offenses considered were murder, attempt to murder, culpable homicide, assaults, threats, use of firearms, and robbery.

d. This desistance probability was not computed for this study.

110

had at least one arrest of the indicated type). Shinnar and Shinnar (1974: 610) also cited other estimates of the total criminal career length that were between two and three times greater than the *UCR* figures presented earlier.

Limited recent research has advanced both conceptually and methodologically beyond earlier efforts. The milestone research in this area by Blumstein et al. (1982) estimated the mean total adult *UCR* index criminal career length using multiple, cross-sectional cohorts of offenders arrested as adults in Washington, D.C., for at least one index offense (except larceny). (The career length spans from the first *UCR* index arrest to the last such arrest.) This mean career length was estimated to be 5.6 years for those offenders arrested for their first *UCR* index offense between ages 18 and 20 (p. 32). The mean residual *UCR* index criminal career length of these offenders—that is, the expected time until the final *UCR* index arrest given the elapsed time already spent active in committing these offenses—was found to be nonlinear: As the elapsed time in the *UCR* index criminal career initially increased from ages 18 to 30, so too did the residual career length; but the residual criminal career length then stabilized between ages 30 and 42 and subsequently declined after age 42 (Blumstein et al., 1982: 38, Figure 12).

Blumstein et al. (1982: Table 4) examined murderers, rapists, aggravated assaulters, and robbers separately: Mean total adult criminal career lengths of those offenders who began their adult *UCR* index criminal careers between ages 18 and 20 were 9.6 years, 5.9 years, 10.3 years, and 4.9 years, respectively.[9] Aggravated assaulters and robbers fell at the upper and lower extremes, respectively, of the total *UCR* index criminal career length spectrum, perhaps reflecting the quite different dynamics of expressive and instrumental violent criminal careers.

Robbers mirrored the overall residual *UCR* index criminal career length pattern described here: Their residual career lengths first increased through age 30 (from 4 years to 7 years), remained stable from ages 30 to 42 (at about 7 years), and declined thereafter through age 60 (from 7 years to 1 year; Blumstein et al., 1982: Figure 20). Murderers and rapists, on the other hand, began with stable residual criminal career lengths ranging between six years and nine years, which then declined rapidly through age 60 from nine years to one year (Figure 21). Rapists began with stable residual criminal career lengths of six to eight years from ages 18 to 37, which then declined steadily through age 60 to one year (Figure 21). Aggravated assaulters displayed an early steep increase in their residual criminal career lengths from about 8 years to 19 years from ages 18 to 22, followed by a sharp drop through age 60 to 1 year (Figure 22).

In view of the importance of both the mean total and mean residual violent criminal career lengths in forging explanations of the maintenance of violent criminal careers and in formulating public policies to focus strategically on those offenders ranking highest on these criminal career measures, it is surprising that precious few investigations have been conducted along these lines. Future analyses will need to augment current research by disaggregating violent criminal careers according to the various violent offense types and their combinations, according to whether the career commences in the juvenile years as opposed to the adult years, and according to the other criminal career characteristics believed to distinguish substantively and conceptually violent criminal careers.

The present findings provide limited evidence in support of a decreasing sequence of violent desistance probabilities, with personal injury offenders experiencing somewhat more elevated violent desistance probabilities than do robbers. Females have a much higher chance of desisting than males. Mean total adult violent criminal career lengths range between 5 and 10 years for robbers and aggravated assaulters, respectively. The length of the mean residual, violent adult criminal career length varies with increasing age according to the type of violent crime.

Age Variation in the Occurrence of Violent Crimes

The total number of violent crimes accumulated over an age or time period of interest by a group of individuals is a function of the individual violent crime rates and violent criminal career durations of those offenders who are actively participating in violent crime over that age or time period. No study has yet linked explicitly to one another these violent career dimensions to permit a detailed analysis of the age-specific production of violent crime. However, despite its multiple determinants, the general age distribution of violent crime is important in its own right, inasmuch as official agencies must respond prudently and differently to the violent criminal activity of offenders across the age spectrum, as the bifurcation of the justice system into its juvenile and adult tiers most clearly attests. Policy responses might certainly differ depending upon whether the age variation in the proportion of violent offenses is a function of differential violence participation or unequal individual violent crime rates, or both. Absent firm information in this regard, which is currently the case, knowledge of the overall distribution of violent offenses nevertheless has at least two beneficial yields. First, distributional peaks and troughs can be identified and targeted for intense study to determine whether violence participation or intensity of involvement in violent offenses is at the root of the observed disparities. Second, the identification of distributional extremes provides justice agencies with information that can be used in the differential allocation of agency resources. Both research and policy concerns, then, can be addressed by the analysis of the age distribution of criminal violence.

Initially we discuss the broad age intervals encompassing the juvenile and adult periods (Table 2.14) and then the age-specific patterns (Table 2.15). The measurement currency in each table is official record. As prelude and background to this discussion, we gauge the proportion of all offenses in different age intervals that are violent.

Regardless of the study, violent and injurious incidents generally comprise modest proportions of all amassed offenses. Robbery, aggravated assault, and, when victim harm is used to describe the incident, injury offenses exhibit the highest proportions of the violent offense types. For example, Tracy et al. (1984) reported that 2.7% and 4.8% of the police contacts sustained through age 18 by all delinquent boys in the 1945 and 1958 Philadelphia birth cohorts, respectively, were for serious personal assaults, including homicide, forcible rape, and aggravated assault (Tracy et al., 1984: Tables 16a-16b). The figures for the constituent assaultive offenses for the 1945 cohort, presented in Table 2.14, range from a low of .1% to a high of 2.2% for homicide and aggravated assault, respectively; the corresponding low and high figures for the 1958 cohort are .4% and 3.7% and pertain to the same two offenses (percentage disaggregations were derived expressly for this chapter). The more recent cohort appears to have been more violently productive with respect to each assaultive crime by a factor of at least one and three-quarters. Rounding out the *UCR* violent index crimes, robberies accounted for 1.9% and 8.5% of all delinquent incidents recorded for the 1945 and the 1958 birth cohorts, respectively. When delinquencies were characterized according to whether they involved only injury (but no property theft or damage) to a victim, less than one in 10 police contacts in each of the two cohorts involved some known degree of physical harm.

TABLE 2.14

Occurrence of Violent Offenses by Age Group: Juveniles (age ≤ 17) and Adults[a] (Official Records)

	Males								Females			Males and Females
	Shannon (1982) % of All Offenses of All Offenders			Tracy et al. (1984)				Facella (1983) 1958 Cohort	Shannon (1982) % of All Offenses of All Offenders			Hamparian et al. (1978)
				1945 Cohort		1958 Cohort						
Offense Type	1942 Cohort	1949 Cohort	1955 Cohort	% of All Offenses of All Offenders	% of All Offenses of Violent/ Injurious Offenders[b]	% of All Offenses of All Offenders	% of All Offenses of Violent/ Injurious Offenders[b]	% of All Offenses Of All Offenders	1942 Cohort	1949 Cohort	1955 Cohort	% of All Offenses of All Offenders
Homicide	d	d	.1	.1	.4	.4	.6	.1	d	d	d	c
Murder	c	c	c	c	c	c	c	c	c	c	c	.4
Negligent homicide	c	c	c	c	c	c	c	c	c	c	c	.1
Rape	c	c	.4	1.1	.7	1.2	c	d	c	c	c	1.2
Aggravated assault	c	c	c	2.2	5.5	3.7	6.4	3.0	c	c	c	2.6
Robbery	d	.5	1.0	1.9	4.8	8.5	14.7	1.2	d	d	d	c
Armed robbery	c	c	c	c	c	c	c	c	c	c	c	1.0
Strong-arm robbery												
Injury[i]	c	c	c	8.6	24.3	8.0	16.4	7.2	c	c	c	d
Assault	.5	1.1	2.1	c	c	c	c	c	d	.9	3.0	c
Simple assault	c	c	c	5.3	13.4	3.8	6.6	5.7	c	c	c	11.1

Adult Males

Offense Type	Miller et al. (1982) (age > 18) % of All Arrests of All Offenders	Weiner[c] 1945 Cohort (ages 18-24) % of All Offenses of All Offenders	Weiner[c] 1945 Cohort (ages 18-24) % of All Offenses of Violent/Injurious Offenders[b]	1958 Cohort (ages 18-24) % of All Offenses of All Offenders	1958 Cohort (ages 18-24) % of All Offenses of Violent/Injurious Offenders[b]	Shannon (1982) (ages 18-20) % of All Offenses of All Offenders 1942 Cohort	1949 Cohort	1955 Cohort	Shannon (1982) % of All Offenses of All Offenders 1942 Cohort (Ages 21-33)	1949 Cohort (Ages 21-26)	1955 Cohort (Age 21)
Homicide	3.3	.8	1.4	1.9	2.9	d	.1	.1	d	d	.4
Murder	c	c	c	c	c	c	c	c	c	c	c
Negligent homicide	c	c	c	c	c	c	c	c	c	c	c
Rape	3.2	2.0	3.6	2.7	4.0	c	c	c	c	c	c
Aggravated assault	7.5	4.1	7.5	11.7	17.2	.2	.4	2.6	.5	.3	.4
Robbery	9.5	5.6	10.2	17.1	25.2	c	c	c	c	c	c
Armed robbery	c	c	c	c	c	c	c	c	c	c	c
Strong-arm robbery	c	c	c	c	c	c	c	c	c	c	c
Injury[f]	c	12.9	24.5	c	c	.2	1.2	2.5	1.2	2.2	2.9
Assault	c	c	c	c	c	c	c	c	c	c	c
Simple assault	c	4.3	7.7	4.4	6.5						

Adult Females

Offense Type	Shannon (1982) (ages 18-20) % of All Offenses of all Offenders 1942 Cohort	1949 Cohort	1955 Cohort	Shannon (1982) % of All Offenses of all Offenders 1942 Cohort (Ages 21-33)	1949 Cohort (Ages 21-26)	1955 Cohort (Age 21)
Homicide	d	d	d	d	d	d
Murder	c	c	c	c	c	c

(continued)

TABLE 2.14 (continued)

Adult Females

Offense Type	Shannon (1982) (ages 18-20) % of All Offenses of all Offenders			Shannon (1982) % of All Offenses of all Offenders		
	1942 Cohort	1949 Cohort	1955 Cohort	1942 Cohort (Ages 21-33)	1949 Cohort (Ages 21-26)	1955 Cohort (Age 21)
Negligent homicide	c	c	c	c	c	c
Rape	c	c	c	c	c	c
Aggravated assault						
Robbery	c	c	c	c	c	c
Armed robbery	d	d	.2	.6	.4	1.3
Strong-arm robbery	c	c	c	c	c	c
Injury[f]	c	c	c	c	c	c
Assault	d	.4	2.2	1.1	d	c
Simple assault	c	c	c	c	c	c

SOURCES: Facella (1983: Tables 13-15); Hamparian et al. (1978: Table 5-1); Miller et al. (1982: Table 4-3); Shannon (1982: Appendix B, Table 1A); Tracy et al. (1984: Tables 16a-b; the percentage of all offenses of just "violent/injurious" offenders was calculated expressly for this chapter); Weiner (see note e).

NOTE:
a. In addition to the studies reported below, Polk et al. (1981: viii) found that "serious violent" offenses accounted for 1.6% and 1.0% of all the court referrals of their cohort for ages 18 or younger and ages 19 to 30, respectively. The definition of "serious violent," while not explicitly given, appears to refer to the UCR violent index offenses.

b. Violent offenders include delinquents who have committed at least one UCR violent index offense (homicide, rape, robbery, and aggravated assault) or a simple assault. Injurious offenders include delinquents who have committed at least one offense in which a victim was physically harmed.

c. This crime category was not designated by this study or for this demographic group.

d. Negligible: < .05%.

e. Prepared expressly for this chapter.

f. Refers to any incident in which at least one victim sustained a physical injury, ranging from minor harm to death.

Shannon (1982) similarly observed that violent offenses accounted for very low proportions of all offenses engaged in by all delinquent males in each of three Racine, Wisconsin, cohorts. Of all the violent offense types, only assault, in the 1949 and 1955 cohorts, exceeded 1.0% of all incidents (Table 2.14).

Females in the 1958 Philadelphia birth cohort studied by Facella (1983) and in the three Racine birth cohorts studied by Shannon (1982) likewise exhibited low proportional accumulations of violent juvenile offenses (Table 2.14). In almost every case, the female accumulation fell beneath its respective male accumulation.

When the calculation of the proportion of juvenile offenses accounted for by the violent subset is restricted to only the violent juvenile male offenders, the resultant figures are still relatively modest, ranging from a low of .4% (homicide) to a high of 5.5% (aggravated assault) for the UCR violent index crimes in the 1945 Philadelphia birth cohort, and from a low of .6% (homicide) to a high of 14.7% (robbery) in the more contemporary 1958 Philadelphia cohort (Table 2.14). Hamparian et al. (1978) reported analogous low proportions for the combination of violent male and female delinquents in the Columbus, Ohio sample, ranging between 0.1% for negligent homicide and 2.6% for aggravated assault (Table 2.14).

The adult data consistently exhibit the same modest proportional accumulations as the juvenile data of violent incidents relative to the total aggregation of incidents, regardless of whether all offenders or just violent offenders are considered (Table 2.14). Although the proportional accumulations are not high with respect to most violent offense types, adult male offenders nevertheless generate higher proportions of violent offenses, relative to all offenses, than do their juvenile counterparts. Adult females almost invariably accumulate less substantial proportions of violent offenses than do adult males.

Other research corroborates the foregoing findings. Farrington (1983) reported that only 4.4% of the conviction charges sustained through age 25 by the boys in a London cohort were for seriously assaultive behavior (p. 44). Polk et al. (1981) found that only a small fraction of the official juvenile court referrals and adult arrests of the Marion County, Oregon cohort boys were for serious violent offenses (inferred to be UCR violent index offenses although not explicitly stated by the authors): 1.6% for their juvenile years and 1.0% for their adult years through age 30 (p. viii).

Some research permits pinpointing with greater accuracy the ages at which violent offenses are most concentrated: The bulk of violent incidents appears to be compressed into the later adolescent and early adult years. For example, Farrington (1983: Table C4) found that the largest mass of the convictions of the cohort males for all offenses between ages 10 and 24 fell between ages 17 and 20, followed by ages 14 to 16 (41.0% versus 33.0%). Assault convictions also peaked between ages 17 and 20 (one conviction per 100 youths, *not* offenders, per year), followed by ages 21 to 24 (.6 convictions per 100 youths per year). Self-reports of fighting were highest for ages 15 to 18, followed by ages 19 to 21 (273.0 and 71.0 per 100 youths per year, respectively; Farrington, 1983: Table C5).

Proportional age distributions of violent offenses are arrayed in Table 2.15. Tracy et al. (1984) reported that the proportion of all police contacts for both the 1945 and the 1958 Philadelphia birth cohort boys increased at each successive age from 11 to 16 and then declined at 17. The concentration of incidents was heaviest across the span of ages 15 to 17 (60.3% and 64.1% in the earlier and more recent cohorts, respectively). The two cohorts displayed the same peak age of overall offense occurrence, 16 (about a quarter of all offenses fell at this age). The decline in all offenses at age 17 observed in the juvenile period continued through age 30 when adult data were tabulated for the follow-up sample of the 1945 Philadelphia birth cohort boys (Wolfgang et al., 1987: Figure 5.3).

More detailed analyses of the juvenile years of the 1945 and the 1958 cohort boys indicated that the proportion of age-specific violent police contacts (the combination of homicide, forcible rape, and aggravated assault) increased to age 16 (which, by itself, comprised nearly one-third of these infractions) in the 1945 cohort and then declined at age 17 (Table 2.15). This pattern was generally reflected in the 1958 cohort, with the peak in violent incidents occurring one year later at age 17, although the level was only slightly above that at age 16. Overall, the great majority of violent delinquencies fell between ages 15 and 17 (more than three-fourths in both cohorts). The violent offense distribution was consistent, then, with the overall offense distribution outlined previously.

Age-specific robbery occurrence departed from the violent offense occurrence in the 1945 birth cohort but closely paralleled the violence occurrence in the 1958 cohort (Table 2.15). No discernible trend was observed in the 1945 cohort, with the age-specific robbery distribution

TABLE 2.15
Occurrence of Violent Offenses by Age: Juveniles (age ≤ 17) and Adults (Official Records)

	U.S. Studies								Foreign Studies	
	Males						Females		Males and Females	
	Tracy et al. (1984)						Piper (1983)		Wikström (1985)	
	1945 Cohort			1958 Cohort			1958 Cohort		Violent[b]	
Age	All Offenses %	Violent Offenses[a] %	Robbery %	All Offenses %	Violent Offenses[a] %	Robbery %	Violent Offenses[a] %	Robbery %	Juveniles[c] %	Juveniles and Adults[d] %
≤10	5.7	2.2	5.2	4.2	1.3	.8	[f] 13.9	14.0	e	e
11	4.3	2.5	5.2	2.5	1.8	1.3			e	e
12	6.5	1.4	7.3	5.8	2.1	4.7	13.9	14.0	e	e
13	9.4	5.8	19.7	10.5	6.6	7.3	18.3	37.2	3.3	.8
14	13.7	9.4	17.6	12.8	11.4	10.8	18.3	37.2	4.3	1.0
15	19.5	18.0	11.9	20.2	19.1	23.5	26.1	23.3	14.9	3.5
16	24.8	32.0	19.7	23.6	28.7	28.8	22.6	20.9	28.1	6.6
17	16.0	28.8	13.5	20.3	29.0	23.0	19.1	4.7	49.5	11.6
18	e	e	e	e	e	e	e	e	g	7.8

(continued)

TABLE 2.15 continued

| | U.S. Studies Males Tracy et al. (1984) | | | | | | Foreign Studies Females Piper (1983) | | Males and Females Wikström (1985) Violent[b] | |
| | 1945 Cohort | | | 1958 Cohort | | | 1958 Cohort | | | |
Age	All Offenses %	Violent Offenses[a] %	Robbery %	All Offenses %	Violent Offenses[a] %	Robbery %	Violent Offenses[a] %	Robbery %	Juveniles[c] %	Juveniles and Adults[d] %
19	e	e	e	e	e	e	e	e	g	13.6
20	e	e	e	e	e	e	e	e	g	9.7
21	e	e	e	e	e	e	e	e	g	7.0
22	e	e	e	e	e	e	e	e	g	7.8
23	e	e	e	e	e	e	e	e	g	9.3
24	e	e	e	e	e	e	e	e	g	7.0
25	e	e	e	e	e	e	e	e	g	7.0

SOURCES: Piper (1983: Table 4.1c); Tracy et al. (1984: Tables 36a–b, 47a–b); Wikström (1985, derived from Figure 6).

NOTE:
a. Violent offenses include homicide, rape, and aggravated assault. Percentages refer to the distribution of just these violent offenses.
b. Violent offenses include murder, manslaughter, and assault. Percentages refer to the distribution of just these violent offenses.
c. Percentages are based on just those violent offenses accumulated during the juvenile period for purposes of comparison with the figures from Tracy et al. (1984).
d. Percentages are based on all violent offenses accumulated during the juvenile and adult years combined.
e. Percentages were not available for this age in the original study.
f. The percentage presented within the brackets pertains to the sum of percentages across all ages within the brackets.
g. Percentages were not calculated for this age for this table.

first increasing (to age 13), then decreasing (to age 15), and subsequently increasing and decreasing (at ages 16 and 17, respectively). The distribution exhibited two peak ages, 13 and 16 (almost 20.0% at each age). In contrast to the fluctuating pattern in the 1945 cohort, the age-specific robbery curve in the 1958 cohort rose steadily through age 16 and then dropped somewhat at age 17. Ages 15 to 17 accounted for three-fourths of the more recent cohort's juvenile robberies in contrast to less than half in the earlier cohort.

Piper's (1983) analysis of the female members of the 1958 Philadelphia birth cohort showed an inclining and then declining pattern in age-specific juvenile violence (the combination of homicide, rape, and aggravated assault) and robbery, in contrast to the males who showed an almost invariant incline across these ages for the corresponding offenses (Table 2.15). In comparison to the cohort males, the females tended to have their violent and robbery incidents concentrated at the lower end of the juvenile age range.

Wikström's (1985) data for the males and females in the 1953 Stockholm birth cohort permitted calculations showing that, through age 25, violent incidents occurred mainly between ages 17 and 20 (Figure 6). Nearly 43.0% of the violent offenses were accumulated over these ages, with the peak age at 19 (13.6% of the offenses; Table 2.15). When only the juvenile ages are considered, a consistent upward slope appeared.

In line with other studies, the majority (70.0%) of the violent infractions recorded by the police for Guttridge et al.'s (1983) three male cohorts born in Copenhagen occurred during the later juvenile and young adult years, between ages 18 and 25 (p. 221). Proportionately, most violent offenses occurred at age 20, which is three years later than when all offenses were considered together.

Overall, violent offenses constitute a modest proportion of the total offense accumulation of all offenders in a population. Furthermore, these offenses constitute a modest percentage of the total offense accumulation even when only violent offenders are considered. Adult accumulations are generally greater than in the juvenile years, although these tallies are still moderate. When only the juvenile period is considered, the bulk of personal injury offenses and robberies are sustained at the more advanced ages. Females generally accumulate lower proportions of violent offenses than do males and these offenses tend to be concentrated at the younger juvenile ages. Although the proportions of violent offenses are usually modest, the proportional barometer of their significance must be weighed against the much greater gravity of harm that they entail relative to other offenses.

Chronic Violent Criminal Careers

The issue of extreme individual persistence in unlawful behavior, measured by an extended sequence of these involvements, has been one of the most studied aspects of the criminal career. Wolfgang et al. (1972) were the first to give research credibility to the often made claim that a few individuals are responsible for disproportionately many offenses. Many other researchers have since confirmed that finding. However, only a handful of studies have focused on whether a few individuals are similarly responsible for disproportionately many violent offenses.

Although involvement in a chronic violent criminal career is a composite measure (the individual-level analogue of the aggregate-occurrence figure), a product either of both a high individual violent crime rate and a long violent criminal career length or of an extreme position on one or the other of these criminal career dimensions, chronic violence nevertheless merits separate treatment because of its important and controversial policy implications. Perhaps foremost among these implications is the potential such analyses hold for the early, prospective identification of repetitive violent offenders for purposes of selective social interventions or enhanced juvenile and criminal justice system processing.

In their research on the 1945 and 1958 Philadelphia birth cohort boys, Tracy et al. (1984) isolated the delinquency pattern in which a few offenders each amassed many offenses. These "chronic" recidivists, who had five or more police contacts of any kind, constituted 6.3% and 7.5% of the 1945 and 1958 cohorts, respectively (18.0% and 23.0% of the delinquents; Tracy et al., 1984: Tables 24a-24b). In the earlier and more recent cohorts the chronic boys accumulated 51.9% and 60.6%, respectively, of the total delinquency output. It is important that in the 1945 cohort this small group accumulated between 70.0% and 80.0% of each of the UCR violent index offenses (Table 2.16). Furthermore, of all incidents in which a victim was injured, nearly three-fifths involved chronic offenders. Similarly, in the 1958 cohort, chronic offenders were responsible for the majority of the UCR violent index offenses, between 60.0% and 75.0% (Table 2.16). These same offenders accounted for two-thirds of the injurious offenses.

Several other studies have since looked at this skewed pattern, focusing, however, on the violent offenders. Results are summarized in

TABLE 2.16

Chronic Offense Careers and the Accumulation of Violent Offenses
in the 1945 and 1958 Philadelphia Birth Cohorts:
Juvenile Offenses, Males (Police Records)

Total Number of Offenses of any Kind[a]	Offenders %	All Offenses %	Homicide %	Rape %	Robbery %	Aggravated Assault %	Injury[b] %
1945 Cohort							
1	46.4	15.8	7.1	9.1	3.1	8.2	11.8
2-4	35.6	32.3	21.4	18.2	15.1	22.7	30.3
5+	18.0	51.9	71.4	72.7	81.8	69.1	57.9
Total	100.0	100.0	100.0	100.0	100.0	100.0	100.0
1958 Cohort							
1	41.8	11.8	10.9	5.9	5.9	8.9	8.3
2-4	35.4	27.6	29.1	18.8	20.9	26.0	25.4
5+	22.8	60.6	60.0	75.2	73.2	65.1	66.3
Total	100.0	100.0	100.0	100.0	100.0	100.0	100.0

SOURCE: Tracy et al. (1984: Tables 24a-b and 27a-b).
NOTE: a. Refers to the total number of offenses of any kind accumulated by a delinquent.
b. Refers to a police contact for an incident in which at least one victim sustained a physical injury, ranging from minor harm to death.

Table 2.17. Piper's (1985) analysis of the 1958 Philadelphia birth cohort boys indicated that the violent chronic recidivists alone (those with five or more police contacts, one or more of which was for a *UCR* violent index offense), although representing just 15.9% of the delinquents, were responsible for nearly three times their proportionate share of all offenses (45.9%; Piper, 1985: Table III). Examining just the violent delinquents, nearly one-fifth of this group participated in three or more *UCR* violent index crimes and accounted for nearly half of all such serious violent crimes (Table 2.17). Clearly, a modest proportion of the most violent boys engaged in a disproportionate share of these most serious delinquencies.

Consistent with Piper (1985), Miller et al. (1982) found that adult males with three or more arrests for *UCR* violent index crimes made up nearly a fourth of the violent offenders and accounted for almost half of the violent arrests (Table 2.17). Guttridge et al. (1983) observed a less pronounced skew over the juvenile and adult years combined for Danish male cohort members: A much smaller proportion of the violent crimes was accumulated by the chronic violent group (three or more violent crimes); nevertheless, this group was still disproportionately involved in these crimes (6.4% of the violent offenders; 18.0% of the violent official contacts).

Two studies have examined males and females combined. Hamparian et al. (1978) found that 3.8% of the delinquents had registered three or more violent arrests and accounted for 10.4% of all such arrests (Table 2.17), a result similar in scale to that of Guttridge et al. (1983). Wikström's (1985) results for a Swedish cohort followed through age 25 are generally consistent with those reported by Piper (1985) and by Miller et al. (1982) rather than with those reported by Guttridge et al. and Hamparian et al.: Offenders with three or more violent offenses represented nearly one-fourth of the violent offenders and amassed nearly three-fifths of the violent offenses.

Overall, these results indicate that among all offenders a small segment accounts for a large proportion of all offenses, including the most violent ones. However, among just the violent offenders the violent incidents appear less extreme in their concentration. Although it is true that a relatively moderate proportion of the violent offenders—the chronic violent group—engages in more than its representative share of the violent offenses, the magnitude of this disproportion is not as marked as that which appears when chronic offenders in general and all of their offenses are examined. These findings indicate that the violent

TABLE 2.17

Chronic Violent Offense Careers (Official Records)

	Males					
	U.S. Studies				Foreign Studies	
	Piper (1985)[a]		Miller et al. (1982)[b]		Guttridge et al. (1982)[c]	
	Juveniles		Adults		Juveniles and Adults	
Offense Rank: Number of Violent Offenses	Offenders %	Offenses %	Offenders %	Offenses %	Offenders %	Offenses %
1	62.2	33.9	48.2	24.7	76.5	56.6
2	19.2	21.0	28.9	29.6	17.1	25.4
3			12.0	18.4		
4			5.9	12.0		
5			2.7	6.9		
6	18.6	45.2	1.2	3.6	6.4	18.0
7			.9	3.1		
8			<.5	.3		
9			<.5	.6		
10+			<.5	.8		

125

	Males and Females				
	U.S. Studies Hamparian et al. (1978)[d]		*Foreign Studies* Wikström (1985)[e, f]		
	Juveniles		Juveniles and Adults		
Offense Rank: Number of Violent Offenses	Offenders %	Offenses %	Offenders %	Offenses %	
1	83.5	68.7	58.9	27.0	
2	12.7	20.9	17.3	15.8	
≥ 3	3.8	10.4	23.9	57.2	

SOURCES: Guttridge et al. (1982: Table 11-2); Hamparian et al. (1978: Table 4-2); Miller et al. (1982: Table 4-9); Piper (1985, derived from Table VIII); Wikström (1985, derived from Figure 7).

NOTE:
a. Violent offenses include police contacts for *UCR* violent index offenses (homicide, rape, robbery, and aggravated assault) or offenses in which a victim was injured.
b. Violent offenses include arrests for *UCR* violent index offenses: homicide, rape, robbery, and aggravated assault.
c. Violent offenses include murder, rape, violence against authority, bodily injury, violence—threat concerning violence, and robbery with violence or threat of violence.
d. Violent offenses include murder, manslaughter, rape and other sexual offenses, robbery, and assault.
e. Violent offenses include murder, manslaughter, assault, robbery, molestation, unlawful threats, and intrusions.
f. The percentages presented are approximations visually extrapolated from Wikström (1985: Figure 7).

career criminal, as represented by official records, is a more widely dispersed group than might have been expected. Should this pattern be confirmed by future research, selective targeting of justice system resources based on official records alone will be reduced in its cost-effective outcome: Identifying a few violent offenders might not lower markedly the overall level of violence occurrence. However, findings relating to the individual violent crime rate reviewed earlier indicate that a small group of offenders report a high rate of violent involvement. Coordinating information about the causes and correlates of violent criminal careers derived from both official and self-report sources may aid in designing the most effective offender-targeting policies.

Using Information About Violent Criminal Careers: Prospects and Problems

This chapter has highlighted some of the structural and dynamic, behavioral features of the individual violent criminal career. Findings indicate that relatively few members of general populations that are at-risk to accumulate official records for seriously violent behavior in fact accumulate such records, regardless of whether one considers the juvenile years, the adult years, or the combined period, through the late thirties and mid-forties. However, substantially larger numbers of people report having participated in seriously violent behaviors that failed to result in an official notation. Cumulative and current serious violent participation rates appear to increase over the juvenile and young adult years and then to decline, although the evidence with respect to this issue is not yet firm. The initial officially recorded violent offense in the criminal career is most likely to occur in late adolescence and early adulthood, with robbery offenders commencing their criminal careers earlier than personal injury offenders. Those individuals who actively participate in seriously violent incidents exhibit, for the most part, very low or modest individual violent arrest and violent offense rates, although a few individuals are so involved at exceedingly high rates. Age patterns in the rates of individual crime are presently unclear.

It appears that the further an offender advances into the sequence of violent crime, the greater is that offender's risk of advancing to the next higher rung in the violence sequence. Stochastic modeling of the observed serious violent recidivism sequence may alter this picture, however, if this modeling mirrors research developments on general individual criminal careers: Violent recidivism probabilities might, in fact, stabilize after initial sequential advancements; and the apparent increases in recidivism risks might reflect an increasingly homogeneous group of a priori high-propensity offenders at the later nodes in the violent criminal career chain. Some specialization in serious violent crime occurs as offenders penetrate further into their criminal careers, mostly at the late juvenile and, more so, early adult ages. This specialization is usually in the form of a violence cluster, or violent crime mixture. Versatility in offending appears, then, to be the dominant configuration of the individual violent criminal career. Escalation in offense gravity has been observed in violent criminal careers, but it is modest and typically comprises an enhanced risk of advancing, as the offense sequence extends, from a less serious to a more serious crime type, including violent types.

The bulk of serious violent crimes occur in late adolescence and, more so, early adulthood. Whether this clustering reflects greater participation at these ages, elevated individual violent crime rates, or both is uncertain. Overall, violent crimes are a modest proportion of all unlawful occurrences: However, the moderate proportional significance of these behaviors must be viewed relative to the substantial physical and related harm inflicted. A small group of chronic violent recidivists—those with multiple violent offenses—accounts for a disproportionate share of the serious violent offenses, but not to the degree that chronic recidivists in general—those with multiple offenses of all types—account for a disproportionate share of all crime, particularly serious violent crime. The average total adult *UCR* violent index criminal career length stretches between half a decade and a decade depending on the criminal type in question. The average duration of the residual, or remaining, adult *UCR* violent index criminal career varies as violent activity progresses, depending, once again, on the violent crime type defining that criminal career. Systematic research has yet to be done that integrates analyses of offenders exhibiting high individual violent crime rates to analyses of offenders exhibiting substantial total individual criminal career lengths: In short, little is currently known about the violent career criminal.

One must bear in mind that this profile of the individual violent criminal career comprises an aggregate depiction of these careers: Consequently, each violent criminal career dimension can be disaggregated into potentially theoretically, demographically, and practically meaningful subgroups, such as by the customary age, gender, and race triad and, among others, the drug, gang, psychopathological, and sexually motivated career continuities addressed by other chapters in this volume. In other words, the profile of the individual violent criminal career presented here comprises diverse constituent types of violent careers; and this composition varies by casual and correlational dynamics, over time, location in the social structure, and so forth.

Findings reported here should caution against any expectation of major intervention breakthroughs that would reduce dramatically the current levels of violent criminal career participation and the frequency of that participation. Difficulties in identifying, prospectively, individuals who will become involved in officially recorded violence are formidable because of the combination of relatively low violence participation levels and the generally low intensity of involvement by participants. Whatever intervention programs might be developed to prevent or control individual violent criminal careers will be rendered less effective to the degree that participants, especially those exhibiting high-rates of violent crimes over extended time periods—the violent career criminals—cannot be identified accurately. Certainly equally as important as the issue of offender identification is that of violence explanation and the policy relevance of violence explanation to prevention and control applications. Enhanced offender identification in the absence of concomitant explanation that possesses some practical utility might perhaps benefit an incapacitation orientation but would likely be impoverished and purely palliative in its rehabilitative and specific deterrent benefits. However, analyses of individual criminal careers in general are in their nascency, with violence analyses, in particular, embryonic. Future research on violence explanation, prediction, and classification will undoubtedly benefit from the systematic approach provided by the individual criminal career paradigm. Some of these programmatic features are outlined next, along with related issues.

As noted at several points in this chapter, intervention strategies can be tailored to address specific stages in and dynamics of the unfolding individual violent criminal career, including the point of initial participation in violent crime, the frequencies with which offenders pursue their violent criminal involvements, the violence specialization and escalation trajectories, the sequential violent recidivism nodes, and the point of desistance from violent criminal activity. These foci can be refined further to concentrate on those career characteristics that productively distinguish different kinds of violent careers from one another—for example, predominantly instrumental from predominantly expressive careers, violent juvenile from violent adult careers, sexually from nonsexually violent careers, psychopathological from nonpsychopathological violent careers, exclusively violent from mixed violent and nonviolent offense careers, and the like.

Approaches to curbing the initiation of a violent criminal career or impeding its maintenance and gravity, should initiation of the violent criminal career nevertheless occur, can be either direct or indirect, proactive or reactive. Direct approaches might include normative and behavioral interventions aimed at the modification of individuals' aggressive and violent conduct and violence-related attitudes at key early developmental ages, perhaps as part of broadly administered and delivered nonselective educational and community programs. Indirect approaches might include modifying substance abuse, breaking the cycle of familial violence, expanding employment opportunities, and diminishing weapons use. While these indirect approaches do not focus on the violent act per se, they do address indirectly other personal and social patterns that, as one of their byproducts, might diminish the chances and gravities of violent conduct. These approaches are proactive insofar as they aim to halt or delay the initiation of the individual violent criminal career. They are reactive insofar as they are intended to respond to violent criminal careers that have already been initiated by reducing the risk that the criminal career will involve further serious and repetitive violent activity.

Should a violent criminal career begin, rehabilitative, deterrent, and incapacitative approaches are potential intervention options. Whichever approach or combination might be selected—based on considerations of feasibility, effectiveness, ethicality, and cost—justification for and success of the selected strategy will depend crucially on the point in the violent criminal career that is targeted and, relatedly, on the capacity of criminal justice system and allied practitioners to implement the strategy through first prospectively identifying those violent offenders who are at greatest risk relative to the criminal career point at issue and then identifying those interventions that are most effective with respect to these offenders.

Effective intervention would require, among other things, the accurate identification of (1) high-rate violent offenders and those times at which these offenders are at greatest risk to commit violent offenses, (2) those offenders who are persistently seriously violent or who will graduate from less serious to more serious violent offenses, and (3) those offenders who will continue for the longest remaining time in their violent criminal careers. Conversely, ineffective strategies would involve the misidentification of high-rate violent offenders as low-rate violent offenders or of low-rate violent offenders as high-rate violent offenders and interventions into those violent criminal careers that are likely either to flag in seriousness or to terminate shortly. Research on the violent criminal career as a *system* of related structures and processes promotes, as just outlined, greater sensitivity to the potential payoffs of these complementary strategies as well as to their potential pitfalls.

Using the individual violent criminal career paradigm as the basis for understanding violent criminal behavior and, based on that knowledge, for developing prevention and control policies raises several ethical and operational issues—for example, the ethical and legal implications of organizing social interventions and imposing criminal sanctions in the face of the inevitable incorrect identification of some high-rate violent offenders, the problem of striking a proper balance between retroactive punishment (retribution) and proactive community protection (deterrence or incapacitation), the justification for disparities in judicial dispositions through violent offender-based or violent charge-based decision-making strategies (that is, using offender attributes or offense attributes, respectively), and the possibility that rules to identify the most serious and persistent violent criminals may disproportionately penalize the disadvantaged and minority group members (Blumstein et al., 1986: 7). Cautious and measured movement across this difficult terrain is required lest the best of policy intentions becomes caught in unforeseen and unintended quagmires.

In broad sweep, future research on individual violent criminal careers might take its lead from the agenda recently advocated by the NRC Panel that called for

> improved measurement of dimensions of criminal careers; measurement of their distributions, which are still known only imprecisely; measurement of the variation of the dimensions over the course of a criminal career; and better identification of the factors that influence criminal careers [Blumstein et al., 1986: 10].

A *theoretically* anchored design; an *interdisciplinary* approach; *multiple partially overlapping or fully contiguous birth cohorts; prospective, repeated-contact follow-up spanning at least ages 6 through 24*; a focus on *high-risk populations* that includes more general populations; *diverse geographical representation* but targeting *urban* areas; a *longitudinal* or over-time design; *multiple instruments and procedures* to measure criminal behavior (for example, self-report, official records, informant contacts, and direct observation): These research pathways will be central to efforts to trace individual violent criminal careers with the precision required for developing a sound and systematic prevention and control policy (Blumstein et al., 1986; Farrington et al., 1986). This core quantitative research thrust should be augmented by other research designs, such as ethnographic studies of the interactional infrastructure of violent criminal encounters, especially those that are repetitive and indicative of entrenched cycles of violence. Important present limitations and deficiencies in the areas of measurement (quantifying violence participation and the intensity and types of such involvement), sampling (selecting representative groups of violent participants), statistical modeling (mathematically depicting violent criminal career dynamics), and administrative record keeping and dissemination (for purposes of conducting policy-related research and implementing intervention strategies) must be confronted and resolved if individual violent criminal careers are to be adequately studied and accurately depicted.

Future research should seek, however, not only to chart more accurately the descriptive contours and correlates of the individual violent criminal career but to search for sequential and, based on this, causal dynamics. Formal and quasi-experimental designs involving, for example, an arrest cohort and an imprisoned cohort have been recommended as study modalities that might add appreciably to our knowledge about causal mechanisms (Farrington et al., 1986). These results can pinpoint criminal career processes that might be modified to prevent or halt the advancement of the violent behavioral sequence. To the extent that there exist various kinds of individual violent criminal careers, further research is needed to reveal their distinctive structural and dynamic features. Firm inferences about individual violent criminal careers will further depend upon research replication.

Special attention will need to be paid to problems confronted by research that focuses on violent and aggressive behavior generally, and on violent criminal behavior specifically. Relative to many other kinds of behavior, violence is *infrequent*. Sampling strategies will need to be devised to net a sufficient number of violent individuals and their violent acts. Relative to many other kinds of behavior, violence is a *sensitive* concern. Data-collection strategies will need to be developed to handle the impediment of reluctant and evasive respondents. Relative to many other kinds of behavior, violence poses formidable *ethical* concerns for experimental research strategies. Proper protections for both subjects and the community will need to be devised to obviate this impediment. However, none of these or corollary problems in conducting research on violent crime are insurmountable. But to be surmounted, the research resolve to conduct these studies must be marshaled; and this resolve must be buttressed by a broad-based consensus that violence studies merit initiation and full follow-through.

The details—and attendant problems and potential pitfalls—of a comprehensive and coordinated program to study general individual criminal careers were presented recently by the NRC Panel (Blumstein et al., 1986) and by others who have been at the vortex of these issues (Farrington et al., 1986). We anticipate that these recommendations, together with other parallel currents in criminology and criminal justice, will galvanize support for research on individual criminal careers. The climate is ripe for developing the details of this core criminological investigation. Surely a central component of this investigation must be a focus on violent crimes, violent criminals, and otherwise serious criminal behavior.

NOTES

1. Because of the limited focus of this chapter on the individual violent criminal career, some controversial conceptual loose ends must unfortunately remain with respect to definitional issues, for example, problems in the operational measurement of violent phenomena: Who decides that a violent act has occurred and how this decision is reached, the nature of "intent" on the part of the violent participants, whether "psychological" force or insult qualify as violence, and whether violence can comprise "acts of omission"? Although these important conceptual strands cannot be pursued in-depth here, their mention is nonetheless important because doing so yields the dual gains of a more fully specified conceptual domain and, as important, lays bare some points of potential analytical disagreement confronting the definitional posture taken in this chapter.

2. Note that the goals and motivations of the person who threatens or applies physical force do not, as the definition indicates, conform to the intentions of the victim. If the motivations of the two parties are consonant, the victim is complicitous of the incident and is perhaps no longer, in strict legal terms, a criminal victim, as might be the case if the victim invites or otherwise precipitates or provokes the application or threat of the injurious physical force—for instance, toward realizing masochistic or, more extremely, suicidal ends. Criminal violence involves, therefore, a victim who does not welcome or consent to the assault or the threat of same. A main component of crimes of violence is, then, the coercive character of the exchange.

3. Berkowitz (1962, 1974, 1978, 1986), among others, has made and worked through the substantive implications of these and other distinctions in studying aggression

generally and both criminal and noncriminal violence specifically. Social scientists have often followed suit with respect to the main distinctions among hostile, expressive, and instrumental violence, although, as indicated in the text, hostile violence is often considered in tandem with the expressive form, usually as a subtype.

4. Few would disagree that the line between interpersonal and collective violence is conceptually and operationally ambiguous. Nevertheless, the dichotomy between these two forms of violence is common in the field and is motivated, as mentioned in the text, by conceptions of their quite different casual and correlative roots and situational dynamics. Similarly, political and other ideologically spawned forms of violence are commonly distinguished from interpersonal violence, mainly with respect to the different organizational and institutional underpinnings of these violent polarities.

5. Should the former approach be chosen, one might examine, for example, the age at initiation into a violent criminal career regardless of whether the initial offense was violent. Should the latter approach be selected, then age at initiation would be marked as the age of the first violent offense. Analysis of other components of the individual violent criminal career can proceed in an analogous fashion.

6. That the individual violent crime rate is calculated on the basis of a year of *actual* time at risk distinguishes it from the *effective* individual violent crime rate that applies to the year after discounting incarceration time or other sources of immobility. For example, an offender may commit violent crimes at a rate of 10 per year while free in the community. If the offender is confined for six months, he can commit violent offenses only at a rate of 10 for the six months while free. The active rate is 10 violent offenses per year, but the effective rate during the entire year is five because he was actively committing violent crimes in the community for only half the year.

7. Transition matrices comprise cross-tabular representations of a pair of successive offenses in an offense sequence—for example, the first to second offense. A transition matrix lists for adjacent offenses in the sequence the set of possible initial, or departure, offense types in the offense pair as the row designations and the set of possible trailing, or destination, offense types in the offense pair as the column designations. For instance, if murder, rape, and robbery comprise, from top to bottom, the set of three-row listings to designate the possible initial offense in the pair, then these same three offenses would comprise, from left to right, the column listings to designate the possible trailing offense in the pair. To illustrate: If a delinquent has been involved in robberies as both the first and second offenses in the career progression, to form a first-to-second offense-transition coupling comprising two robberies, then that delinquent would fall into the transition matrix at the intersection of the third row and third column of the cross-tabular offense array just described.

8. If, for example, 25 violent delinquents in a group of 100 delinquents commit their first violent delinquent acts at age 15, the age-specific violent initiation rate is .25 (that is, 25/100). If 25 other violent delinquents in the group commit their first violent delinquent acts prior to age 15, then only 75 of the violent delinquents overall did not commit their first violent offenses by the start of the fifteenth year, producing an age-specific violent hazard rate of .33 for those 25 who committed their first violent delinquency acts at age 15 (that is, 25/75).

9. Criminal career length refers to the time span from the first *UCR* index arrest (between ages 18 and 20) of any type (except larceny) to the last arrest of the designated type for offenders active in that type—for example, from the first *UCR* index arrest of any type to the final robbery of robbers. The same measurement rule applies to the following discussion of the residual criminal career length.

REFERENCES

Bachman, J. G., P. M. O'Malley, and J. Johnston (1978) Youth in Transition, Vol. 6. Ann Arbor: University of Michigan Institute for Social Research.

Baker, T., F. Mann, and C. J. Friedman (1975) "Selectivity in the criminal justice system." Prison Journal 55 (1): 22-34.

Barnett, A., A. Blumstein, and D. P. Farrington (1987) "Probabilistic models of youthful criminal careers." Criminology 25: 83-107.

Berkowitz, L. (1962) Aggression: A Social Psychological Analysis. New York: McGraw-Hill.

Berkowitz, L. (1974) "Some determinants of impulsive aggression: role of mediated associations with reinforcements for aggression." Psychological Review 81: 165-176.

Berkowitz, L. (1978) "Is criminal violence normative behavior? Hostile and instrumental aggression in violent incidents." Journal of Research in Crime and Delinquency 15: 148-161.

Berkowitz, L. (1986) "Some varieties of human aggression: criminal violence as coercion, rule-following, impression management, and impulsive behavior," pp. 87-103 in A. Campbell and J. J. Gibbs (eds.) Violent Transactions: The Limits of Criminality. New York: Basil Blackwell.

Blumstein, A. and J. Cohen (1979) "Estimation of individual crime rates from arrest records." Journal of Criminal Law and Criminology 70: 561-585.

Blumstein, A., J. Cohen, and P. Hsieh (1982) The Duration of Adult Criminal Careers; Final Report to the National Institute of Justice. Pittsburgh: School of Urban and Public Affairs, Carnegie-Mellon University.

Blumstein, A., J. Cohen, J. A. Roth, and C. A. Visher [eds.] (1986) Criminal Careers and "Career Criminals." Washington, DC: National Academy Press.

Blumstein, A., D. P. Farrington, and S. Moitra (1985) "Delinquency careers: innocents, desisters, and persisters," pp. 187-219 in N. Morris and M. Tonry (eds.) Crime and Justice: An Annual Review of Research, Vol. 6. Chicago: University of Chicago Press.

Blumstein, A. and E. Graddy (1981-1982) "Prevalence and incidence in index arrests: a feedback model." Law and Society Review 16: 265-290.

Blumstein, A. and M. A. Greene (1976) "Analysis of crime-type switching in recidivism." Urban Systems Institute, School of Urban and Public Affairs, Carnegie-Mellon University, Pittsburgh. (preliminary draft)

Blumstein, A. and S. Moitra (1980) "The identification of 'career criminals' from chronic offenders in a cohort." Law and Society Quarterly 2 (July): 321-334.

Booth, E. (1929) Stealing Through Life. New York: Knopf.

Buikhuisen, W. and R. W. Jongman (1970) "A legalistic classification of juvenile delinquents." British Journal of Criminology 10: 109-123.

Bursik, R. J. (1980) "The dynamics of specialization in juvenile offenses." Social Forces 58: 851-864.

Cernkovich, S. A. and P. C. Giordano (1979) "A comparative analysis of male and female delinquency." Sociological Quarterly 20: 131-145.

Chaiken, J. M. and M. R. Chaiken (1982) Varieties of Criminal Behavior. Santa Monica, CA: Rand Corporation.

Chaiken, M. R. and J. M. Chaiken (1984) "Offender types and public policy." Crime and Delinquency 30: 195-226.

Chambliss, W. J. and R. H. Nagasawa (1969) "On the validity of official statistics: a comparative study of white, black, and Japanese high-school boys." Journal of Research in Crime and Delinquency 6: 71-77.

Clarke, S. N. (1975) "Getting 'em out of circulation: does incarceration of juvenile offenders reduce crime?" Journal of Criminal Law and Criminology 65: 528-535.

Cohen, J. (1983) "Incapacitation as a strategy for crime control: possibilities and pitfalls," pp. 1-84 in M. Tonry and N. Morris (eds.) Crime and Justice: An Annual Review of Research, Vol. 5. Chicago: University of Chicago Press.

Cohen, J. (1986) "Research on criminal careers," pp. 292-418 in A. Blumstein, J. Cohen, J. A. Roth, and C. A. Visher (eds.) Criminal Careers and "Career Criminals," Vol. 1. Washington, DC: National Academy Press.

Denno, D. J. (1982) "Sex differences in cognition and crime: early developmental, biological, and sociological correlates." Ph.D. dissertation, University of Pennsylvania.

Elliott, D. S., S. S. Ageton, D. Huizinga, B. Knowles, and R. Canter (1983) The Prevalence and Incidence of Delinquent Behavior: 1976-1980. National Youth Survey Report No. 26. Boulder, CO: Behavioral Research Institute.

Elliott, D. S. and D. Huizinga (1984) The Relationship Between Delinquent Behavior and ADM Problems. National Youth Survey Report No. 28. Boulder, CO: Behavioral Research Institute.

Elliott, D. S., D. Huizinga, and B. Morse (1986) "Self-reported violent offending: a descriptive analysis of juvenile violent offenders and their offending careers." Journal of Interpersonal Violence 1: 472-514.

Facella, C. (1983) "Female delinquency in a birth cohort." Ph.D. dissertation, University of Pennsylvania.

Farrington, D. P. (1983) Further Analyses of a Longitudinal Survey of Crime and Delinquency; Final Report to the National Institute of Justice. Washington, DC: Government Printing Office.

Farrington, D. P., L. E. Ohlin, and J. Q. Wilson (1986) Understanding and Controlling Crime: Toward a New Research Strategy. New York: Springer-Verlag.

Figueira-McDonough, J., W. H. Barton, and R. C. Sarri (1981) "Normal deviance: gender similarities in adolescent subcultures," pp. 17-45 in M. Q. Warren (ed.) Comparing Female and Male Offenders. Beverly Hills, CA: Sage.

Frum, H. S. (1958) "Adult criminal offense trends following juvenile delinquency." Journal of Criminal Law, Criminology, and Police Science 49: 29-49.

Gold, M. (1966) "Undetected delinquent behavior." Journal of Research in Crime and Delinquency 3: 27-46.

Greenberg, D. F. (1975) "The incapacitative effect of imprisonment: some estimates." Law and Society Review 9: 541-580.

Greene, M. A. (1977) "The incapacitative effect of imprisonment policies on crime." Ph.D. dissertation, Carnegie-Mellon University.

Greenwood, P. W. and A. Abrahams (1982) Selective Incapacitation. Santa Monica, CA: Rand Corporation.

Guttridge, P., W. F. Gabrielli, Jr., S. A. Mednick, and K. T. Van Dusen (1983) "Criminal violence in a birth cohort," pp. 211-224 in K. T. Van Dusen and S. A. Mednick (eds.) Prospective Studies of Crime and Delinquency. Boston: Kluwer-Nijhoff.

Hamparian, D. M., R. Schuster, S. Dinitz, and J. P. Conrad (1978) The Violent Few: A Study of Dangerous Juvenile Offenders. Lexington, MA: Lexington.

Hindelang, M. J., T. Hirschi, and J. G. Weis (1981) Measuring Delinquency. Beverly Hills, CA: Sage.

Høgh, E. and P. Wolf (1983) "Violent crime in a birth cohort: Copenhagen, 1953-1977," pp. 249-267 in K. T. Van Dusen and S. A. Mednick (eds.) Prospective Studies of Crime and Delinquency. Boston: Kluwer-Nijhoff.

Klockars, C. B. (1974) The Professional Fence. New York: Free Press.

Kratcoski, P. C. and J. E. Kratcoski (1975) "Changing patterns in the delinquent activities of boys and girls: a self-reported delinquency analysis." Adolescence 10: 83-91.

Lab, S. P. (1985) "Patterns in juvenile misbehavior." Crime and Delinquency 30: 293-308.

Martin, J. B. (1952) My Life in Crime: The Autobiography of a Professional Thief. New York: Knopf.

McCord, J. (1980) "Some child-rearing antecedents of criminal behavior in adult men," pp. 121-130 in E. Bittner and S. L. Messinger (eds.) Criminology Review Yearbook, Vol. 2. Beverly Hills, CA: Sage.

Miller, S. J., S. Dinitz, and J. P. Conrad (1982) Careers of the Violent: The Dangerous Offender and Criminal Justice. Lexington, MA: Lexington.

Mitchell, S. and P. Rosa (1981) "Boyhood behaviour problems as precursors of criminality: a fifteen-year follow-up study." Journal of Child Psychiatry and Psychology 22: 19-33.

Petersilia, J., P. W. Greenwood, and M. Lavin (1977) Criminal Careers of Habitual Felons. Washington, DC: Government Printing Office.

Peterson, M. A., H. B. Braiker, and S. M. Polich (1981) Who Commits Crimes: A Survey of Prison Inmates. Cambridge, MA: Oelgeschlager, Gunn & Hain.

Peterson, R. A., D. J. Pittman, and P. O'Neal (1962) "Stabilities in deviance: a study of assaultive and non-assaultive offenders." Journal of Criminal Law, Criminology, and Police Science 53: 44-48.

Piper, E. S. (1983) "Patterns of violent juvenile recidivism." Ph.D. dissertation, University of Pennsylvania.

Piper, E. S. (1985) "Violent recidivism and chronicity in the 1958 Philadelphia cohort." Journal of Quantitative Criminology 1: 319-344.

Polk, K., C. Alder, G. Bazemore, G. Blake, S. Cordray, G. Coventry, J. Galvin, and M. Temple (1981) Becoming Adult: An Analysis of Maturational Development from Ages 16 to 30 of a Cohort of Young Men; Final Report of the Marion County Youth Study. Eugene, OR: University of Oregon, Department of Sociology.

Porterfield, A. L. (1946) Youth in Trouble: Studies in Delinquency and Despair with Plans for Prevention. Fort Worth, TX: Leo Potishman Foundation.

Robins, L. N. (1966) Deviant Children Grown Up. Baltimore: Williams & Wilkins.

Rojek, D. and M. L. Erickson (1982) "Delinquent careers: a test of the career escalation model." Criminology 20: 5-28.

Shannon, L. W. (1982) Assessing the Relationship of Adult Criminal Careers to Juvenile Careers. Iowa City: Iowa Urban Community Research Center, University of Iowa.

Shaw, C. (1930) The Jack Roller: A Delinquent Boy's Own Story. Chicago: University of Chicago Press.

Shaw, C. (1931) The Natural History of a Delinquent Career. Chicago: University of Chicago Press.

Shinnar, S. and R. Shinnar (1974) "The effects of the criminal justice system on the control of crime: a quantitative approach." Law and Society Review 9: 581-610.

Short, J. F., Jr. and F. I. Nye (1958) "Extent of unrecorded juvenile delinquency: tentative conclusions." Journal of Criminal Law, Criminology, and Police Science 49: 296-312.

Smith, D. R. and W. R. Smith (1984) "Patterns of delinquent careers: an assessment of three perspectives." Social Science Research 13: 129-158.

Sutherland, E. H. (1937) The Professional Thief. Chicago: University of Chicago Press.

Tittle, C. R. (1980) Sanctions and Social Deviance: The Question of Deterrence. New York: Praeger.

Tracy, P. E., Jr., M. E. Wolfgang, and R. M. Figlio (1984) Delinquency in a Birth Cohort II: A Comparison of the 1945 and 1958 Philadelphia Birth Cohorts; Final Report Submitted to the National Institute of Justice. Philadelphia: Center for Studies in Criminology and Criminal Law, University of Pennsylvania.

Visher, C. A. and J. A. Roth (1986) "Participation in criminal careers," pp. 211-291 in A. Blumstein, J. Cohen, J. A. Roth, and C. A. Visher (eds.) Criminal Careers and "Career Criminals," Vol. 1. Washington, DC: National Academy Press.

Walker, N., W. Hammond, and D. Steer (1967) "Repeated violence." Criminal Law Review 1967: 465-472.

Weiner, N. A. (1985) Violent Recidivism Among the 1958 Philadelphia Birth Cohort Boys; Report Submitted to the National Institute of Justice. Philadelphia: Sellin Center for Studies in Criminology and Criminal Law.

Weis, J. G. (1976) "Liberation and crime: the invention of the new female criminal." Crime and Social Justice 6: 17-27.

Wikström, P. O. H. (1985) Everyday Violence in Contemporary Sweden: Situational and Ecological Aspects. Stockholm: National Council for Crime Prevention.

Williams, J. R. and M. Gold (1972) "From delinquent behavior to official delinquency." Social Problems 20: 209-229.

Wolfgang, M. E., R. M. Figlio, and T. Sellin (1972) Delinquency in a Birth Cohort. Chicago: University of Chicago Press.

Wolfgang, M. E., T. P. Thornberry, and R. M. Figlio (1987) From Boy to Man, From Delinquency to Crime. Chicago: University of Chicago Press.

3

Race and Violent Crime

Toward a New Policy

LYNN A. CURTIS

[Blacks are] inferior to whites in the endowments both of body and mind.

—Thomas Jefferson

The nation's inner cities can be reclaimed. Argus, created by ghetto residents, staffed by them, managed by them, with help from the outside, teaches children how to heal their pain, reach for a broader world and live in it. Their achievement can be a reference point for efforts on a larger scale.

—Elizabeth Sturz

Sturz is right and Jefferson was wrong. We will show that this is so by briefly profiling the extent and character of violent crime in America, summarizing explanations on the role of race, and then spending the better part of this chapter reviewing concrete programs that can become the basis for a new policy to reduce violent crime among inner city minorities.

Extent and Character

Based on both crimes reported to the police and on U.S. Census Bureau victimization surveys of household samples, we can reasonably conclude that rates of serious violent crime—murder, assault, rape, and robbery—have increased since the late 1960s (Weiner and Wolfgang, 1985). Today, the chance of becoming a victim of violent crime is greater than the chance of divorce, the risk of being in an automobile accident, or the probability of dying from cancer (Curtis, 1985b: 3).

The level of violent crime in the United States remains astronomical—much higher than in other industrialized democratic nations (Curtis, 1985b: 3).

Considerably more than half of all murders, assaults, and rapes continue to be committed by minorities on minorities. In robbery, offenders are disproportionately minority, though nationally victims are about as likely to be white as minority (Curtis, 1985b: 3).

Both victims and offenders are disproportionately young in serious violence, with the exception of robbery where the distribution between younger and older victims is more equal (Curtis, 1985b: 3).

The evidence from decades of research shows an almost linear relationship between economic deprivation and serious crime (Currie, 1985: 146). But social class and income level do not account for all the disparity between minorities and whites in rates of committing serious violent crime and delinquency. For example, when Wolfgang et al. compared different groups in their Philadelphia cohort study of boys born in 1945, no other variables emerged quite so clearly as did race as a determinant of contrast (1972: 245-249). Poor boys were involved in more reported delinquencies than were middle- or upper-class boys; but even within the lower class, nonwhite boys were involved in significantly more delinquencies than white boys. A later Philadelphia cohort study, of boys born in 1958, found that the racial imbalance remained pervasive and startling and that the second cohort was significantly more violent than was the first (Wolfgang and Tracy, 1982).

Overall, the most typical murder or assault is committed for an ostensibly trivial motive by a young, poor, inner-city, minority male against someone with the same characteristics. Murder is the number one cause of death in the United States for young black men. The murder and assault victim-offender patterns hold for forcible rape, except, of course, for the gender of the victim. In robbery, there are two dominant patterns—young, poor, inner-city, minority males who victimize persons with similar characteristics and also victimize older whites. A very large proportion of all violent crime is committed by a very small proportion of the offending population (Curtis, 1974b, 1985a; Wolfgang and Tracy, 1982).

Levels of fear also have increased since the 1960s for both minorities and whites. Among whites, fear often is associated with the assumption that blackness indicates criminality (even though most minority members are not violent criminals). In the late 1980s that presumption led a Louisiana sheriff to order deputies to stop and question all blacks on sight; produced a debate in Washington, D.C. over whether local stores, fearing robbery, should refuse to admit black men; and resulted in signs on the doors of small shops on the Upper East Side of Manhattan that say, "Men by appointment only." Although the incidence of violent acts by whites against blacks may or may not be as high today as in Thomas Jefferson's time (we have no valid and reliable historical data), we have experienced an increase in the 1980s of well-publicized examples—like the killing and beating of blacks by a gang of teenagers armed with bats in Howard Beach, Queens; the firebombing that destroyed the home of a black family that had moved into a predominantly white Philadelphia suburb; and the shooting of four blacks in a New York subway by Bernhard Goetz (Curtis, 1985b; New York Times, 1986; Milwaukee Journal, 1986).

Explanations

In the late 1960s, the National Commission on the Causes and Prevention of Violence (hereinafter referred to as the Violence Commission), concurring with the findings of the National Advisory Commission on Civil Disorders 1968 (hereinafter referred to as the Kerner Commission), concluded that:

> To be a young, poor male; to be undereducated and without means of escape from an oppressive urban environment; to want what the society claims is available (but mostly to others); to see around oneself illegitimate and often violent methods being used to achieve material success; and to observe others using these means with impunity—all this is to be burdened with an enormous set of influences that pull many toward crime and delinquency. To be also a Black, Mexican or Puerto Rican American and subject to discrimination adds considerably to the pull [National Commission on the Causes and Prevention of Violence, 1969: 35].

Violent crime is too complex for any brief statement to be entirely accurate in explaining disproportionate minority involvement in violent and related crimes. But no explanations since the Violence and Kerner Commissions better explain the available statistics on levels of violence, trends in violence, the role of relative economic deprivation, and the independent determinant of race.

Continuity with the Commissions

This is not the place for an extensive review of the literature since the Violence and Kerner Commissions. But the work of Rainwater (1970), Silberman (1978), and Currie (1985) illustrates explanations of disproportionate violent crime by inner city minorities that are consistent with and build on the conclusions of the Commissions.

After carefully examining the Pruitt-Igoe public housing project in St. Louis, Rainwater (1970) concluded, in a complementary way, that

> White cupidity
> creates
> structural conditions highly inimical to basic social
> adaptation (low income availability, poor education,
> poor services, stigmatization)
> to which Blacks adapt
> by
> social and personal responses which serve to sustain
> the individual in his punishing world but also
> generate aggressiveness toward the self and others
> which results in
> suffering directly inflicted by Blacks on themselves
> and on others [p. 4].

Acquisitive violence by minorities can thus be an attempt, however illusory or symbolic, to take back that which has been denied—a poor minority male's form of income redistribution. Assaultive behavior by young men, even if inflicted predominantly by minorities on other minorities, can reflect an acceptance of violence in everyday life as an available means of expressing anger, frustration, and masculinity. A lethal outcome is all the more likely, given the easy availability of handguns in the United States and traditions of weapons carrying as further proof of masculinity among poor minority youth (Curtis, 1975, 1985b). In some parallel ways, motherhood is a means by which some teen minorities perceive that they can express their womanhood in a society with opportunities blocked to them.

Consistent with Rainwater, Silberman (1978: 118, 163) pointed out that this is not the first time in the history of American ethnic groups that it has become necessary to dispute those who see no relation between crime, relative poverty, and discrimination. In the last part of the nineteenth century and the first part of the twentieth, many of the people most responsible for street crime were Irish-, German-, Italian-, and Polish-Americans. During each period there were academic "experts" who were certain that reducing poverty would have little effect on crime because the poor, they said, actually preferred their crime-ridden way of life. Yet each of these groups moved out of crime as they moved into the middle class.

The continuity of such thinking carried through to the mid-1980s and was expanded with Currie's statement that:

> If we wanted to sketch a hypothetical portrait of an especially violent society, it would surely contain these elements: It would separate large numbers of people, especially the young, from the kind of work that could include them securely in community life. It would encourage policies of economic development and income distribution that sharply increased inequalities between sectors of the population. It would rapidly shift vast amounts of capital from place to place without regard for the impact on local communities, causing massive movements of population away from family and neighborhood supports in search of livelihood. It would avoid providing new mechanisms of care and support for those uprooted, perhaps in the name of preserving incentives to work and paring government spending. It would promote a culture of intense interpersonal competition and spur its citizens to a level of material consumption many could not lawfully sustain [1985: 278].

This portrait is particularly striking for poor urban minorities for whom there are few job opportunities in the inner city. Historically, high unemployment has been made worse by capital movements into higher technology, which intensifies work skill deficits among minorities. As government spending has been cut in the 1980s (for example, 50% for the employment and training of disadvantaged minorities), the rate of poverty has increased, adding further pressures to families in which the unchanged national welfare system encourages fathers to live apart (Henderson, 1987: 130). If, in light of the interpersonal competition that street life and the electronic media bring into focus, a young inner-city minority male can find no legal labor-market job to match the material consumption of the white suburbs, he can mug or sell cocaine to whites coming in from the suburbs for it.

The "Underclass"

But why can't poor blacks, in particular, climb up into Currie's material consumption role as did all of Silberman's other ethnic groups in American history? As Comer (1985) eloquently noted, unlike other immigrant groups that were allowed to use kinship and family as a source of security and basis for development, West African culture was "broken in the enslavement process and replaced by the powerlessness and degradation of the slave culture" (p. 76). The fashionable contemporary (yet also very Jeffersonian) version of the slave culture is called the underclass—those who were unable to rise to the middle class during the last two decades. Underlying so much modern commentary on the urban underclass, like the work of Lemann (1986) and Murray (1984), are the assumptions that poor minorities created it, are responsible for perpetuating it, and would not change if the economic and racial inequalities causing it were dissolved. As has been said about one observer of the underclass, "He confuses the symptoms of deprivation, concentration, isolation, abysmal education, and limited opportunity with the causes" (Glasgow, 1987: 134).

Stated another way, the modern Jeffersonian chooses to concentrate on Rainwater's (1970) "social and personal responses which serve to sustain the individual in his punishing world" and ignores the fact that, causally, Rainwater began his paradigm with "white cupidity," which "creates structural conditions highly inimical to basic social adaptation" (p. 4). The modern underclass was, in truth, created by whites through slavery, and perpetuated by whites through continued class and racial inequities. Although there were many failures, the programs of the 1960s and 1970s did provide opportunities for some to escape and suggested how future programs might be constructed to facilitate further progress. Yet, at the national public sector level, at least, many of the successful or partially successful programs (for example, the Job Corps) were eliminated or reduced; their replacements (for example, the Job Training Partnership Act) have not been directed at those in most need; promising new private sector initiatives (for example, the Competing Competencies Program and JobStart) have not been adapted as public policy on a broad scale; and destructive old policies (for example, federal welfare regulations) have been maintained. At the same time, the public state and local sectors have not filled the void left by the federal pullout. Nor has the private sector been able to carry anywhere near the burden placed on it. Nonetheless, many whites, believing that the civil rights movement was a "complete success," see no need for continued "agitation" by minorities (Williams, 1987: C1).

In addition, contemporary underclass observers do not adequately understand the continued breadth and functioning of the minority extended family and the role in the inner city of minority working-class residents who manage "to support themselves and their children, maintain positive social values, and offer beneficial socialization influences to others around them" (Glasgow, 1987: 133).

As Glasgow (1987) admits, none of this is to deny the need for the minority community to take responsibility for improving conditions in inner city ghetto-slums. The "crime is not part of our black heritage" programs being implemented by Gary Mendez (1980) at the National Urban League are a positive step in this direction. But we must also acknowledge the limits of minority self-help when disproportionate opportunity is controlled by whites. We need to remember that greatly expanded funding is needed even with public policy reforms that empower poor minorities to structure their own solutions at the grassroots level.

Critiques

Some researchers and social commentators have asserted that poverty and race could not have been responsible for the increase in violent crime in the 1960s and 1970s because blacks had made "great advances." There were, indeed, some gains. Perhaps most publicized was the increase in the number of blacks and other minorities in managerial and professional jobs. By the 1980s, over 1.5 million blacks held such jobs—a doubling in one decade. These changes appear to have resulted primarily from federal education, employment, and affir-mative-action programs targeted at minorities. Yet the gains were limited, and economic deprivation continued or increased for those in the group who were disproportionately involved in violent crime— young, poor, inner-city, minority males. The National Urban League's (Williams, 1984) estimates of unemployment among this group during the 1970s were in the range of 50% to 60%; and this rate increased over many of the same years when the crime rate increased (Curtis, 1985b: 5).

As proof that poverty is not a cause of crime, some researchers have advanced the curious argument that we have a high crime rate in the United States even though our poorest people are materially better off than the poorest people in countries with lower crime rates. But there is no evidence that a poor black in Harlem compares himself to a poor black in Tanzania rather than to a rich white on Park Avenue. The logic of this "proof" follows the position of the government of South Africa, which has argued that income and living conditions in Soweto, the all-black suburban ghetto compound outside Johannesburg, are better than those found in black-ruled African states. Are Soweto blacks, whose violent crime rates are so much higher than those of blacks in American cities, really thinking of other African states? Or might they have been comparing the privilege and luxury of Johannesburg to their own political disenfranchisement and to the reality, for example, that only 20% of their houses have electricity and only 15% have toilets (Curtis, 1977: 10)?

Biology and Race

Thomas Jefferson underscored his perception of the importance of constitutional differences by concluding that, "The improvement of blacks in body and mind, in the first instance of their mixture with the whites, has been observed by everyone, and proves that their inferiority is not the effect merely of their condition of life" (Higginbotham, 1978: 10).

We might have expected Jefferson to continue that "distributions of crime within and across societies may, to some extent, reflect underlying distributions of constitutional factors." But the latter quote comes from two contemporary commentators in the now-fashionable school of genetic and biological criminology—Wilson and Herrnstein (1985: 103). Some of the inferences in their book, *Crime and Human Nature,* are instructive as lessons in how "snippets of data are plucked from a stew of conflicting and often nonsensical experimental results" and used in the manner of a lawyer who builds a case by anecdote. "The data do not determine the conclusions reached by the lawyer. Instead the conclusions toward which the lawyer wants to steer the jury determine which bits of data he presents." For example, in trying to correlate biologically linked personality traits to crime, Wilson and Herrnstein pointed to low crime rates and low paper and pencil test scores on introversion in Japan. Yet they failed to tell the reader that the same personality test showed the Japanese scoring higher than people of other countries on a personality trait associated with "brutality and insensitivity of feelings for others" (Kamin, 1986: 24).

As did Jefferson, Wilson and Herrnstein confused genetic correlation and genetic causation. For example, the logic of their position was that, should blacks make up a disproportionate share of the unemployed, we are on the trail of a genetic correlate of unemployment—just because black skin has a genetic basis. Yet "there is no meaningful sense in which the genes of black people cause their unemployment. We can easily imagine a society in which skin color would no longer be a correlate of unemployment" (Kamin, 1986: 26).

Along similar lines, Wilson and Herrnstein cited research to show that blacks are less "normal" than whites in their personality test scores, have lower I.Q.s, and are more likely to be of low birth weight. Despite their ostensibly qualifying discussion admitting the role of environmental determinants of black crime, they went on to imply that certain genes, frequent in blacks, interact with environmental conditions to cause crime. "The fatal (and insensitive) confusion between correlate and cause is again obvious. If blonds are subject to persuasive discrimination and committed crimes, would it make sense to talk of their genes as causing both blondness and crime?" (Kamin, 1986: 27).

The underlying and unsubstantiated theme implied in Wilson and Herrnstein's book is that when genes and environment are correlated, causation resides in the genes. This fallacy of confusing correlation and causation is compounded by the suggestion that behaviors with a genetic correlate cannot be changed by conscious policy. Thus Wilson and Herrnstein (1985) wrote that the "underpinnings of the sexual divisions of labor . . . go so deep into the biological substratum that beyond certain limits they are hard to change" (p. 125). Kamin (1986) has replied, "Tell that one to the Marines—the women Marines, that is" (p. 26).

Such selective use of poor data to support a muddled theory of biological determinism is not unrepresentative of a social science that is influenced, and perhaps even caused, by the political climate of the 1980s. As Wilson and Herrnstein admitted, sometimes theories are chosen not through an inductive process but for "political and ideological reasons" (Kamin, 1986: 27). The Violence Commission's Task Force on Individual Acts of Violence, after an extensive review, concluded that, "Although we find differences among age, sex, and racial groups in the tendency to violent behavior, there is no evidence to link these variations to genetic or biological difference" (Mulvihill et al., 1969: xxx). Later updates, like those of Currie (1985) and Silberman (1978), have concurred on the lack of evidence. Is there really any reason to replace these conclusions with a criminology that, one might expect, next will seek a theory of genetic difference that explains the disproportionate involvement of blacks in robbery, Italians in organized crime, and Jews in insider trading on Wall Street? Not uncommonly, these contemporary constitutional interpretations are combined with lamentations about the unchangeability of the underclass—to reach the conclusion that, in effect, nothing can be done about minority crime except to invoke law and impose order.

Deterrence, Rationality, Incapacitation, and Folly

Accordingly, contemporary Jeffersonians argue that deterrence by the criminal justice system can increase the costs of assaultive violence, acquisitive violence, and other illegal labor-market employment enough so that disproportionately involved minority offenders will be dissuaded.

One trouble with this philosophy of raising the costs of illegal labor-market employment is at its front end: The risk of apprehension by the police is very low. Only half of all crimes are reported to the police. Arrests are made in less than 20 of every 100 reported burglaries, larcenies, and auto thefts (with the apprehension rate for robbery only a little higher. Curtis, 1984: 94).

So let us improve police apprehension rates. The Law Enforcement Assistance Administration (LEAA) of the 1970s granted considerable hardware, including a submarine to the San Diego police for shore patrols and tanks to the Mobile, Alabama, police for riot protection. Indeed, Ball-Rokeach and Short (1985) suggested that high-tech command and control did "gulag" the ghetto, instilling enough fear among minorities to minimize the type of civil disorder prevalent in the late 1960s.

But illegal-market behavior, like mugging and street crime, is a form of slow rioting. It is also safer from hardware because it is more individualized and less public. So it is not surprising that apprehension rates in the 1970s did not improve and crime rates did not decrease. Only LEAA declined, a victim of the expectations raised by the war on crime of the early 1970s and the budget-cutting of the late 1970s and the 1980s.

Parallel to the effort to improve police apprehension rates was an attempt, evolving partly out of the President's Commission on Law Enforcement and Administration of Justice (1967; hereinafter the Katzenbach Commission) and the Violence Commission's (1969) recommendations, to provide swifter, surer punishment. Through grants, LEAA tried to improve court efficiency, and often its recommendations were carried out locally. Sentencing became more severe for those apprehended for predatory violence, and the rate of state prison incarcerations doubled during the 1970s. Today, America's incarceration rates are higher than those of any other industrialized country except, notably, South Africa and the Soviet Union. This is especially true in the case of black males, who constitute about 50% of the prison population. At current rates, every fifth black man in America will spend some time in a state or federal prison, with the proportion much higher for specific inner-city communities. The prison is now one of the few institutions in the United States dominated by blacks—or, in some regions, Hispanics (Currie, 1985: 91; Curtis, 1985a: 222).

Despite the high incarceration rates, however, our extraordinarily high levels of violent crime have persisted since the 1960s. As Currie

(1985) concluded, on the basis of both this practical experience and prestigious academic studies, the theory of deterrence has not been borne out. That is, there is little useful evidence that raising the costs of crime by inflicting more (or speedier or more severe or more certain) punishment results in less violent crime.

The failure of the theory of deterrence is related to the inaccuracy of the notion of "rational" behavior by offenders. As used by white academic deterrence theorists, like Wilson and Herrnstein (1985), rational behavior is based on the nineteenth-century, middle-class, English utilitarian economics of Jeremy Bentham: Economic man maximizes benefits and minimizes costs. Thurow (1983) is well known for his criticism of this rationality assumption in econometric modeling. Etzioni (1987) is the cofounder of a new perspective, socioeconomics, that rejects it.

Examples abound of minority criminal behavior that does not seem rational to white academics. For example, a large proportion of robberies are committed by young, poor, minority men whose most common victims are other young, poor, minority men who tend to have the least money and are the most likely to fight back with lethal weapons. To an academic it might appear "irrational" to try to rob such young men; but on the street this might seem reasonable to a young man who seeks the approval of his peers to gain admittance to a gang.

Similarly, some academics, like Banfield (1970), deplore the apparent disregard by minorities of deferred gratification (like saving money) in favor of immediate gratification (like spending or mugging). As Rainwater (1970) noted, this ignores the fact that the choice is often between immediate gratification and no gratification at all.

In addition, only a few empirical studies can be cited to support the notion of immediate versus delayed gratification, and these works are deeply flawed. For example, Wilson and Herrnstein (1985: 452) pointed to a 1961 study in Trinidad in which two groups—school children and delinquents—were asked to choose between receiving a small candy bar immediately or a larger one in a week. The proportion of delinquents choosing the smaller, immediate reward was significantly greater. But, typically, the authors also failed to note that the experimenters made two additional observations that largely vitiated the findings. First, a child's decision is dependent upon who the experimenter is. Presumably, this is because experimenters, consciously or unconsciously, communicate different messages to their subjects—messages influenced by the experimenter's biases. Second, a child's decision depends on the type of reward being tested. Hence, the same child who takes a small candy bar today rather than wait a week for a candy bar five times as large may nonetheless prefer to forego watching one television program today if in return she can watch five next week. "That is, there is no evidence for (and considerable evidence against) a general personality trait such that some individuals more than others consistently delay gratification in order to obtain larger rewards of all sorts" (Kamin, 1986: 23).

A rational (older, richer, white) man can carefully consider his (foregone) opportunities—alternative streams of benefits and costs— before making a decision. The best research, by the Vera Institute of Justice (Thompson et al., 1981) concluded that this "rational" process is irrelevant to undereducated, unemployed, young minority men who have no stake in the future and nothing to lose by illegal-market employment.

To an intelligent young man who has a substandard education, few legal-market heroes, and an address in a public housing project with an 80% youth unemployment rate, it is often "rational"—that is, consistent with his values and experiences—to pick up one or more of the illegal options. Both the written literature (for example, Freedman, 1987) and personal interviews with incarcerated youth to whom this writer has had access suggest this kind of reasoning: If I'm successful with the crime, I win; if I'm killed, I don't have to worry about tomorrow; and if I'm caught, I'll have food, shelter and continuing (illegal labor-market) education in prison. To an inner-city youth, prison is "an inevitability, or at least a probability, accompanied by nothing more than the mild apprehension or anxiety that attends, for instance, a bar mitzvah, joining the Marines or any other manhood initiation ritual in any normal society" (Freedman, 1987: B2).

Accordingly, unless white advocates of deterrence take greater care to understand how their values and experiences differ from those of inner-city residents, policy action against minority crime will continue to be misdirected—to the detriment, of course, of minorities.

If we believe that society should be protected from serious offenders and that punishment is a valid reason for incarceration (this author's position on both counts), the notion of incapacitation—taking criminals off the street to prevent them from committing more crimes—seems to be a commonsense alternative to the failure of deterrence. Yet careful research on incapacitation shows that "the potential reduction in serious crime is disturbingly small, especially when balanced against the social and economic costs of pursuing this strategy strenuously enough to make much difference to public safety" (Currie, 1985: 88). It has been estimated that to have any significant effect on the rate of serious crime—say, to try to reduce it by 20%—we would have to triple this prison population. The cost is about $70 billion in new construction (American prisons being filled to capacity) and, conservatively at present prices, $14 billion in new annual operating costs. The $70 billion is well over *double* the amount needed to lift *every* poor family above the poverty line. The $14 billion could provide one million unemployed inner-city youths with solid jobs at an entry-level wage of $7 an hour (Currie, 1985: 88-91). In addition, "Not only do a greater number of those who receive punitive treatment . . . continue to violate the law, but they also commit more serious crimes with greater rapidity than those who experience a less constraining contact with the judicial and correctional systems" (Wolfgang et al., 1972: 252).

Even though crime and fear have risen dramatically despite the vast sums of money that have been poured into criminal-justice social engineering over the last 20 years, we still observe state legislatures churning out laws to "lock them up and throw away the key," and similar advocates arguing that if we just got still tougher, we would see some light at the end of the tunnel. In reality, the net result of deterrence and incapacitation policies against minority-dominated street crime is the kind of folly described by Pulitzer prize historian Barbara Tuchman (1984):

> [Folly] is the pursuit by governments of policies contrary to their own interests. . . . In its first stage, mental standstill fixes the principles and boundaries governing a political problem. In the second stage, when dissonances and failing function begin to appear, the initial principles rigidify. . . . Rigidifying leads to increase of investment and the need to protect egos; policy founded upon error multiplies, never retreats . . . until it causes . . . the fall of Troy . . . [or] the classic humiliation in Vietnam [p. 383].

As Federal Appeals Court Judge Irving R. Kaufman, chairman of the President's Commission on Organized Crime, said, with regard to drugs, "Law enforcement has been tested to the utmost, but let's face it, it just hasn't worked" (Brinkley, 1986: E10).

Program Models for a New National Policy

If we accept the explanations of disproportionate minority violence by the Presidential Commissions, Rainwater, Silberman, and Currie, and recognize the folly of a policy response based on the criminal justice system alone, where do we turn?

In this section, some specific programmatic alternatives are reviewed that have been attempted and evaluated in real-world settings since the Presidential Commissions. Community-based crime prevention initiatives like block watches, patrols, and citizen organizing have gained national attention. However, in and of themselves, such programs have not been successful in addressing the causes of minority inner-city violent crime. Consistent with the research findings of the Vera Institute, other community-based programs have better addressed ways of overcoming economic deprivation and racial discrimination. These programs—like the Argus Community, Centro Isolina Ferre, and the House of Umoja—have reduced recidivism and increased economic and psychological self-sufficiency among minority youth who are at risk of violence and related crime. The common principles underlying such programs provide the basis for a new national policy to reduce violence among inner-city minorities.

Community-Based Opportunity Reduction

One response to the failures of deterrence and the limitations of incapacitation has been "opportunity reduction" in the community—as typified, for example, by block watches, citizen patrols, police foot patrols, and escort services that make potential victims "harder targets."

Whether led by citizens or the police, opportunity-reduction programs have resulted in equivocal evaluations, when there have been reputable evaluations at all. There is only limited evidence that opportunity reduction consistently reduces crime (although the exemplary Seattle Community Crime Reduction Program, which organized block watches against burglary, is an exception). Sometimes fear is reduced; but there is partial evidence (at least for police-led opportunity reduction) that the effect is more apparent in white, middle-class, homeowner neighborhoods than in minority, inner-city, renter neighborhoods (Curtis, 1987).

One explanation for marginal outcomes among poor minorities may be that opportunity-reduction programs usually are designed to keep criminal "invaders" out of the neighborhood. Yet, in the inner city, the offender is often just as likely to live next door or be in the family as to attack from an outside perimeter. In addition, citizen opportunity reduction disproportionately involves volunteers; however, it is often difficult to organize volunteers among those who already are dealing with a great many inner-city problems (though it can be done). Podolefsky and DuBow (1981) suggested that the minority poor perceive, rightly, that opportunity reduction, at least when implemented by itself without coordinated programs in economic justice, is really just a form of surrogate policing that addresses symptoms and "keeps the lid on."

The existing partial evidence of greater success, at least in fear reduction in police-led programs among white, middle-class home-owners, is more consistent with a mentality of keeping invaders out—especially when coupled with the white stereotypical perceptions that invaders are minorities and minorities are criminals. Block-club organizing by middle-class whites can serve many purposes besides crime prevention—such as assuring that homes are not purchased by minorities. This is not to deny the rights of all citizens to protect themselves nor to downplay crime by minorities (even though most minority crime is disproportionately committed in *minority* neighborhoods). But, in the extreme, we have experienced Howard Beach, the white homeowner neighborhood in Queens, New York, where white youths killed one young black and injured several others. At Howard Beach, "civic pride mingles with an insular spirit and concern over crime that has led to the creation of private street patrols that stop and question strangers" (Milwaukee Journal, 1986: 19).

Without doing something about the causes of crime, then, opportunity reduction potentially can become a vehicle for racism—and worse—an excuse to violate the individual rights of minorities in the name of community cohesion:

> At what point, if ever, should needs of the community as a whole be allowed to harm an innocent minority? John Rawls, the philosopher, suggests one widely respected answer: No one ought to endorse a social order that he could not accept if he were in the shoes of the most disadvantaged [New York Times, 1986: E10].

Over the last few years there has been a trend to evaluate opportunity reduction programs like block watches and citizen patrols as successful if they reduce fear, even if they do not reduce crime. Fear reduction appears easier to achieve and so can help justify the budgets of criminal-justice and other agencies that are unsuccessful in reducing actual crime. In some instances, programs have been labeled as successful—in reducing fear—at the same time that there have been increases in reported crime rates (Curtis, 1987). What might it mean if people feel less fearful, even though crime rates are very high or even increasing?

Are we merely altering their perceptions through public relations gimmickry—while making them more vulnerable? Are we forgetting substance and concentrating on public relations "spin control"? To the extent that opportunity reduction is more successful in lowering fear in white neighborhoods than minority neighborhoods, do we not potentially have a policy of white appeasement that does nothing about actual crime—to the detriment of both minorities *and* whites?

Almost all urban dwellers in the United States know the feeling of intimidation that comes from approaching a group of youths in an isolated location late at night. Fear reduction *is* a legitimate goal to which we can all relate. But if we are unsuccessful at simultaneously reducing crime, as much of the empirical evidence suggests, then perhaps we can begin to plan more systematically for fear-reduction programs that are also part of a broader plan to address the causes of crime. For example, in the Bronx over the last three years, the Mid-Bronx Desperadoes Community Housing Corporation has used citizen patrols to reduce fear and improve the quality of life, as measured through in-person pre- and postinterviews in a careful evaluation design (Curtis, 1987). Fear reduction has been used to help continue to stabilize the neighborhood for housing rehabilitation, economic development, and business retention—leading, one hopes as a result, to more employment of minority youths in the area and to settlement by more working- and middle-class families. This is a process to which future opportunity reduction can aspire.

Employment, Discipline, Life Skills, and Familylike Sanctuary

Other community-based programs since the Presidential Commissions have better addressed the causes of disproportionate minority violence. These programs begin with the employment of minority youth and all that is needed educationally, socially, and emotionally to ensure the effectiveness of that employment. From a research point of view, most community programs that have been successful along these lines have been consistent with the findings of the Vera Institute of Justice in its exhaustive review of the relationship between employment and crime. Accordingly, it will be helpful first to review Vera's research findings before describing programs that have been successful on the street.

The Vera Institute of Justice

Vera concluded that, particularly for the highest-risk age group—school drop-outs between ages 14 and 18—we cannot assume a direct, one-to-one, short-term relationship between employment alone and a reduction in crime rates by those employed. Rather, Vera suggested that a number of components are necessary to reduce successfully robbery (and related income crime) rates by those employed (Thompson et al., 1981).

Employment training and actual jobs for high-risk youth ideally should provide a "bridge" from less secure and promising "secondary" labor-market employment to more secure "primary" labor-market employment, in which the work is steady and holds promise of upward mobility.

Employment opportunities must exist. Training and bridge employment mean nothing if the private and public sectors cannot supply the jobs. Of importance for our focus on poor minorities in the inner city, Vera found that the private supply was much more limited for poor black than for poor white youth. Therefore, although more private-sector employment needs to be identified for minority youth, we cannot rule out the public-sector sources that, in recent years, have often been more accessible to poor minorities than have private-sector opportunities. Examples are local government, civil service, and postal service jobs.

Employment networks are crucial for linking the demand for bridge employment of high-risk youth to the supply of jobs. Vera found that black high-risk youth have far fewer contacts than do white high-risk youth with family, friends, and others who provide access to opportunities. In the absence of such contacts, alternative sources, such as community organizations in which high-risk youth feel comfortable, are seen as needed to make the linkages between the youth and employers.

Vera found that family support is helpful in finding legal labor-market employment for high-risk youth and in dissuading them from illegal labor-market employment. When such support is not present, Vera noted, ways must be found to either strengthen the control of natural families or provide both discipline and psychological support through alternative, extended families. Vera also found that high-risk youth need more hands-on, accessible role models, who have made it in legal labor markets, to work with them. As youth grow older, the formation of their own families can be a stabilizing influence both by making employment more important to them and by encouraging a noncriminal life style.

Peer networks must be tapped. Vera's findings suggest that it is naive to deny, try to break up, or try to compete with peer influence, as most past job training programs have done. Rather, a crucial lesson was that the influence of peers needs to be incorporated into an employment program as another essential support to the job itself.

Although Vera found considerable variations among ethnic groups, there were clear payoffs associated with high school graduation or more advanced education. However, while school was seen as valuable, the schools for minorities that were studied often were disorganized, full of conflicts, and unhelpful in providing personal contacts and job opportunities. This raises the possibility of alternative community settings, like community organizations, that can provide more order and a refuge for G.E.D. (Graduation Equivalency Diploma) study—or at least counselors and role models who can assist and motivate high risk youth who remain in high school. Alternative schools are needed as well.

Vera's work is more than just theory. Already there are real-world programs, operating in inner cities with high-risk minority youth, that incorporate most of Vera's principles and that have been successful in increasing income *and* reducing recidivism by the young people (and not just fear among their potential victims). Three such programs are the Argus Community, Centro Isolina Ferre, and the House of Umoja.

The Argus Learning for Living Community

The Argus Community is physically located in a former school in the South Bronx. Begun in the late 1960s, it has an eight-hour nonresident program as well as a resident program. The Argus Community works with young males and females ages 13 to 21, mostly black and Hispanic chronic underachievers, runaways, addicts, and criminals. Many are directed from the juvenile justice and school systems, while others walk in from the neighborhood.

The Argus Community provides an extended family of staff and peers; a safe and therapeutic environment; a moral climate with strict rules, discipline, and daily routines; and a concrete program that includes counseling, street-savvy therapy, high school and vocational education, recreation, practical job training, and job placement. A great deal of the work is remedial—emotionally, socially, academically, and vocationally.

Led by its founder, Elizabeth Lyttleton Sturz, and a staff who themselves often were runaways, addicts, and criminals, the Argus Community seeks to provide for these young people what their natural families and the other schools in New York City often do not—an opportunity for bonding (forming two-way trust relationships), a safe and orderly place (sanctuary), encouragement in the airing of emotions, and a strong emphasis on the accumulation of knowledge (Sturz, 1983).

At any one time, the Argus Community has between 100 and 200 youths working through one of two phases. Phase one involves becoming part of the Argus Community's extended family, working in the classroom, accepting the rules, learning to trust the staff and controlled peer feedback, gaining a sense of responsibility, and developing self-esteem. Phase two—training, work, and eventually a non-subsidized job—is not pegged to academic progress but to behavioral, attitudinal, and emotional growth. For those who are not academically talented, there are alternative avenues to knowledge and self-esteem (such as being an artist or peer group trainer; Sturz, 1983: 45).

The Argus Community measures outcomes in terms of reduced crime and improved ability to function self-sufficiently at a personal level and in real-world legal labor markets. By these standards it has been successful. For example, studies by the Vera Institute and the Criminal Justice Coordinating Council have shown lower recidivism rates—including violent crime rates—for the Argus Community graduates than for participants in almost all other programs in New York City that work with such high-risk offenders. In addition, 67% of the Argus Community's enrollees attained nonsubsidized job placement in 1980. This is a much higher job-placement rate than for similar "high-risk" youth who are not involved with the program (Sturz, 1983: 46, 310; Sturz, personal communication, July 10, 1986).

Centro Isolina Ferre

Centro was begun in 1970 in Ponce, Puerto Rico's second largest city, by Sister Isolina Ferre, a Catholic nun who studied at Fordham University.

The La Playa community where Sister Isolina began her program was, at that time, almost written off by the public and private sectors: It had high levels of poverty, unemployment, crime, and physically deteriorated housing.

Centro started with 10 full-time "advocates"—local residents trained to work with and represent young people in trouble with the law. Eventually, the number of advocates increased, and their role embraced the larger community. They began to organize, led recreational and cultural programs, encouraged residents of La Playa to become involved in community issues, and served as brokers between the people in need and the services provided by El Centro.

Today, El Centro's goal is to enhance self-respect and reduce dependency among young people in trouble with the law. Primarily a daytime program, though there is temporary housing for young people, El Centro involves young Puerto Rican men and women—many diverted from the juvenile court but also many high-risk nonadjudicated teenagers from La Playa.

Community as well as individual competence is developed so that all in La Playa can gain greater control over their lives. The view is that, in the last analysis, it is the disorganization of the community at large—the evidence that their parents are unable to control their children's lives and are unable to impose sanctions on people who threaten their own or their community's well-being—that persuades the young that the cards are stacked hopelessly against them. These youth believe that fate will not permit them to "make it" in any legitimate form, thereby allowing crime to seem a rewarding alternative (Silberman, 1978: 424-455). This is a variety of the community social cohesion that is fundamental to opportunity reduction programs. But at El Centro, while the community is supportive, the more basic process is to facilitate opportunity and self-respect in individual young people.

Beyond the extended family of the advocates and other immediate staff, El Centro has over 30 programs that include:

- *Education:* An alternative school has been established for young people who are dropouts or need more individualized instruction.
- *Family counseling and support:* Counselors work with young people and families in crisis.
- *Vocational skills:* Training is provided to youth in cosmetology, horticulture, sewing, electrical engineering, computer technology, and nursing assistance.
- *Enterprise development:* Some of the activities that were begun in the early years of El Centro have become employment opportunities for youth and adults in La Playa (where, as in the South Bronx, the unemployment rate is over 50%). These small industries include bookbinding, silk-screened Christmas cards, calendars, agricultural products, ceramics, landscaping, and laminating.

Silberman (1978) called El Centro the "best example of community regeneration I found anywhere in the United States" (p. 434). He reported that over the 1970s the number of adjudicated delinquents had been reduced by 85%, and the delinquency rate, including violent acts, was cut in half, "despite an exploding teenage population" (p. 435).

The House of Umoja

The House of Umoja—begun in the late 1960s by David and Falaka Fattah—is now known as the first inner-city Boys' Town in the United States. Up to 40 teenage males—mostly black—are in residence at any one time along a city block of rehabilitated row houses in West Philadelphia. (A nonresident program was operated in the past.) Most of these residents are adjudicated offenders (for any offenses, including murder and other violence but excluding sex crimes), though some are high-risk youth who walk in from the community.

The House of Umoja (from the Swahili word for "unity") defines its notion of the extended family in terms of the African culture: The African mother and father are mother and father to all children. Applying this belief to the urban situation, the House of Umoja considers all teenagers living therein to be sons of Sister Falaka and David Fattah and therefore brothers (Curtis, 1985a: 207). Within this context, the House of Umoja creates a sanctuary—a sheltered environment that

- requires adherence to a strict sense of house rules and order, underscored through a signed contract between each resident and the House of Umoja;
- assures individual counseling to each youth to help determine his immediate and life goals, define his educational needs, and resolve his internal conflicts and problems;
- involves the youth in the operation of the house—including household chores and food preparation;
- ensures that youth attend a regular school or an in-house G.E.D. program;
- assists youth in securing employment or enrolling in a training program;
- fosters a sense of togetherness and group unity by imparting the values inherent in African culture; and
- addresses each youth's well-being—including regular health check-ups, clothing, food, and recreation.

At the House of Umoja, the house parents (the Fattahs), "Old Heads" (graduates), peer pressure by other young men in residence, and African ethnic identity all operate to build self-respect, a sense of control, and a willingness to channel one's energy into a future based on education, employment, and family.

There is classroom training in emerging House of Umoja youth enterprise ventures and job placement. Some young men train at the

Umoja Security Institute, which is accredited for training in the private security industry.

Youth enterprises that are being planned within the Boys' Town—including a restaurant, a moving company, and a printing company—will provide sheltered training opportunities. For the most part, they cannot (yet) provide full-time employment for all House of Umoja youth who, with the aid of counselors, often eventually seek work outside the House of Umoja community in the course of becoming self-sufficient. The black youth unemployment rate in West Philadelphia is above 50%, so job placements require extensive work by the counselors.

The House of Umoja is geared to independent living after six months to one year of residence if family reunion is not a realizable goal.

Success at the House of Umoja is defined mainly in terms of frequency of recidivism for adjudicated offenders who pass through. Most cited is the study by the Philadelphia Psychiatric Center, which reported a 3% rearrest rate for the first 600 youths who lived at the Boys' Town, including violent offenders—compared with a rate of 70% to 90% for young people released from conventional juvenile correctional facilities (Curtis, 1985a: 208).

Discussion

While we still require many more careful, cohort-based measures of these model programs and several other such examples from around the nation, there is consensus among a broad political spectrum of observers that the models are on the right track and are cost-effective, compared with the alternatives. For example, measured in terms of recidivism, the Argus Community, El Centro, and the House of Umoja are much more effective than is prison. And in terms of money, the cost per year per person is $30,087 for New York State prisons, $24,186 for Minnesota prisons, $22,433 for a federal maximum-security prison, $19,339 for California prisons, $16,000 for Argus Community residents, $16,000 for House of Umoja residents, $2,000 for Argus Community nonresidents, and $200 for El Centro nonresidents (Curtis, 1987).

In each of these cases, the minority community organization takes the lead. While the criminal justice system does not control, it may support. The House of Umoja began in Philadelphia *despite* opposition from then-police chief Frank Rizzo. The Argus Community has always used police support, which varies over time based on the attitudes of South Bronx precinct captains. The Puerto Rican police initially were hostile to and suspicious of El Centro. Today, the police rely more and more on El Centro's advocates. Unless a crime is very serious, the police will avoid arrest and will instead bring a juvenile to an advocate for counseling. When police are asked to settle a domestic dispute, they often will ask an advocate to meet them in the barrio to help mediate. Several advocates have police "hot lines" in their homes so they can be contacted immediately when there is trouble after hours (Curtis, 1987).

These programs make clear that the criminal justice system need not conclude from Wolfgang et al.'s (1972) cohort findings—that a very small proportion of all offenders commit a very large proportion of violent crimes—that these chronic offenders are the prime candidates for incapacitation. *Many of these same kinds of high-risk youth have made the transition successfully to responsible, married, tax-paying citizens—at lower cost—via the Argus Community, El Centro, the House of Umoja, and other such model programs around the nation.*

Each of these programs carries through all of the Vera Institute's advice for making minority youth employment an effective vehicle for reducing violent and other crime rates (Thompson et al., 1981). Despite their overall successes, each program has considerable difficulty when it comes to the Vera Institute's conclusion that employment opportunities must exist. Employment training and support have little meaning if the white-dominated public and private sectors fail to supply the jobs. Each of these groups follows the same underlying principle: to create an extended-family setting with strict rules and nurturing through which self-respect is instilled, education is pursued, training is undertaken, and employment is found. The ultimate measures of success are reduced crime rates, reduced welfare dependency, and increased personal and economic self-sufficiency. Each of these examples shows how—if the structural conditions in Rainwater's paradigm are skillfully and sensitively addressed—adaptions to them, in terms of values and behavior, will change, the assertions of white underclass theorists notwithstanding. Each extended-family program demonstrates the silliness of academics who profess that they have never seen the causes of crime; who claim that the employment-crime relationship is too complex for any public policy to handle; and who ask, rhetorically, "What agency do we create, what budget do we allocate, that will supply missing parental affection and restore to the child consistent discipline by a stable and loving family?" (See Currie, 1985, and Curtis, 1978, 1987, for critiques of such academics.)

For the future, we must better define and understand the relationship among the terms in the equation that extended family plus employment equals less crime and dependency. For example, to what extent, if any, are residential programs more cost effective than nonresidential programs and for what kinds of minority youth? (Both seem to have their place.) What is the significance of El Centro's drawing the entire community into its extended family, compared with the Argus Community and the House of Umoja, where the surrounding community appears less involved (though each has fledgling businesses serving the community)?

Can we replicate the principles underlying these successes and facilitate new varieties of the Argus Community, El Centro, and the House of Umoja that are tailored to local circumstances? It has become a cliché for observers to say that one cannot replicate a Sturz, Ferre, or Fattah. But all these pioneers say that natural leaders are present in every minority community and that we need only the financial and political mechanisms to nurture their development. The author of this chapter is presently associated with an attempt to replicate modestly these principles at a number of locations around the nation. For example, in the Adams-Morgan neighborhood of Washington, D.C., the first step was to negotiate a supportive role by the police in an effort to organize opportunity reduction against drug dealing, thus creating a more secure setting for low-income housing rehabilitation and for local business people. As a kind of *quid pro quo,* the local business people then helped support a home rehabilitation and weatherization business that employs minority youth who are ex-offenders. The federal government followed by better capitalizing the business. The employees hold regular "team leader" meetings where they supply one another with mutual support (and sometimes discipline). This is a kind of extended family, helpful in keeping employees "straight" and in avoiding illegal employment (like drug dealing). Many employees act as role models for youngsters in the community. The program's objectives are to reduce crime rates and recidivism by those employed, increase their economic self-sufficiency through the jobs, and establish the business itself as financially self-sufficient. Preliminary process and impact evaluation findings suggest that the program has had considerable success in meeting these objectives (Curtis, 1987).

National Public and Private Policy

In sum, it does appear feasible to suggest a new national policy, consistent with the Presidential Commissions of the 1960s, that addresses the causes of disproportionate minority inner-city violence by replicating such successes as the Argus Community, El Centro, and the House of Umoja. We must encourage inner-city leaders to create such programs themselves by providing resources and putting new groups in touch with existing ones. We must facilitate a "bubble-up" process, not mandate another "top-down" program. The goal must be true economic and social empowerment of inner-city minorities, based on the targeted employment-education-extended-family formula that has worked elsewhere.

Other Employment and Education Breakthroughs

The formula behind the programs described here is emerging in other, related national innovations. For example, the Summer Training and Education Program (STEP), the Jobs for America's Graduates Program, and the JobStart Program all provide remedial education leading to job training for at-risk youth. They also integrate in life skills training that ranges from counseling on responsible sexual behavior to money management and how to interview for a job. In some locations, the JobStart Program incorporates the highly successful Comprehensive Competencies Program, an individualized, computer-based learning system that teaches basic skills. These demonstrations are carried out by private local and national intermediate institutions and are funded by both the private and public sectors (Brown, 1986). A not unrelated initiative also has gained national prominence: The "I Have a Dream" program began in 1981, when philanthropist-businessman Eugene Lang returned to his elementary school in Harlem and promised to pay the college tuition of every graduating class member who finished high school and qualified for higher education. As a result, almost all class members have stayed in high school and out of the criminal justice system. Some are receiving college scholarships from sources other than Mr. Lang, who has combined his incentives with familylike social supports that his "adopted" kids missed at home. Variations on the program have spread rapidly throughout the nation, with private benefactors as well as public ones (Shanker, 1987).

Federal Leadership

Private sponsorship and innovation are essential; but only through a return to significant federal public leadership and resources can we hope to create a significant impact on a large number of at-risk minority youth who might otherwise become involved in violent and related crimes. Given staggering budget deficits, this will require trade-offs with federal military defense programs. Yet the levels of needed spending are not dramatic in a trillion-dollar economy. For example, *Business Week* put the cost of expanding (nonresidential) employment and extended-family programs to reach everyone who needs them (minority and white) at about $13 billion per year (compared with Currie's estimate of $70 billion in new prison construction costs and $14 billion per year in prison maintenance costs to reduce serious crime by 20% through incapacitation). This estimate, which would reach 3.5 million poor Americans, is considerably higher than the $3 billion currently spent on job training and employment; but it is also considerably less than the $20 billion per year currently spent on welfare programs (Brown, 1986).

Federal, state, and local public-sector institutions would do well to consider more use of private intermediate institutions for administration, technical assistance, and evaluation of new initiatives. The justification is that the cost effectiveness of existing private intermediate institutions appears superior to public entities and that the intermediate institutions could then directly empower community-based organizations. An example of such success is the Local Initiatives Support Corporation (LISC), the largest private sector facilitator of inner-city economic development. Other programs could continue to be run by the public sector. For example, the federal residential Job Corps—with its affinities to the Argus Community, El Centro, the JobStart Program, and the House of Umoja—is one of our most successful crime prevention efforts. According to Department of Labor statistics, during the first years after the experience, Job Corps members were a third less likely to be arrested than nonparticipants. Every $1 spent on Job Corps results in $1.45 in benefits to society, including reduced crime and substance abuse (which alone account for 42 cents in benefits); reduced welfare dependency; and increased job production, income, and taxes. The most sophisticated evaluation of Job Corps (which costs $13,000 per year per participant, compared with the $22,000+ per year figure for federal security-prison incarceration) concluded that, "Naysayers who deny that labor market problems are real and serious, that social interventions can make a difference, or that the effectiveness of public programs can be improved, will find little to support their preconceptions" (Taggert, 1981: 49).

Even with existing federal programs, more coordinated federal policies from the Department of Education for remedial education, from the Department of Labor for training and placement for the structurally unemployed, from the Department of Commerce and Department of Housing and Urban Development for economic development, and from the Department of Health and Human Services for family support and life skills could easily result in greater crime prevention than has any other national effort to date, among many other benefits. Whenever possible, job placement should be linked to inner-city economic development that can be secured through opportunity-reduction type crime prevention. The same improved coordination is needed at the state, city, and neighborhood levels.

Macro Policy

To reduce violence in inner cities through remedial education, employment, and extended family programs, we are advocating a very targeted policy—at the "ships in the mud." But the "rising tide" philosophy to lift all ships is relevant in that we need a macro economic framework that ensures sufficient employment opportunities. This means the kind of demand-side economic policy of the early 1960s that produced 4% unemployment and low inflation. It does not mean the supply-side economics of the 1980s that has fostered further segmentation of America into two societies—one rich and prospering and one becoming poorer. Affirmative action is still needed to ensure opportunity. A more effective national policy, along the lines suggested by Alperowitz and Faux (1984), is needed to end the erosion of the American industrial structure and to reduce capital movements that disrupt local labor markets and separate the resulting job searchers from family and community anchors. In ways that follow Edelman's proposals (1987), the present welfare system must be reformed to encourage nuclear-family formation and continuation, the completion of high school, and the opportunity for employment.

National public-sector leadership that legitimately opens opportunities and acknowledges the need for more resources will have little difficulty inspiring inner-city institutions—such as churches—with large voluntary networks to renew their dedication to spiritual and value restorations simultaneously. We speak, for example, of "the value of dignity, respect for our elders, for our family; the disciplining of our children always by blacks' love for children; the strength of our pulling together; and our commitment to go just a little farther to make it in a race controlled by unequal rules" (Glasgow, 1987: 144).

Law and Order Reconsidered

Most policy observers still do not understand that the criminal justice system—police, courts, and prisons—merely reacts to crime and cannot do much to prevent it. At the federal level, therefore, the Department of Justice can lead in opportunity reduction but does not have the mandate to address the causes of crime—except, perhaps, for enforcement of equal opportunity. We need to continue improving the equity and efficiency of the criminal justice system, as advocated by the Katzenbach Commission (1967) and the Violence Commission (1969), because, among other reasons, victims require better treatment and society deserves more protection from those who have committed crimes. (After being robbed by four minority males, this author certainly wanted criminal justice protection and punishment for the perpetrators.) In addition, some criminal justice-related policies (neglected here, but important in a comprehensive policy against violent crime that is sensitive to minorities) need to be pursued—including effective control of handguns in urban areas and expanded domestic violence prevention, mediation, and victim-witness initiatives in inner cities. Nonetheless, we must learn from the 1970s and 1980s that massive new investments in the justice system will not reduce our historically high levels of violent crime.

We must better recognize the relationship between white-collar activities and minority street crime. White middle- and upper-class males control the institutions that block opportunities, to which poor minorities adapt. Whites control the organizations that distribute narcotics and manufacture Saturday night specials. The U.S. Chamber of Commerce has estimated that whereas street crime, disproportionately involving minorities, costs $88 billion per year, white-collar crime, disproportionately involving whites, costs $200 billion per year (Mendez, 1980). If we are to establish justice better, how can we send a poor minority member who steals several hundred dollars worth of property to prison but let off with a light fine bank officials who steal hundreds of thousands of dollars from trusting depositors?

Political Feasibility

On September 14, 1769, Thomas Jefferson placed this ad in the *Virginia Gazette:*

Run away from the subscriber in *Albemarle*, a Mulatto slave called Sandy, about 35 years of age . . . he is a shoemaker by trade, in which he uses his left hand principally, can do coarse carpenters work . . . in his conversation he swears much, and his behaviour is artful and knavish. He took with him a white horse ... of which it is expected he will endeavour to dispose; he also carried his shoemakers tools, and will probably endeavour to get employment that way. Whoever conveys the said slave to me in *Albemarle*, shall have 40 s. reward.... [Higginbotham 1978: 478]

Jefferson limited Sandy's job opportunities to the secondary labor market; did not allow training beyond "coarse" carpentry; chose, as a "rational" man of the European Enlightenment, to label Sandy's adaptations to reality as "artful and knavish"; and defined as a crime Sandy's decision to express himself as a human being by seeking freedom.

Politically, some would say that it is not feasible to create reform by reminding the American electorate that even (or especially) our Founding Fathers held beliefs and promulgated policies that were insensitive to the reasons behind minority violence. Indeed, there are more constructive routes, and I believe they must be traveled. For example, we can remind the majority that, in terms of absolute numbers, more white males than black males live in poverty (Gibson, 1987). More dramatically, we might point out that a conservative president has praised the House of Umoja before the National Alliance of Businesses, saying that the House of Umoja has done "what all the police and social welfare agencies have failed to do" (MacNeil-Lehrer Report, 1981). Similarly, the Argus Community has been praised by business leaders as an inner city school that works (Sturz, 1983). The advocate who sought "community action" and sponsored "mobilization for youth" in the 1960s came from a different philosphic position than the observer who today wants people to "pull themselves up by their bootstraps" (Curtis, 1985a: 223). Yet there is some political common ground here, a certain shared support of "self-help" by progressives and conservatives—and it should be built upon (even though self-help and related buzzwords have all too apparent limitations when it comes to resource levels needed and implementation of barriers on the street).

Still, Americans also respect the truth. We should not conclude, uncourageously, that bringing reality to the fore in the 1990s, as Martin Luther King, Jr., did in the early 1960s, will necessarily backfire as a political strategy. Historically, the nation has cycled between public action and private interest. Ralph Waldo Emerson observed that both lead to excess over time—though we also can conclude reasonably from American history that periods of uncontrolled private interest generally are holding actions, whereas democratic reforms produce enduring change (Schlesinger, 1986: 47).

At the end of the period of private interest and material retrenchment, history has taught, neglected problems become acute and demand remedy. People grow weary of materialism as their ultimate goal. They ask not what their country can do for them but what they can do for their country. With the cycles of the twentieth century as a guide and the knowledge that those who learned at the knee of the reformer later come of political age, Schlesinger has concluded that at "some point, shortly before or after the year 1990," the nation will return to reform, "comparable to that of Theodore Roosevelt in 1901, Franklin Roosevelt in 1933 and John Kennedy in 1961" (1968: 47).

In a speech in Houston the night before he was assassinated, President Kennedy quoted Proverbs: "Where there is no vision, the people perish" (quoted in Manchester 1983: 276). Our times await that vision with renewed anticipation. The political will to deal with the American Dilemma and the causes of violence has been dormant. But the dream has not perished. We are undiminished in our capacity to empower the minority poor with youthful vigor and noble purpose.

REFERENCES

Alperowitz, G. and J. Faux (1984) Rebuilding America. New Haven, CT: Pantheon.

Ball-Rokeach, S. and J. F. Short, Jr. (1985) "Collective violence," pp. 155-180 in L. A. Curtis (ed.) American Violence and Public Policy. New Haven, CT: Yale University Press.

Banfield, E. (1970) The Unheavenly City. Boston: Little, Brown.

Brinkley, J. (1986) "Fighting narcotics is everyone's issue now." New York Times (August 10): E10.

Brown, D. (1986) "Promising, promising." Youth Policy (July): 18-19.

Comer, J. P. (1985) "Black violence and public policy," pp. 63-86 in L. A. Curtis (ed.) American Violence and Public Policy. New Haven, CT: Yale University Press.

Currie, E. (1982) "Crime and ideology." Working Papers Magazine 9 (3): 26-35.

Currie, E. (1985) Confronting Crime. New York: Pantheon Books.

Curtis, L. A. (1974) Criminal Violence. Lexington, MA: D.C. Heath.

Curtis, L. A. (1975) Violence, Race and Culture. Lexington, MA: D.C. Heath.

Curtis, L. A. (1977) "The new criminology." Society (March-April): 8-11.

Curtis, L. A. (1978) "Violence and youth." Testimony to the Committee on Science and Technology, U.S. House of Representatives, January.

Curtis, L. A. (1980) "What's new in murder." New Republic (January 26): 19-21.

Curtis, L. A. (1981a) "Inflation, economic policy and the inner city." Annals 456: 46-58.

Curtis, L. A. (1981b) "Violence in America." Keynote address at the Forum on Preventing Violence in America, John F. Kennedy Library, Boston, September 9.

Curtis, L. A. (1984) "Underclass, structural unemployment and labor markets: legal and illegal." Corrections Today (June): 94-106.

increases, have they occurred across all societies; and (4) do any changes appear to be associated with women's changing educational and occupational statuses?

Review of the Literature

A major difficulty in integrating studies on women and violent crime stems from the absence of gender as a major analytic variable in contemporary theoretical approaches. As Harris noted, "This failure is more than merely methodological, precisely because it means that purportedly general theories of criminal deviance are now no more than special theories of male deviance" (1977: 3). Criminological theories offer scant explanation for the long-observed disparity in the proportions of men and women who are arrested for violent and nonviolent crimes.[2] Consequently, these theories have not guided research on female criminal behavior, and the set of theoretically derived rival hypotheses is small.

The women's liberation movement of the mid-1960s generated a number of theoretical perspectives to fill the void. Building on Lombroso and Freud's arguments that female criminal behavior reflected role reversal, a number of scholars proposed what Weis (1976) labeled the "liberation theory" of female crime. Lombroso claimed that women who engage in crime are more masculine than are their conformist sisters. Freudian theory holds that women who are not content with their roles as mothers and wives are maladjusted, and that any manifestations of deviance, including their participation in criminal acts, reflect a "masculinity complex," that is, penis envy. Adler (1975), as one of its chief proponents, wrote of the "liberation theory" perspective:

> The social revolution of the sixties has virilized its previously or presumably docile female segment. . . . The emancipation of women appears to be having a twofold influence on female juvenile crimes. Girls are involved in more drinking, stealing, gang activity, and fighting— behavior in keeping with their adoption of male roles [pp. 87, 95].

A variant of this approach is the "human liberation" or "role convergence" theory of criminal behavior that argues that criminal behavior is least frequent in settings in which boys are taught traditionally feminine values (for example, violence is never appropriate) and girls traditionally masculine values (for example, self-sufficiency;

see Wise, 1967). This perspective was developed to account for the similarity and relative pettiness of deviant acts of middle-class boys and girls and the dissimilarity and violence apparent in the deviance of working-class boys and girls. Both of these approaches focus on the magnitude of differences in the socialization of women and men.

In contrast, the opportunity or "role validation" perspective proposes that women's criminal behavior is an illegitimate extension of the female role rather than a sign of masculinity (Weis, 1976). For example, shoplifting and petty theft are extensions of the domestic consumption role of women; prostitution is an extension of the sexual role (Davis, 1961). Hoffman-Bustamante (1973), Pollak (1950), and Simon (1975) argued that opportunities for criminality are determined by sex roles. Women have committed primarily petty property crimes (for example, shoplifting) because these are the only opportunities available to house-bound women whose major social role is that of consumer. This perspective suggests that as women expand their roles, enter the labor force, and increase their education, they will experience the same opportunities and motivations as men to commit property crimes. Advancements in the status of women per se should be associated with increases in their criminal conduct, which should, in turn, be reflected in an increase in the numbers of women arrested.

Hill and Harris (1981) labeled the opportunity explanations "objectivist" (that is, stemming from women's roles and statuses) and advocated a "subjectivist" explanation that stresses attitudes and interprets increases in women's criminality as reflecting changes in their self-perceptions. This dismissal of role (that is, social structural) approaches is in line with Harris's (1977) earlier contention that structural models cannot readily account for (1) the crime rate of women being much lower than that of men or (2) the greater propensity of women to commit nonviolent property crimes rather than violent personal and property crimes. Durkheim (1951) and Merton's (1968) structural strain theories would predict higher crime rates among women than among men because the former's traditional roles deny access to legitimate means of achievement, forcing them to become criminal "innovators." Similarly, Harris contended, differential opportunity theory would interpret traditional sex roles as blocking access to both legitimate and illegitimate means. In their frustration, women would be expected to commit relatively more violent crimes than men. Neither of these expectations is borne out in official U.S. police data or in the profile of offenders sketched by victimization surveys.

The women's liberation and opportunity hypotheses continue to direct the bulk of research on women and crime today. Both perspectives argue that female crime rates should increase as women move toward greater equality with men in the social, economic, and political spheres in their societies. The opportunity approach, however, views changes that free women from solely home-based activities (such as getting a job and going to school) as simultaneously presenting opportunities for criminal—especially property—misconduct. The liberation perspective is more psychological and hypothesizes increases in female crime as women's self-definitions change. Self-definitions are likely to change before actual changes in labor force and educational status occur. The research design typically followed correlates changes in the status of women in the United States with the *Uniform Crime Reports* (*UCR*) statistics over time. (*UCR* have been published annually by the Federal Bureau of Investigation since 1930 and present data obtained from over 10,000 law enforcement agencies across the country, including the number of arrests per year, the offenses for which suspects have been arrested, and the age, sex, and racial backgrounds of those arrested.) The problem with this design is that the study is couched within only one society, thus offering little variance in crime statistics and in the social, economic, or psychological factors thought to influence these statistics. A richer design maximizes social structural variation by comparing national crime data derived from a large number of countries. Several researchers have followed this design (for example, Hartnagel, 1982; Widom and Stewart, 1986) but have drawn comparisons across a number of countries for only one year, which is a cross-sectional design. As discussed more fully in the next section, this strategy is problematic. A more rigorous approach, and the one employed here, involves both comparative and longitudinal data: Crime rates are analyzed by country and across time, and conclusions are based on the empirical evidence from a widely varying set of countries for a lengthy period.

Method

The data were drawn from the Correlates of Crime Archive (Bennett and Lynch, 1986), which contains crime data printed in the International Police Organization's (Interpol) biannual *International Crime Statistics*. Member countries voluntarily report the number of crimes recorded in total and by type (homicide, major larceny, minor larceny, fraud, and so on), the number of crimes cleared by arrest, and the number of offenders arrested (by gender and adult/juvenile status).

The validity and reliability of the Interpol data have been criticized severely by numerous researchers. Archer and Gartner (1984: 18) depicted Interpol data as "by far the least satisfactory." They were especially critical of the organization's arbitrary definitions of offense categories that constitute a more serious threat to validity than the well-known tendency of member countries to use different operational definitions of types of crimes (Wellford, 1974) or to underreport systematically (International Police Organization, 1980, cited in Bennett and Lynch, 1986; Vigderhouse, 1978). Archer and Gartner's (1984) contention was refuted by Bennett and Lynch's (1986) comparison of Interpol data (used in the Correlates of Crime Archive) with the figures Archer and Gartner collected directly from the nations. A test of the comparability between the two data sources found them virtually identical.

Whatever biases and inconsistencies exist in the Interpol figures, they are minimized when crime figures are analyzed for one nation over a considerable period. The data set analyzed in this chapter contains information on each of 31 countries over the period from 1962 to 1980.

Six crime measures were defined using the Interpol data. The first three were total crimes (the total number of crimes reported to the police), overall arrests (the number of women and men arrested in all the crime categories reported to the police), and female arrests (the number of women arrested in all the crime categories). Each of these three measures was converted to an annual rate through division by the nation's population for each year.[3] The three remaining crime measures separately calculated women's arrests for homicide, major larceny, and minor larceny. For each measure, the denominator was the number of women and men arrested for that offense category; and the resulting figure was the percentage of women among those arrested for the offense. Increases in these measures were interpreted as greater proportions of women and therefore lesser proportions of men, among arrested offenders.

There are known inconsistencies in what nations report as arrests. Some countries count only the people apprehended and others report only those formally arrested. The within-nation design of this study makes this cross-national variation acceptable if we assume that member nations do not change their definition of an arrested offender over time. We make precisely this assumption.

Four social and demographic measures were examined. Female enrollment in secondary educational institutions was measured as the percentage of all secondary education students who were women in a given country. Female labor-force participation was calculated as the percentage of women in the national labor force. Two other indices measured social structural characteristics of the countries. The level of economic opportunity was measured by the per capita private consumption of the gross national product (GNP); and the level of industrialization was indicated by the percentage of the labor force in industry. Other factors useful for testing the liberation and opportunity hypotheses described here—such as the percentage of women employed in managerial and professional positions; the percentage of women who have completed the equivalent of four years of college or more; and statutes pertaining to women's rights to hold and inherit property, to divorce, to vote, to obtain an abortion—were not available over a period of years and for a large enough group of countries to be analytically useful.[4]

Analysis and Findings

The first step in the analysis was to collapse the 19 years' worth of data into three time frames—period A: 1962-1965, period B: 1969-1972, and period C: 1977-1980—to stabilize the rates by averaging out their minor year-to-date fluctuations.[5] The time periods were selected to represent the beginning, middle, and end of the nearly two decades for which data were available.

Crime Rates

Table 4.1 presents the total crime rates for the 31 nations over the three time periods, in descending order, based on the crime rate in period A. The data show that crime rates rose in 23 of the 31 nations and that there was a steeper increase in crimes reported between periods B and C than between periods A and B. Australia, the United States, Finland, and the Netherlands, all highly industrialized countries, showed the largest increases across the three periods. The eight countries in which crime rates fell (including Burma, Cyprus, the Ivory Coast, and Kuwait) are developing nations.

TABLE 4.1
Total Crime Rates over Three Time Periods

Country	Period A (1962-65)	Period B (1969-72)	Period C (1977-80)	Group Means: Periods A, B, C	Rate Change Periods A-B %	Rate Change Periods B-C %
Sweden	4885.58	7853.51	10235.68	7658.26	+ 60.75	+ 30.33
New Zealand	4696.58	6291.36	9634.57	6874.17	+ 33.96	+ 53.14
Korea	3580.52	1404.41	1486.84	2157.26	− 60.78	+ 5.87
Austria	3297.63	3634.55	4285.04	3739.07	+ 10.22	+ 17.90
West Germany	3157.27	3982.67	5707.56	4282.50	+ 26.14	+ 43.31
Israel	3147.78	4469.45	5977.00	4531.41	+ 41.99	+ 33.73
Denmark	3059.91	5704.32	6958.66	5240.96	+ 86.42	+ 21.99
Canada	3052.67	5375.08	7149.32	5189.02	+ 75.75	+ 33.26
Finland	2899.60	6137.32	10132.46	6389.79	+111.66	+ 65.10
Fiji	2456.23	4275.79	6059.49	4263.84	+ 74.08	+ 41.72
Libya	2372.21	1693.84	1154.28	1740.11	− 28.60	− 31.85
Japan	2035.25	1311.92	1267.68	1538.28	− 35.54	− 3.37
England/Wales	1892.15	2617.75	4631.06	3046.99	+ 38.35	+ 76.91
Australia	1807.76	2887.35	8190.29	4295.13	+ 59.72	+183.66
France	1772.48	2805.01	4308.39	2961.96	+ 58.25	+ 53.60

Kuwait	1772.39	1067.66	647.30	1162.45	− 39.76	− 39.37
Luxembourg	1619.12	1990.07	2649.29	2086.16	+ 22.91	+ 33.13
Jamaica	1592.44	1756.17	2461.58	1936.73	+ 10.28	+ 40.17
Zambia	1283.16	2243.99	2580.39	2035.85	+ 74.88	+ 14.99
United States	1269.96	3058.11	5309.87	3212.65	+140.80	+ 73.63
Netherlands	1269.35	2390.63	4339.49	2666.49	+ 88.33	+ 81.52
Norway	1241.43	1919.28	2636.73	1932.48	+ 54.60	+ 37.38
Hong Kong	992.75	1223.52	1474.13	1230.13	+ 23.25	+ 20.48
Cyprus	783.58	461.98	387.73	544.43	− 41.04	− 16.07
Burma	744.26	752.91	171.46	556.21	+ 1.16	− 77.23
Philippines	690.05	66.07	121.92	292.68	− 90.43	+ 84.53
Malawi	635.17	745.98	998.47	793.21	+ 17.45	+ 33.85
Ivory Coast	300.15	251.28	184.38	245.27	− 16.28	− 26.62
Malaysia	292.89	349.45	568.27	403.54	+ 19.31	+ 62.62
Sri Lanka	266.88	483.85	704.67	485.13	+ 81.30	+ 45.64
Nigeria	146.33	173.28	247.38	189.00	+ 18.42	+ 42.76
Median for time period	1721.33	2253.34	4381.99	2785.55	+ 30.91	+ 94.47
Mean for time period	1903.66	2560.28	3634.24	2699.39	+ 34.49	+ 41.95

Arrest Rates

Table 4.2 shows the overall arrest rates in those same countries during the three time periods. Similar to the trend of the crime rates, the arrest rates increased in 20 of the 31 nations, but more steeply between periods A and B than between periods B and C. The nations showing the greatest increases continued to be largely industrialized—Sweden, Canada, and the United States. Similarly, four of the nations with decreasing total crime rates—Kuwait, Cyprus, Burma, and the Philippines—showed the greatest declines in arrest rates as well.[6]

Female Arrest Rates

The total crime rate and the overall arrest rate figures provide some measure of the magnitude of offenses by men and women and the ability of police organizations to apprehend offenders. Within the national context provided by these data, it is interesting to examine the female arrest rates separately. The data in Table 4.3 show a steady increase in 13 of the 31 countries. Only three nations—Kuwait, Israel, and the Ivory Coast—showed consistent declines in female arrests. Across the 31 countries, women's arrests accounted for about one-eighth of the total arrests in each time period.

The repeated appearance of several countries (West Germany, Austria, and New Zealand) on the three lists of nations showing the greatest increases across the three periods in Tables 4.1 to 4.3 led us to examine the extent to which female arrest rates rose or fell in accordance with total crime and overall arrest rates. The Pearson's r (a statistic that equates 1.0 at perfect correlation and zero at perfect independence) between total crime and female crime rates was similar to those reported for the overall arrest rates: $r = .63, .68,$ and $.73$, in periods A, B, and C, respectively. As could be expected, the correlations between overall arrest rates and female arrest rates were even higher: $r = .72, .88,$ and $.90$ in periods A, B, and C, respectively. The strength of the association among the three variables suggests that the factors influencing changes in a nation's crime and arrest rates also affect that nation's female arrest rates.

We turn next to an analysis of female arrests for homicide and major larceny. For purposes of comparison, we also report the percentage of female arrests for a nonviolent offense—minor larceny, which includes theft and receiving stolen goods.

TABLE 4.2
Total Arrests over Three Time Periods

Country	Period A (1962-65)	Period B (1969-72)	Period C (1977-80)	Group Mean: Periods A, B, C	Rate Change Periods A-B %	Rate Change Periods B-C %
Israel	989.53	1072.24	457.96	839.91	+ 8.36	− 57.29
West Germany	769.39	944.93	1287.40	1000.57	+ 22.82	+ 36.24
New Zealand	719.54	1063.83	1740.67	1174.68	+ 47.85	+ 63.62
Burma	585.79	459.38	313.72	452.96	− 21.58	− 31.71
Luxembourg	545.05	504.49	438.20	495.91	− 7.44	− 13.14
Austria	526.72	577.66	598.02	567.47	+ 9.67	+ 3.52
Finland	465.09	680.79	834.39	660.09	+ 46.38	+ 22.56
Kuwait	460.43	190.00	109.39	253.27	− 58.73	− 42.43
Korea	417.15	291.62	319.34	342.70	− 30.09	+ 9.51
Australia	397.73	544.57	572.71	505.00	+ 36.92	+ 5.17
England/Wales	342.75	496.49	676.07	505.10	+ 44.85	+ 36.17
Netherlands	334.11	463.27	526.87	441.42	+ 38.66	+ 13.73
France	326.25	788.21	721.60	612.02	+141.60	− 8.45
United States	325.39	539.43	896.40	587.07	+ 65.78	+ 66.18
Cyprus	290.58	188.33	125.19	201.37	− 35.19	− 33.53

(continued)

TABLE 4.2 continued

Country	Period A (1962-65)	Period B (1969-72)	Period C (1977-80)	Group Mean: Periods A, B, C	Rate Change Periods A-B %	Rate Change Periods B-C %
Canada	278.56	379.17	791.55	483.09	+ 36.12	+108.76
Jamaica	276.03	725.11	918.12	639.75	+162.69	+ 26.62
Libya	269.77	224.38	176.89	223.68	− 16.83	− 21.16
Sweden	264.78	437.68	1002.08	568.18	+ 65.30	+128.95
Zambia	263.68	208.38	206.49	226.18	− 20.97	− 0.91
Japan	259.45	189.13	198.10	215.56	− 27.10	+ 4.74
Fiji	212.74	355.35	453.12	340.40	+ 67.03	+ 27.51
Norway	154.96	198.22	194.72	182.63	+ 27.92	− 1.77
Hong Kong	147.10	185.47	239.84	190.80	+ 26.08	+ 29.31
Ivory Coast	130.02	161.96	115.91	135.96	+ 24.57	− 28.43
Sri Lanka	121.08	239.20	153.11	171.13	+ 97.56	− 35.99
Denmark	104.26	150.41	251.09	168.59	+ 44.26	+ 66.94
Philippines	102.82	55.09	43.83	67.25	− 46.42	− 20.44
Malawi	100.97	110.42	158.54	123.31	+ 9.36	+ 43.58
Malaysia	50.84	45.52	65.36	53.91	− 10.46	+ 43.59
Nigeria	30.43	45.93	51.01	42.46	+ 50.94	+ 11.06
Median for time period	281.72	430.87	611.62	441.40	+ 52.94	+ 41.95
Mean for time period	331.06	403.76	472.18	402.34	+ 21.96	+ 16.95

TABLE 4.3
Total Female Arrest Rates over Three Time Periods

Country	Period A (1962-65)	Period B (1969-72)	Period C (1977-80)	Group Mean: Periods A, B, C	Rate Change Periods A-B %	Rate Change Periods B-C %
West Germany	134.27	197.26	290.91	207.48	+ 46.91	+ 47.48
Austria	84.91	94.37	107.89	95.72	+ 11.14	+ 14.33
New Zealand	75.65	202.88	390.83	223.12	+168.18	+ 92.64
Luxembourg	66.92	77.35	69.65	71.31	+ 15.59	− 9.95
Israel	63.32	53.32	51.84	56.16	− 15.79	− 2.78
England	52.42	72.90	151.37	92.23	+ 39.07	+107.64
Netherlands	48.63	67.01	67.92	61.19	+ 37.80	+ 1.36
Finland	48.02	77.81	97.34	74.39	+ 62.04	+ 25.10
United States	47.19	97.29	215.79	120.09	+106.17	+121.80
France	46.37	148.18	143.58	112.71	+219.56	− 3.10
Australia	43.37	88.34	142.92	91.54	+103.69	+ 61.78
Japan	40.15	37.82	60.28	46.08	− 5.80	+ 59.39
Sweden	36.11	62.01	138.11	78.74	+ 71.73	+122.72
Jamaica	34.38	157.06	62.49	84.64	+356.84	− 60.21
Korea	32.32	26.69	31.67	30.23	− 17.42	+ 18.66

(continued)

TABLE 4.3 continued

Country	Period A (1962-65)	Period B (1969-72)	Period C (1977-80)	Group Mean: Periods A, B, C	Rate Change Periods A-B %	Rate Change Periods B-C %
Canada	26.70	60.16	115.60	67.49	+125.32	+ 92.15
Cyprus	19.02	8.94	9.11	12.36	− 53.00	+ 1.90
Burma	15.92	17.57	26.14	19.88	+ 10.36	+ 48.78
Denmark	13.54	12.66	17.94	14.71	− 6.50	+ 41.71
Norway	13.52	20.04	17.73	17.10	+ 48.22	− 11.53
Libya	10.75	4.28	4.79	6.61	− 60.19	+ 11.92
Fiji	7.21	12.80	19.28	13.10	+ 77.53	+ 50.63
Kuwait	7.16	7.09	4.85	6.37	− 0.98	− 31.59
Hong Kong	6.55	5.43	24.41	12.13	− 17.10	+349.54
Zambia	4.46	3.20	5.01	4.22	− 28.25	+ 56.56
Ivory Coast	4.28	4.12	3.78	4.06	− 3.74	− 8.25
Philippines	3.78	1.69	1.96	2.48	− 55.29	+ 15.98
Sri Lanka	3.67	8.87	8.39	6.98	+141.69	− 5.41
Malawi	2.17	2.73	4.80	3.23	+ 25.81	+ 75.82
Nigeria	1.11	3.08	2.67	2.29	+177.48	− 13.31
Malaysia	0.77	0.69	0.79	0.75	− 10.39	+ 14.49
Median for time period	34.27	28.18	46.09	36.18	− 17.76	+ 63.52
Mean for time period	32.09	52.70	73.87	52.88	+ 64.24	+ 40.17

Commenting first on the homicide data, we note that the percentages decreased an average of 10% across the three time periods and that the decline was slightly steeper between periods A and B than between periods B and C (Table 4.4 and the mean percentage figures at the bottom). The percentages for major larceny increased an average of 10% across the three time periods (Table 4.5). Nevertheless, women accounted for only about 10 in 100 and 4 in 100 homicide and major larceny arrests, respectively.

As hypothesized, an examination of the statistics in Table 4.6 reveals a higher percentage of females arrested for minor larceny than for homicide (except in period A) and major larceny and a steady increase across the three time periods. On the whole, women accounted for about 13 of every 100 arrests for minor larceny.

Even for minor larceny, the most frequent of the three offense types, the female arrest rate was only one-eighth that of males. The expectations of the "liberation theorists" that by the 1980s women would be involved in property offenses at a level comparable to that of men were far from realized. Even in nations with the highest female minor larceny arrest rates—the United States, West Germany, and Japan—women accounted for less than one-third of such arrests.[7]

The data presented thus far show that crime rates and arrest rates increased at about the same levels and the female arrest rates correlated strongly with the overall arrest rates. Examination of the data on female involvement in the major violent offense category revealed a slight decline in the overall percentage of female homicide arrests across the three time periods. Female arrests for major larceny remained steady at a relatively low percentage. Female arrests for minor larceny increased more steeply than for major larceny but did not attain the levels anticipated by many researchers in the 1970s.

Societal Correlates of Crime

The opportunity, liberation, and social structural perspectives provide hypotheses about the relationship between the percentage of women arrested for violent and property offenses and the socioeconomic and demographic characteristics of their societies. The demographic variables of interest are the percentages of women in the labor force and in institutions of higher education. These are direct indicators of women's freedom from their traditional domestic role. The socio-

(text continued p. 192)

TABLE 4.4

Percentage of Females Arrested for Homicide over Three Time Periods

Country	Period A (1962-65)	Period B (1969-72)	Period C (1977-80)	Group Mean: Periods A, B, C	Rate Change Periods A-B %	Rate Change Periods B-C %
Norway	30.10	2.50	11.40	14.67	− 91.66	+354.18
Denmark	25.00	14.00	12.40	17.13	− 44.00	− 11.43
England/Wales	23.40	15.80	13.70	17.63	− 32.48	− 13.29
Austria	23.20	18.80	20.70	20.90	− 18.97	+ 10.11
New Zealand	22.90	14.00	10.30	15.73	− 38.86	− 26.43
Korea	21.70	17.50	17.30	18.83	− 19.35	− 1.14
West Germany	18.50	12.90	11.00	14.13	− 30.27	− 14.73
United States	18.20	15.60	13.70	15.81	− 14.21	− 12.07
Libya	18.00	15.90	9.70	14.53	− 11.67	− 38.99
Australia	16.60	12.80	14.00	14.47	− 22.89	+ 9.38
Fiji	16.00	8.30	6.10	10.13	− 48.13	− 26.51
Jamaica	14.90	7.80	2.80	8.50	− 47.65	− 64.10
Japan	14.60	18.00	21.40	18.00	+ 23.29	+ 18.89
France	14.20	14.40	13.40	14.00	+ 1.41	− 6.94

Finland	13.20	16.00	8.80	12.67	+ 21.21	− 45.00
Netherlands	10.50	6.00	5.70	7.40	− 42.86	− 5.00
Canada	8.70	11.70	10.50	10.30	+ 34.48	− 10.26
Malawi	7.50	4.80	11.90	8.07	− 36.00	+147.92
Kuwait	7.00	6.40	11.50	8.30	− 8.57	+ 79.69
Luxembourg	6.40	14.50	5.70	8.87	+126.56	− 60.69
Ivory Coast	5.90	9.60	7.40	7.63	+ 62.71	− 22.92
Israel	5.20	4.60	3.30	4.37	− 11.54	− 28.26
Nigeria	4.70	7.30	3.80	5.27	+ 55.32	− 47.95
Sri Lanka	4.70	5.50	6.10	5.45	+ 17.87	+ 10.11
Sweden	4.10	12.10	9.70	8.63	+195.12	− 19.83
Hong Kong	3.80	5.00	9.60	6.13	+ 31.58	+ 92.00
Malaysia	3.30	1.80	3.30	2.80	− 45.45	+ 83.33
Zambia	2.80	1.00	0.30	1.37	− 64.29	− 70.00
Cyprus	2.10	23.30	12.50	12.63	+1009.52	− 46.35
Philippines	1.60	1.40	2.00	1.67	− 12.50	+ 42.86
Burma	0.90	1.10	1.70	1.23	+ 27.59	+ 53.15
Mean percentage	11.92	10.34	9.41	10.56	− 13.31	− 8.97

TABLE 4.5

Percentage of Females Arrested for Major Larceny over Three Time Periods

Country	Period A (1962-65)	Period B (1969-72)	Period C (1977-80)	Group Mean: Periods A, B, C	Rate Change Periods A-B %	Rate Change Periods B-C %
Denmark	16.00	7.90	5.10	9.66	− 50.53	− 35.19
Austria	10.30	8.50	5.30	8.03	− 17.33	− 37.34
Jamaica	9.10	23.90	4.70	12.55	+162.95	− 80.21
France	9.00	8.70	7.30	8.32	− 3.67	− 15.38
Korea	6.80	2.40	1.40	3.51	− 65.15	− 43.04
Canada	4.80	6.10	5.70	5.49	+ 27.52	− 6.92
Luxembourg	4.30	7.80	12.40	8.16	+ 79.03	+ 59.20
West Germany	4.00	3.60	5.40	4.30	− 11.03	+ 51.27
Cyprus	3.90	2.20	4.50	3.53	− 44.27	+104.11
United States	3.90	5.20	6.40	5.14	+ 33.42	+ 24.27
Netherlands	3.70	4.40	4.80	4.27	+ 18.48	+ 9.40
Finland	3.60	3.50	9.30	5.46	− 3.31	+164.86
Israel	3.60	2.20	3.60	3.11	− 39.83	+ 65.28
Norway	3.20	3.60	5.20	3.99	+ 13.25	+ 44.05

Australia	3.20	3.40	5.80	4.11	+ 7.62	+ 71.09
New Zealand	2.60	5.30	11.80	6.58	+101.52	+123.02
England/Wales	2.50	2.90	4.40	3.23	+ 15.85	+ 53.33
Sweden	2.10	2.70	4.60	3.14	+ 30.62	+ 68.50
Sri Lanka	2.00	3.40	6.40	3.93	+ 67.66	+ 90.50
Nigeria	2.00	2.10	2.10	2.07	+ 5.00	+ 0.95
Ivory Coast	1.80	3.00	1.90	2.26	+ 64.13	− 36.42
Libya	1.60	2.30	2.80	2.24	+ 43.75	+ 22.61
Philippines	1.40	1.60	1.90	1.59	+ 15.44	+ 17.83
Hong Kong	1.20	0.80	0.60	0.87	− 27.83	− 25.30
Japan	1.10	1.70	6.80	3.21	+ 48.67	+305.95
Kuwait	1.10	1.80	2.20	1.68	+ 73.58	+ 16.85
Malawi	0.80	1.60	1.40	1.27	+ 92.68	− 11.39
Burma	0.60	0.30	0.50	0.47	− 50.79	+ 51.61
Fiji	0.60	0.80	0.90	0.75	+ 31.03	+ 21.05
Zambia	0.30	0.50	1.10	0.63	+ 35.29	+139.13
Malaysia	0.20	0.00	0.10	0.07	−100.00	0.00
Mean percentage	3.58	3.99	4.39	3.99	+ 11.40	+ 10.09

TABLE 4.6

Percentage of Females Arrested for Minor Larceny over Three Time Periods

Country	Period A (1962-65)	Period B (1969-72)	Period C (1977-80)	Group Mean: Periods A, B, C	Rate Change Periods A-B %	Rate Change Periods B-C %
West Germany	21.60	31.20	29.70	27.50	+ 44.08	− 4.59
Netherlands	20.90	25.20	22.00	22.68	+ 20.65	− 12.63
Austria	20.80	25.90	25.30	23.98	+ 24.40	− 2.05
Sweden	20.40	19.80	21.60	20.58	− 3.04	+ 9.31
United States	20.30	22.40	30.60	24.43	+ 10.66	+ 36.49
England/Wales	19.40	19.10	28.40	22.31	− 1.39	+ 48.46
Japan	18.80	22.30	34.30	25.11	+ 18.60	+ 54.25
Luxembourg	18.20	24.60	17.60	20.14	+ 35.00	− 28.61
Jamaica	14.90	18.60	11.50	14.98	+ 25.13	− 38.51
France	14.90	17.70	18.10	16.89	+ 19.39	+ 2.09
Finland	14.40	16.30	11.50	14.07	+ 13.12	− 29.45
Norway	13.60	18.50	14.30	15.47	+ 35.36	− 22.38
Australia	12.10	19.20	31.90	21.07	+ 58.20	+ 66.23
New Zealand	11.70	25.80	25.30	20.96	+120.10	− 2.09

Cyprus	10.20	6.00	10.00	8.72	− 41.64	+ 67.00
Canada	9.70	16.50	15.00	13.70	+ 69.69	− 9.17
Korea	9.50	9.20	8.10	8.95	− 2.94	− 12.34
Israel	8.10	7.10	13.20	9.46	− 12.00	+ 85.65
Burma	6.00	6.90	14.10	8.98	+ 15.03	+104.21
Philippines	5.30	5.10	7.60	6.03	− 3.75	+ 48.54
Denmark	4.90	4.70	5.90	5.16	− 3.49	+ 25.96
Hong Kong	4.50	4.10	18.20	8.93	− 10.13	+345.34
Fiji	4.30	4.50	5.90	4.90	+ 5.59	+ 29.58
Nigeria	4.10	7.60	6.10	5.93	+ 84.88	− 19.26
Sri Lanka	3.90	3.60	4.30	3.92	+ 6.49	+ 19.44
Ivory Coast	3.20	1.90	3.00	2.68	− 41.25	+ 56.91
Libya	3.10	1.60	2.80	2.51	− 47.57	+ 74.07
Malawi	2.60	2.80	3.40	2.90	+ 5.77	+ 21.82
Zambia	1.90	2.70	4.50	3.04	+ 38.14	+ 67.91
Kuwait	1.80	4.70	5.00	3.80	+161.80	+ 6.22
Malaysia	1.70	1.60	1.50	1.59	− 8.19	− 4.46
Mean percentage	10.90	13.10	14.80	13.00	+ 31.70	+ 31.50

191

economic variables are levels of industrialization and economic opportunity that measure the societywide possibilities for women and men alike. Durkheim and Merton's structural strain theory predicts higher violent female crime rates in those societies in which there is greater suppression of women's rights. As women feel more downtrodden and blocked in their aspirations for social and economic equality with men, they are more likely to "innovate" by committing violent acts against those whom they view as the sources of their oppression. Thus women in societies that do not allow divorce, that forbid them to inherit or hold property, that bar them from participation in institutions of higher education or in various labor markets, and that are not highly industrialized and offer few economic opportunities to their citizens are hypothesized to be more likely to commit homicide and major larceny than are women in societies in which they enjoy the full rights of citizenship.

Conversely, societies in which there are high rates of female property offenders are likely to be those that support female participation in higher education and the labor force, provide economic opportunities generally and as the result of industrialization, and give women political rights (for example, the right to vote), social rights (for example, divorce), and other economic rights (for example, inheritance and the right to hold property in one's own name).

This phase of the analysis was directed at testing two hypotheses: (1) women's propensities to commit violent offenses are negatively correlated with their labor force participation, enrollment in secondary education institutions, the nation's level of industrialization, and its level of economic opportunity; and (2) women's propensities to commit property crimes are positively related to these same indicators.

Examining first, in Table 4.7, the correlations between female labor force participation and the percentage of females arrested for the three offenses, we found no strong correlations (0.5 or above) in any of the three time periods. The strongest relationship was between minor larceny and female labor force participation ($r = .43$) in period C. The table also shows a strong relationship between females attending institutions of secondary education and female homicide arrests ($r = .50$) in period A. Overall, the top half of Table 4.7 shows little support for either hypothesis.

In addition to the two demographic indicators we also arrayed societies by levels of economic opportunity (the private consumption of

TABLE 4.7
Pearson Product Moment Correlations Between
Crime and Societal Variables over Three Time Periods

Variables	Period A (1962-65) r =	Period B (1969-72) r =	Period C (1977-80) r =
Correlations between female labor participation and			
female homicide arrests	–0.07	0.12	0.10
female major larceny arrests	0.23	0.12	0.18
female minor larceny arrests	0.28	0.26	0.43
Correlations between female enrollment in secondary education and			
female homicide arrests	0.20	0.14	0.56
female major larceny arrests	0.22	–0.01	0.19
female minor larceny arrests	0.51	0.45	0.36
Correlations between level of industrialization and			
female homicide arrests	0.37	0.40	0.51
female major larceny arrests	0.50	0.40	0.46
female minor larceny arrests	0.68	0.66	0.70
Correlations between level of economic opportunity and			
female homicide arrests	0.31	0.35	0.54
female major larceny arrests	0.57	0.42	0.65
female minor larceny arrests	0.56	0.53	0.65

the gross domestic product divided by the population) and industrialization (the percentage of the work force engaged in industry). Societies that are industrialized and measure high in economic opportunity offer women more important roles outside the home, which may in turn provide opportunities for criminal activities. Computing correlations between each of those measures and female homicide, major larceny, and minor larceny, we found many more strong relationships than for the demographic variables. Consistently high positive correlations were found between female minor larceny and both societal indicators in all three time periods. The data provide strong support for the second hypothesis. The first hypothesis, that job and labor force opportunities are negatively related to violent crimes by women, is clearly not supported. Not only are the correlation coefficients not negative, as the hypothesis would predict, but they are occasionally strongly positive.

Conclusion

The data show that over the 19-year time span there were comparable levels of increase among crime, arrest, and female arrest rates from 1962 through 1980. The fears raised in the late 1960s and early 1970s that women's participation rates in crime would soon be commensurate with their representation in the population clearly were not realized. For homicide and major larceny, the percentage of female offenders actually decreased slightly. Thus at least among the 31 countries for which longitudinal data were available, women continued to play relatively minor roles in those societies' violent criminal activities.

We found little support for the social structural hypothesis of Durkheim and Merton that women would commit more violent crimes in the less socially and economically progressive nations. We also discovered that the nonviolent crime of minor larceny is much less correlated with changes in women's educational and work status, as the liberation and opportunity perspectives hypothesized, than with more general measures of societal economic opportunity. Interestingly, female arrests for the violent offenses of homicide and major larceny were also positively related to societal opportunity.[8]

The data presented here are an improvement over what has appeared in much of the comparative literature on women's participation in criminal activities in that we have marshaled longitudinal crime statistics over a 19-year time span for 31 countries. In addition to the crime and arrest statistics for violent offenses and one form of property offense, we presented data on four social and demographic characteristics: the percentage of women enrolled in secondary educational institutions, the percentage of females in the labor force, the level of economic opportunity as measured by the per capita private consumptions of the gross national product, and the level of industrialization as measured by the percentage of the labor force in industry. We used these measures because they permit hypothesis tests about female crime rates under different conditions and because they were available over the 19-year time span and for the 31 countries for which we had crime data. But we recognize that these are not the best of all possible measures. In order to make a more definitive test of the relationship between women's statuses and their crime patterns and rates in different societies over time, we need better statistics (for example, the number of women in each country's population so that the female arrest rates can be calculated on the basis of the total female population) and more sensitive socioeconomic and sociopolitical indicators, such as women's rights to hold and inherit property, to testify in court, to divorce, to abort unwanted babies, to vote, to hold public office, as well as the percentage of women in the labor force in professional and managerial positions, the percentage of women who have completed at least four years of postsecondary education, and marriage and birth rates. All of these measures together over two or three decades and for a wide range of countries would provide more definitive answers to questions we and many other researchers ask about the relationship between the status women occupy in a society, the roles they play, the political, social, and economic rights they enjoy, and the types and levels of crime they commit. With a sufficiently long time period, the changes in women's statuses and roles could be related to changes, or the lack thereof, in their participation in crime. These data are being collected in a more systematic manner and, we hope, future researchers will make use of them.

NOTES

1. Major larceny is considered a violent offense because it includes robbery with dangerous aggravating circumstances.

2. In addition to homicide, major larceny, and minor larceny, the other offense categories are fraud, counterfeiting, drug offenses, and a miscellaneous category of other offenses not including the six cited here.

3. Unfortunately, data on the number of women in each nation's population were not routinely available, so the female arrest rates were calculated using total population as the denominator.

4. The World Bank and United Nations publications were the sources for the annual data on the number of women enrolled in secondary educational institutions, the level of economic opportunity, and the level of industrialization in a nation. The International Labor Organization published the data on female labor force participation.

5. Grouping the data in this fashion reduced the autocorrelation effect present in the time-series data and enabled unbiased correlation coefficients to be calculated between two data trends grouped in identical time period categories.

6. Pearson product moment correlation coefficients were calculated between the crime rates and the overall arrest rates for the three time periods. The coefficients were quite strong: $r = .73, .73$, and $.75$ for periods A, B, and C, respectively.

7. In computing Spearman's rank order correlation between the percentages of female arrests for homicide, major larceny, and minor larceny within each time period we found the following:

	Periods		
	A	B	C
Homicide and major larceny	.44	.45	.39
Homicide and minor larceny	.38	.47	.47
Major and minor larceny	.65	.59	.59

Overall, the strongest relationship in each time period was between major and minor larceny. The former category, as we have noted, involves both violent and property offenses.

8. This study did not explore lagging variables during the analysis. The correlations were calculated within the same year, such that women's larceny in Sweden in 1976 was correlated with the arrest, demographic and socioeconomic variables as measured for 1976. It may be that criminal behavior is a response to a preexisting condition and the crime data for 1976 should be correlated with the other variables as measured for 1975, or even earlier.

REFERENCES

Adler, F. (1975) Sisters in Crime. New York: McGraw-Hill.

Archer, D. and R. Gartner (1984) Violence and Crime in Cross-National Perspective. New Haven, CT: Yale University Press.

Austin, Roy L. (1982) "Women's liberation and increases in minor, major and occupational offenses." Criminology 20: 407-430.

Bennett, R. B. and S. Baxter (1983) "Investigating the effect of police on the incidence of criminality: a cross-national study." Criminal Justice Review 8: 32-39.

Bennett, R. R. and J. P. Lynch (1986) "Does a difference make a difference: comparing cross-national crime indicators." Washington, DC: American University.

Bowker, L. H. (1978) Women, Crime, and the Criminal Justice System. Lexington, MA: D.C. Heath.

Bunge, M. (1981) "Development indicators." Social Indicators Research 9: 369-385.

Davis, K. (1961) "Prostitution," in R. K. Merton and R. A. Nisbet (eds.) Contemporary Social Problems. New York: Harcourt Brace Jovanovich.

Durkheim, E. (1951) Suicide. (G. Simpson, ed.). New York: Free Press.

Harris, A. R. (1977) "Sex and theories of deviance: toward a functional theory of deviant type-scripts." American Sociological Review 42: 3-16.

Hartnagel, T. F. (1982) "Modernization, female social roles, and female crime: a cross-national investigation." Sociological Quarterly 23: 477-490.

Hill, G. D. and A. R. Harris (1981) "Changes in the gender patterning of crime, 1953-1977: opportunity vs. identity." Social Science Quarterly 62: 658-671.

Hoffman-Bustamante, D. (1973) "The nature of female criminality." Issues in Criminology 8: 117-136.

International Police Organization (1980) "International crime statistics." 92-Saint Cloud, France, 1962-1965, 1969-1972, 1977-1980.

Klein, D. (1973). "The etiology of female crime: a review of the literature." Issues in Criminology 8: 3-30.

Merton, R. (1968) Social Theory and Social Structure. Glencoe, IL: Free Press.

Pollak, O. (1950) The Criminality of Women. Philadelphia: University of Pennsylvania Press.

Simon, R. J. (1975) Women and Crime. Lexington, MA: D. C. Heath.

Simon, R. J. (1976) "American women and crime." Annals 423: 31-46.

Simon, R. J. and N. Sharma (1979) "Women and crime: does the American experience generalize?" pp. 391-400 in F. Adler and R. J. Simon (eds.) The Criminology of Deviant Women. Boston: Houghton Mifflin.

Steffensmeier, D. J. (1978) "Crime and the contemporary woman: an analysis of changing levels of female property crime, 1960-1975." Social Forces 57: 566-584.

Steffensmeier, D. J., R. H. Steffensmeier, and A. S. Rosenthal (1979) "Trends in female violence, 1960-1977." Sociological Focus 13: 217-226.

Vigderhouse, G. (1978). "Methodological problems confronting cross-cultural criminological research using official data." Human Relations 31: 229-247.

Weis, J. G. (1976) "Liberation and crime: the invention of the new female criminal." Crime and Social Justice 6: 17-27.

Wellford, C. R. (1974) "Crime and the dimensions of nations." International Journal of Criminology and Penology 2: 1-10.

Widom, C. S. and A. J. Stewart (1986) "Female criminality and the status of women." International Annals of Criminology 24: 137-162.

Wise, N. B. (1967) "Juvenile delinquency among middle-class girls," pp. 179-188 in E. W. Vaz (ed.) Middle-Class Juvenile Delinquency. New York: Harper & Row.

5

Street Gang Violence

MALCOLM W. KLEIN
CHERYL L. MAXSON

During an interval of a few days in the mid-1960s, a reputed gang area near downtown Los Angeles was subjected to seemingly random gunfire during which a young woman was wounded by a shot from a passing car. Police earnestly sought information leading to the assailant or assailants; but their information sources and gang intelligence capacities were not equal to the task. Yet in a neighboring gang area, a street worker assigned to the local gang knew soon thereafter that the "Garcia Cousins" (pseudonym) were responsible for the shooting and the "random" gunfire; he knew why the gunfire had taken place and had corroboration from other gang members. And because the episode was seen as a threat to the successful disbanding of the Garcias' gang following an intensive street intervention program, an anonymous tip from program staff led to the Garcias' arrest by the grateful police.

Over the course of a few weeks in the early 1980s, a street worker program agreed to provide a university research team with a list of gangs, gang cliques, territories, and rosters in order to help evaluate the effect of the program. The information provided by the workers was pitiable in contrast to what was routinely provided in the mid-1960s. Meanwhile, police information on these same gangs was so extensive and detailed that it generated a successful ACLU lawsuit to regulate gang intelligence-gathering, recording, and retention by the police.

AUTHORS' NOTE: Some of the material reported in this chapter was collected with the support of grants from the National Institute of Justice (#81-IJ-CX-0072 and #84-IJ-CX-0052). Points of view expressed herein are those of the authors and do not necessarily represent the official position or policies of the U.S. Department of Justice.

The contrast between these two situations, separated in time by less than 20 years, symbolizes a number of fundamental changes in relation to street gangs and what can be known about them. During this period, the growth of law enforcement gang expertise, specialized gang units, and information-gathering activities has produced increased reliance on police data as the major source for information on street gangs and gang activity. Gang programs have shifted focus, goals, and intervention strategies. And, not surprisingly, current research on gangs—the questions asked, the modes of scholarly investigation, and the knowledge about gangs and gang crime that results—contrasts substantially with research from prior decades.

The most recent major review of writings on street gangs (Quicker, 1983b) lists 170 reports on gangs published through October 1981; and one might well wonder if there can be any legitimate reason for continuing to investigate an area already covered so extensively. The answer is an emphatic yes for a variety of reasons.

First, there has been a decline in scholarly attention to gang developments during a period when the available evidence suggests that significant changes have taken place. Quicker's review yielded an interesting pattern of published materials on gangs. Starting with a book published early in this century—J.A. Puffer's *The Boy and His Gangs* (Boston: Houghton Mifflin, 1912)—Quicker listed seven scholarly articles and books prior to 1950, 20 in the 1950s, 55 in the 1960s, and then a decrease to about 25 in the 1970s. Reasons for the decline have been attributed to civil rights developments, drugs, and other factors that might "drain off" gang activity and therefore gang research (Galea, 1982; Recktenwald and Sheppard, 1984; Stafford, 1984). It has also been suggested that it is not a decline in gang activity but changes in political and research paradigms that have yielded the decrease in research activity (Bookin-Weiner and Horowitz, 1983; Maxson and Klein, 1983). Given some of the findings about the spread of gang activity in the 1970s (Miller, 1975, 1980; Stapleton and Needle, 1982), we are inclined toward the latter explanation.

What do we know from the research undertaken since the early 1970s? Not much, according to several analyses. Bookin-Weiner and Horowitz (1983) and Stafford (1984) commented specifically on the decline in new information and new theory. Quicker (1983b) was quite explicit on this point:

Most of the theoretical statements had been made and most of the testing of those statements had been completed by the end of the 1960's. In the

1970's and 1980's, we find very little new theory, and certainly nothing on the order of opportunity theory, or its immediate predecessors. The research in this decade and the 1980's is somewhat more amorphous, since, for the most part, it was not part of a national trend as it was during the 1960's. Research during this period reflects more of a response on the part of researchers to particular interests or to particular trendy issues rather than to major theory testing and policy development [p. 82].

A somewhat different interpretation is that current gang research reflects a national trend of political and ideological conservatism that stresses immediate policy concerns of controlling gang crime and, particularly, gang violence. While loosely tied to deterrence theory, this policy emphasis and the intervention programs it has spawned have presented few opportunities for theoretical tests or advancement. Law enforcement personnel have been the spearheads in the latest efforts to control gang violence. As a byproduct, they have established substantial repositories of gang information that present different opportunities for researchers, with theoretical and methodological limitations.

Summarizing a broad range of gang topics, Quicker concluded from his review, "Nothing which has been produced discredits or seriously undermines the vast storehouse of knowledge generated in the 1960s although some new dimensions have been added" (1983b: 120). One such new dimension is the increasing research on female gangs (Bowker, et al., 1980; Campbell, 1981; Miller, 1973; Quicker, 1983a). However much of this—for example, Bowker et al. (1980), and Miller (1973)—is delayed reporting of data collected in the prior two decades. As the reader will see in the pages to follow, Quicker's conclusion will require some modification. The "vast storehouse" requires some alterations to fit the picture of street gangs being revealed by the most recent research.

Scholarly attempts to integrate the more recent material into existing theoretical perspectives or to develop altogether new conceptual approaches have not yet emerged to span the theoretical gap between the 1950s and the 1960s and the 1980s. For instance, in years past, the well-known gang cities were the urban maelstroms of New York, Chicago, Boston, Philadelphia, and Los Angeles. Now gangs are said to be all too evident in "clean-living" smaller cities such as Denver, Minneapolis, St. Paul, Evanston, Salt Lake City, Riverside, and San Diego. Indeed, one recent report provides an estimate of between 600 and 800 gangs operating in various cities throughout the state of California (California Council on Criminal Justice, hereinafter CCCJ, 1986). There is the question of how we got here from there.

If recent changes in gang patterns require our renewed attention, so also do other aspects of the gang arena. Much of what is known remains to be translated successfully into programs to control and reduce gang-related crime and gang violence in particular. As our introductory paragraphs suggest, things have changed substantially in gang programming since the 1960s. Some 20 years ago we were assessing rehabilitation programs for misguided group members; today we are seeking ways to control gang violence. Again, there is the question of how we got here from there and, moreover, where do we go from here?

Conceptual Issues

The reported increase in gang violence and the appearance of gangs in smaller urban areas provide reasons enough to maintain our interest. Beyond that, however, the gang arena incorporates features of conceptual importance to criminologists. First, gangs provide an extreme form of group criminality; and most criminologists are agreed that youthful crime is primarily a group phenomenon (using the term *group* rather loosely). Accordingly, gangs, it is thought, have much to teach us about the role of group or subcultural processes in the etiology of criminal behavior as well as about the group properties of crime events. Second, gang members commit more crime—and thus more violent crime—than do their nongang counterparts. To the extent that this is attributable to their gang membership per se, understanding the specific gang component should contribute to our capacity to reduce violent offending. Third, there are important definitional issues yet to be resolved, specifically the meaning of *gang* and the behavior to be included under the rubric of *gang-related offenses*. We will review these three issues briefly before moving on to questions of continuities and changes in various aspects of the street gang problem.

The Group Issue

When the comment is made, as it commonly is, that delinquency is a group phenomenon, it is seldom accompanied by data on the prevalence of group offending and almost never by explication of the meaning assigned to the "group" in group offending. Too often "gang" and "group" are used interchangeably. This issue was highlighted in a review of relevant literature and a discussion of misconceptions perpetuated by reference to various types of companionate offending as group offending

(Klein, 1969). Use of the term *group* requires specifying parameters of the relationship such as cohesiveness, longevity, group identification, commonness of goals and values, and boundaries. Nonetheless, Erickson and Jensen (1977) reasserted the preponderance of group offending, citing data on admitted delinquency and companionship. The latest and most comprehensive statement on the topic has been provided by Reiss (1985) who suggested that the common view that most offenders are group offenders is based on the group composition of crime *events* rather than on criminal histories of *offenders:*

> When all of the events in a criminal history are considered, a large proportion of offenders exhibit neither exclusively lone nor group offending. Rather, most offender histories are characterized by a mix of offending alone and with accomplices [p. 8].

Offender histories provide a different picture of group offending than is obtained from a population of events. In discussing several parameters of group offending, Reiss cited Swedish data regarding the lack of stability of group affiliations and the small size and short duration of accomplice groupings, drawn more often from small cliques than from large networks. These data parallel findings in various American gang studies. Turning to patterns in group offending (based on the U.S. data for 1982) Reiss found group offenders to be younger, on the whole, than sole offenders and more likely to be black than white. Victims of major *crimes* against persons, with the noteworthy exceptions of robberies and assaults, report single offender victimization as the mode; but the majority of *offenders* in major crimes against persons, except homicides and certain sexual offenses, are with accomplices.

An important point emerges in analyses of both violent offenders and violent events: There is a positive relationship between violence and cooffending. Nowhere does this relationship seem more prominent than in the setting of the street gang. Thus continued and improved studies of gang behavior of the sort pioneered by Short and Strodtbeck (1965) may well be the quickest route to highlighting and understanding the social dynamics of much violent behavior, including the causal and reciprocal relations between companionship and violence.

Gangs and Violence Escalation

There are two ways in which street gang membership can lead to a greater level of violence than that found among nongang offenders.

First, gang membership may be related to higher levels of offending generally, with violent offenses merely being a part of this pattern. Second, particular features of gangs may encourage or facilitate violent forms of behavior disproportionately. There is evidence to support both propositions, none of it conclusive as yet.

The evidence from literally dozens of studies (reviewed by Klein, 1984) yields the conclusion that youthful offenders, including gang members, show predominantly versatile patterns of offending rather than specialization. Thus lower levels of offending would yield lower levels of violence, while increased offending would include increased violence.[1] Since gang members offend at higher rates than do their nongang counterparts (Tracy, 1979), gang members *ipso facto* should be involved in higher levels of violence.

On the second point, gang ethnographers (Erlanger, 1979; Horowitz, 1983; Vigil, 1983, 1985) have concluded from extended observations that violent activities among gang members serve important social and psychological functions in asserting masculinity. Especially among Hispanic gangs, the emphasis on machismo and honor have been seen as legitimating and thus facilitating violent behavior in circumstances that challenge gang members' courage or territory. The constraints against violence that might lead others into avoidance behaviors are thus greatly weakened among gang members.

The gang as a critical reference group, therefore, may contribute to violence escalation, an issue still deserving of closer empirical investigation. Violent offending must be examined relative to individual career offending and, optimally, within categories of solitary, companionate, and, specifically, gang offending.

The Definitional Issues

Increasingly over the past two decades, definitional problems have surfaced with conceptual and operational dimensions of relevance to policymakers, law enforcement personnel, gang program implementers, and researchers. There are two facets to the issue: What should be called a "gang-related" crime?

Gangs. It is commonplace for writers on gang matters to decry the ambiguities that inhere in the term gang. It is less common to find serious attempts to achieve clarity. A few examples of the problem will suffice. Tracy's (1979) otherwise very careful analysis of gang offense patterns compared with nongang patterns was reported without any definitional attempt. Since it was based on Philadelphia Police Department reports, presumably the designation as a gang offense was taken from some comment in the reports. But Philadelphia's official reports of gang activity have been the object of much skepticism for years. Savitz et al. (1977) noted that the police department's Juvenile Aid Division limited its records to "high profile" gangs, records that contained identification of gang membership for fewer than 10 of 1,000 boys in the study cohort. "Structural" gang criteria included stable leadership and turf. "Functional" criteria were an emphasis on intergroup fighting and defense. But the data on gang members so defined leave one in doubt that either approach to a definition is very useful.

Reiss (1985) cited Sarnecki's (1985) definition for Swedish gangs as "a group of juveniles who were linked together because the police suspected them of committing crimes together" (p. 11). As useless as this definition might seem, it is almost identical to that reported a decade and a half ago (Klein, 1971) as the operational definition employed by the Los Angeles Police Department, which, when applied to departmental records, provided the basis for policy decisions about the size and deployment of police resources to control gang activity.

A more illuminating and discouraging example of the problem is provided in Morash's much-cited study (1983). Suggesting that to define gangs by including their criminal involvement as a definitional component would be tautological, Morash undertook her analysis of ganglike behavior by looking at groups without reference to this definitional component. The result was that her gangs, by the criteria she retained, could have included adolescent church groups or school clubs. To think of modern street gangs independent of their criminal involvement is to ignore the very factor that makes them qualitatively different from other groups of young people.

But the most sincere attempt to solve the definitional riddle to date is in its failure to achieve its aim, perhaps the most telling evidence of the inherent difficulties. Miller was one of the principal theorists and researchers in the heyday of gang research during the 1950s and 1960s. His attempt to update what was known about gangs in the mid-1970s brought him once again to the definitional problem: How do you investigate the problem of gang prevalence throughout the nation without first delineating what is and is not a gang?

Miller produced an admirable summary in which he decried the absence of attention given to "collective youth crime," even finding evidence (questionable, in our view) of "a studied effort to minimize its importance" (1980: 115). But he then set aside the gang issue to develop the concept of *law-violating youth groups,* which he defined as "an association of three or more youths whose members engage recurrently in illegal activities with the cooperation and moral support of their companions" (p. 118). Obviously, this approach does little to advance our thinking and fails to recognize the turnover of membership within gangs, the relatively short duration of most offense accomplice pairings, and out-of-group teaming highlighted in Reiss's review (1985).

Miller then listed 20 types or subtypes of law-violating groups, which had the unintended effect of reifying temporary appearances of companionship, of reifying undefinable and unmeasurable nuances separating the 20 types, and of contradicting well-established empirical findings on offense versatility and within-gang cliquing.

Perhaps most discouraging, however, was Miller's approach to determining which of his 20 types may be called gangs. This approach applied criteria that represented the consensus of opinions from a survey of various types of practitioners—police, judges, criminal justice planners, youth workers, politicians, ex-offenders, gang members, probation officers, and others. This voters' approach was no more definitive or valid than any other; it was the result of a respondents' centrifuge, not a conceptual construct.

We do not mean by this critique to be unusually negative toward Miller's attempt. Rather, the point is to emphasize just how difficult and arbitrary the definitional task can be. We are trapped by a typical problem of attempting to operationalize nominal definitions of hypothetical constructs, an inherently unsatisfying task. For the purposes of the discussion to follow, we will adopt a slight variation of the definition suggested by Klein (1971) over a decade ago:

> For our purposes, we shall use the term [street gang] to refer to any denotable . . . group [of adolescents and young adults] who (a) are generally perceived as a distinct aggregation by others in their neighborhood, (b) recognize themselves as a denotable group (almost invariably with a group name) and (c) have been involved in a sufficient number of [illegal] incidents to call forth a consistent negative response from neighborhood residents and/or enforcement agencies [p. 13].

It should be noted that, unlike many definitions employed by enforcement agencies, this working definition does not require turf mentality or intergang hostilities.[2] Some gangs, especially Asian gangs, do not feature territoriality. Other gangs, especially in cities where the gang problem is emergent, do not require rivalries to develop or maintain their existence.

Notwithstanding the variation among gang definitions preferred by researchers, police gang intelligence gathering and enforcement practices usually require them to translate their notions of what *gang* means to an operational level. Inadequate specification of the term limits the utility of jurisdictional reports regarding numbers of gangs, membership size, and gang activity for both enforcement and research purposes.

Gang-related offenses. No matter how one defines *gang,* a concern for the criminal activity associated with gangs raises a second definitional ambiguity, the designation of an offense as *gang-related.* If gang member Frank kills rival gang member Arthur in retaliation for an earlier shooting, few would have difficulty calling this a gang-related incident. But what if the killing results from a love triangle rather than a retaliation? Or what if the victim was a known gang member but the assailant, if known, was not? Any serious attempt to count gang-related crimes, whether for purposes of measuring street gang crime or evaluating the implementation or outcome of gang control programs, requires decision making about these and similar variations.

Official police reporting procedures incorporate these decisions but not always systematically, not always according to reliable criteria, not always with adequate information regarding the motive or circumstances of the crime, not always with extensive gang membership information on file, and—most clearly—not by the same criteria from city to city. For those doing gang research and using official designations of events as gang-related or not, the definitional issue can be severe, but some form of official definitional policy usually can be obtained. Researchers relying on unofficial designations—their own, for instance—must find some conceptually rational criteria for separating gang events from others. As with definitions of the term gang, uniformity is hardly likely, yet our attempts to aggregate findings and distill gang patterns make the implicit presumption of definitional uniformity. We compare cross-study findings based on noncomparable events. The effect can be dramatic, as we will indicate.

The point can be made by contrasting the definitional stances and procedures of the Los Angeles Police Department and the Los Angeles Sheriff's Department, on the one hand, with those of the Chicago Police Department, on the other. All three departments have sophisticated gang intelligence and control units with many years of experience. For a number of years the two Los Angeles jurisdictions have employed almost identical criteria for designating an incident as gang-related. If either the assailant or victim is a gang member or, failing clear identification, elements of the event, such as motive, garb, characteristic gang behavior, or attribution by witnesses, indicate the likelihood of gang involvement, the incident is counted and reported as gang-related. Gang unit personnel review crime incident reports for all violent and some property, drug, and weapons offenses. Only homicides are labeled and logged by incident throughout both jurisdictions.[3] This approach to gang designation is quite inclusive. The definitional criteria capture gang member involvement in violent crime without regard to gang motive or function.

In Chicago a definitional distinction is made between homicides and general gang activity. Regarding the latter, the Chicago Police Department will apply the gang label if the investigation reveals a gang name, gang membership of the victim or offender, a gang-related motive (usually retaliation or territoriality), or some action on either side that "reasonably indicates" member involvement. Incidents are labeled as gang activity by the reporting officer and reviewed for evidence by crime analysts who request assistance from the gang unit if necessary. Among the offense types not considered for the gang activity designation are narcotics cases and, according to a local researcher (Spergel, 1985a), car theft, burglary, forgery, and arson.[4]

Among homicides a more restrictive definition is used. To be labeled gang-related by Chicago police, a homicide must be based upon gang motives (this usually involves gang members on both the assailant and victim sides but can be one-sided—motive, rather than membership, is the key). Thus in her research on homicides in Chicago from 1965 to 1981, Block (1985a) found that of 672 gang homicides, 670 resulted from assaults (presumably gang-on-gang in most instances), leaving virtually none resulting from robberies or other confrontations. Similarly, Spergel's (1983) analysis of gang homicide offenders (1978-1981) suggested that few, if any, incidents with unapprehended suspects were labeled gang-related (that is, no suspect, no motive).

Thus Chicago uses different review and recording procedures than does Los Angeles in its compilation of gang crimes; and with respect to homicide in particular, it employs a far more restrictive criterion. What would happen if Chicago's definition of gang-related homicides were to be applied to the Los Angeles data? We have undertaken an analysis of the Los Angeles data for the period of roughly 1978 to 1981, when gang homicides ranged between just over 200 to a peak of 351 annually. The Chicago definition would reduce the Los Angeles figures by over 50. The implications for comparative research and for policy development are considerable. The assumption of dealing with common phenomena from city to city is not only inappropriate, it is grossly inaccurate.

Recent research carried out by this chapter's authors in five additional cities offers some corroboration. These are smaller cities, of the sort alluded to earlier as part of the gang expansion beyond the traditional urban homes of street gangs. In one city designations of gang violence (the focus of our recent research) were restricted by policy to gang-on-gang situations, that is, those with gang victims and gang assailants. However, our review of the gang-designated events revealed a number of robberies with gang members as perpetrators only. Nonetheless, this city adopted (at least nominally) a restrictive definition closer to that for Chicago's gang homicides and did so for the explicit purpose of including only the most "pure" gang cases.

The four cities all defined gang-related offenses far more broadly, as those involving a member on either side. In two cities only violent offenses were designated as gang-related, while in the other two more latitude was found. In fact, in one of the latter two cities a gang-related offense was specifically defined as "any crime committed by a gang member" although the gang unit limited itself principally to gang assaults. In another city, two homicides reported as gang-related were rejected by the gang unit, one because the victim was a girlfriend and the other because the homicide resulted from an intragang fight.

In brief, four of these five cities employed a rather broad definition in terms of membership criteria but also tended to limit gang labeling to the assaultive types of incidents. They mirrored neither the Chicago nor the Los Angeles approaches. Our data collectors noted, in addition, a considerable number of instances in which policy was belied by practice (as seen in gang unit logs) and noted that working definitions were often determined by the mandate of the investigative team (assault, robbery, narcotics) rather than by policy—that is, what is called gang-related depends, in part, on which police unit gets the case assignment. Does all of this matter? Certainly it does if we are seeking generalizations, an oft-cited goal of science. Using police-designated gang cases is unlikely to yield valid generalizations unless we can explicitly account for the interjurisdictional differences in definitional operations. Spergel's (1984) finding, for instance, that Chicago gang homicides accounted for 5.3% of that city's total homicides over a 15-year period might have grown considerably if the broader Los Angeles definitions had been applied. One in nine begins to take on the character of an important conceptual and policy-related phenomenon.

On a practical, operational level, consider the plight of the New York City Police Department's gang specialist, John Galea (1982): "My responsibility is to keep tabs on 40 active gangs [in Brooklyn South] with 3,400 members, and to investigate 52 other 'gangs' to determine if they are, in fact, gangs" (p. 216). Galea's task could be greatly diminished by sheer definitional sleight of hand, leaving him to concentrate on the sorts of grisly assaults and homicides he chose to include in his discussion.

Or consider the problem for criminal justice planners charged with the task of allocating two precious resources: time and personnel. The San Diego Association of Governments found, in an area now beset with some serious gang problems, a lack of clarity and agreement across operating agencies on both gang definitions and member identification criteria (Pennell and Curtis, 1982). How do you prevent or control a problem you can't identify?

Finally, we note Miller's (1975) comment on one of the more unfortunate consequences of definitional ambiguity:

> With regard to the manipulability of gang-related statistics, descriptions of the process of deriving figures for each of the four largest cities—New York, Chicago, Los Angeles, and Philadelphia—suggest that in all four cities the process of deriving publishable statistics involves objectives other than that of providing systematic and accurate data. In all four cities at least some of these influences can appropriately be designated as "political" [p. 33].

Then and Now Continuities

We reported earlier Quicker's conclusion that the data on gangs reported in the 1960s have not been significantly invalidated by more recent research. While there are several important exceptions to that conclusion, the shift in research paradigms mentioned earlier precludes a systematic comparison between gangs then and gangs now. The 1960s gang programs, which permitted detailed description of gang structure and activity patterns, are now largely absent. Prior to delving into the areas in which change is evident, it will be useful to review those features that seem to present continuities between the 1960s' and 1980s' gang pictures. Unfortunately, the current picture is based on evidence that is largely hearsay rather than empirical.

Structure

Street gangs come in numerous forms.[5] Most common, perhaps, are "spontaneous" gangs of youths that come together for periods of weeks, months, or as long as a year, but then disintegrate. Presumably the advantages of gang involvement are assessed and found wanting in the face of negative responses from parents, other peers, and enforcement agencies.

Less common are "specialty cliques" that arise around common illegal pursuits such as car theft, burglary, or drug use. Flying in the face of normal criminal versatility, such cliques usually will remain small, will be reabsorbed into larger structures, or will dissolve under enforcement pressure.

Horizontal "alliances," such as the original Blackstone Rangers and Disciples in Chicago or the old Slausons and the Crips in Los Angeles, are even rarer but highly visible loose confederations of many gangs. Their massive numbers (in the thousands) and hydra-headed structures can effectively defeat attempts at control, and they maintain a meta-morphic existence over many years.

The "violent gang," as described by Yablonsky (1963), while it has captured the public imagination, is perhaps the rarest form of all. The large size, sociopathic leadership, and commitment to violent encounters described by Yablonsky have not been observed by other social science researchers. Indeed, the two gangs described by Yablonsky existed for only a few weeks in one case and eight months in the other.

Spontaneous gangs, specialty cliques, horizontal alliances, and violent gangs, because of their rarity or limited duration, have not been the subject of most gang research. Rather, most of what is known of gangs comes from intensive and extensive research on what have been called "traditional," "vertical," or "area" gangs. These traditional gangs have also proven to be the greatest cause of concern for those interested in either prevention or control and probably account for the preponderance of gang crime. The discussion in this chapter is based principally on traditional gangs, which have the following characteristics:

(1) They are normally territorially bounded and self-identified as such.

(2) Age distributions have run roughly from 11 years of age to the early twenties, although we will note an apparent change in this pattern in a later section of this chapter.

(3) Sex and ethnic homogeneity are commonly found. In the case of females, it is not unusual to find "auxiliary" girls' groups associated with the traditional gang, which is otherwise a predominantly male collectivity.

(4) The traditional gang is, in fact, a "cluster" of vertically distinguishable, age-graded subgroups. As few as two or as many as five

such age-homogeneous subgroups may coexist, using different subgroup names or age-designating nomenclatures (pee-wees, babies, juniors, seniors, veterans, and the like). Members affiliate principally with their age peer groups but identify with the overall cluster.

(5) One can distinguish three general categories of membership. "Fringe" members are distinguished from "core" members. A principal axis factor analysis of Los Angeles data (Klein, 1971) yielded two major factors related to the fringe/core distinction. The first, accounting for 34% of the variance, showed core members to be high on "deficient-aggressive" items; they had personal deficits, both intellectual and psychological, closely tied to lower impulse control and aggressiveness. The second factor, accounting for 13% of the variance, was clearly a group involvement factor stressing greater gang participation and group involvement. Core members were far more delinquent as well. The third category is "clique" membership, consisting primarily but not exclusively of core members. It is the cliques that embody the principal friendship patterns with the gangs, provide the more cohesive foci that resist attempts at gang control or dissolution, and probably constitute the principal magnets for membership recruitment.

(6) Contrary to common perceptions among many enforcement officials and the general public, gang leadership tends *not* to reside only in older members or in the toughest or most criminally inclined members. Gang leadership is shifting and age-related. It changes by activity and time period, is to be found in each age-graded subgroup, and is closely related to clique structures. In many ways, gang leaders are more often modeled than followed.

(7) Because gang cohesiveness is *not* generally high, by and large gangs do not act as gangs; rather, temporary groups and cliques are normally the functional units of activity beyond the individual level (see Reiss, 1985, on co-offending patterns generally). For control and prevention efforts, this means that "the" gang presents a shifting, elusive target, permeable and elastic, and thus inherently resistant to outside intervention. It presents not a cohesive force but, rather, a spongelike resilience. To the extent that recent research has concerned itself with structural depictions, the foregoing description seems to pertain to the situation in the 1980s relatively unchanged since the 1960s (Horowitz, 1983; Spergel, 1983, 1984; Stumphauzer, Veloz, and Aiken, 1981).

Criminal Patterns

Despite both theoretical and empirical attempts to build the case for gangs organized around categories of criminal pursuits (for example, violence, theft, or drug use), the predominant trend for gang members, and for most nongang offenders as well (Klein, 1984), remains involvement in a wide variety of minor illegal activities ("cafeteria-style" delinquency). With respect to crimes against persons, gang members tend to have rival gang members (or suspected rivals) as their principal victims. Stranger victims, in the sense of innocent bystanders totally unconnected with the gang scene, are rare. Gang crime, then, tends to be unpatterned and locally exhibited. Pictures of marauding bands invading quiet neighborhoods and attacking strangers for "kicks" are, with occasional but rare exceptions, distortions that play better in movie houses than in responsible reports.[6]

New Developments

In this section, we will indicate some areas in which gang matters are reported to have changed. One change not noted in most reports, but important for this discussion because of the available data sources, is the growth in intelligence about gangs among large, urban police departments and some prosecutors' offices as well. We have noted elsewhere (Maxson and Klein, 1983) that changes in the focus of gang intervention programs from rehabilitation to deterrence perspectives have resulted in changes in gang expertise. In the earlier decades, street gang workers were a major source of information on gangs. Much of the data upon which social science gang knowledge was based came from street worker programs, since the workers were intimately associated with gang members and their neighborhoods. By contrast, police information on gangs was, as noted at the beginning of this chapter, minimal at best.

The 1980s have brought a reversal. Street worker programs are less common. When they do exist, they concentrate less on specific gangs, thus yielding less data of value to gang researchers. But enforcement agencies have become far more sophisticated. Both the Los Angeles Police Department and Sheriff's Department have gang units with literally scores of officers and updated gang roster information capable of yielding highly significant information for case investigation and clearance. A similar unit is to be found in Philadelphia and other smaller ones in New York and San Francisco. In Chicago the police department's Gang Crimes Section, with 385 officers, maintains a similar intelligence file and involves itself in a myriad of gang intervention activities. The department has published a 175-page manual, "Guide for the Identification of Chicago Street Gangs," offering incredible details on locations, ethnicity, clothing, emblems, hand signals, tattoos, graffiti, allied gangs, and rivals.

With the emergence of gangs in a number of smaller cities, specialized gang units have been developed in these cities as well, although our contacts with such units (ranging in size from one to a dozen or so officers) suggest that their level of expertise is highly variable. Still, it is from such sources that a greater portion of gang information now comes to the gang researcher; the credibility and intentions of enforcement data sources must be kept in mind in comparing "the good old days" to the present. Only *reported* crimes are in the enforcement-derived data: Observed and self-reported gang offenses, commonly employed in earlier gang research, are now seldom available.

With this disclaimer we can review several areas of interest.

Age Distributions

While there have been occasional claims that the lower limit of gang members' ages has dipped to include youngsters as young as 8 years of age—the Chicago Police Department lists ages from 8 to 55—most reports find little change at the lower age levels but significant expansion at the upper levels. Data from Chicago (Spergel, 1984), Los Angeles (Maxson et al., 1985), and San Diego (Pennell and Curtis, 1982) confirm numerous informal reports that gangs now include a larger proportion of members in their twenties and even beyond in selected cases. The median gang age in San Diego is placed at 19. In Chicago and Los Angeles, gang homicide perpetrators average between ages 19 and 20. As Spergel (1984: 199-200) stated, "gang violence is primarily a young adult rather than a juvenile problem." Horowitz (1983) neatly portrayed how membership matures into adult male relations rather than gang membership per se, although to the outsider these relations may look very much like a continuation of gang involvement.

Ethnicity

Although gangs remain principally a minority problem and are ethnically homogeneous, ratios of ethnic involvement seem to vary quite a bit (Block, 1985b). In particular, Asian gangs are now encountered more commonly in Los Angeles, San Francisco (CCCJ, 1986), New York (Rice, 1977), and reportedly in other cities as well. Often these reports suggest that Asian gangs are more likely to consist of first-generation youths (often from Hong Kong, Taiwan, and Vietnam), to involve a higher ratio of young adults than is found among black and Hispanic groups, and to be involved more narrowly in racketeering forms of crime such as gambling and extortion. To date, reliable information on this group is skimpy and—according to police informants—very difficult to obtain owing to the close-knit organizational forms exhibited by Asian gangs and their reportedly lower tendency to proclaim gang status during the course of criminal activity.

Gangs in Schools

Reports from school officials often comment on gang involvement on junior and senior high school campuses, and some schools develop unenviable reputations (for example, "Fort Crenshaw"). Supportive data are hard to find. The Safe Schools Research (Gottfredson and Daiger, 1979) found most on-campus disruptions to be attributable to enrollees; gang members are more often among the nonenrolled category. Nonetheless, both Miller (1975) and the California Council on Criminal Justice (1986) have cited positive evidence. Miller employed such phrases as "frantic," "devastating," and classroom "takeovers" to describe school officials' perceptions of the problem. He warned about such exaggerations but concluded, nonetheless, that the problem had increased rather dramatically. The CCCJ's task force report concluded, "Studies support the finding that many modern gangs are extending their areas of control into schools. One apparent fact from current research is that students who are gang-involved play a disproportionate role in acts of violence, threats, and extortion on public school campuses" (CCCJ, 1986: 12).

Finally, a special school project in Chicago has added some data. Spergel (1985b) cited police department data showing that 10.5% of the city's gang incidents occurred on school property in 1984. About 8.6% of the violent crimes in the schools was due to gang activity. Overall, 18% of serious student incidents reported by the Bureau of Student Safety, Chicago Public Schools, were gang-related. "Approximately 10 percent of high school students are probably gang members" (p. 194), with rates up to 80% in the worst schools. It is interesting that Spergel reported that the number of gang members does not correlate with the severity of gang problems. This depends upon school factors and drop-out levels.

Gangs in Smaller Cities

Gangs have appeared in a wide assortment of American cities differing markedly from the urban centers of New York, Chicago,

Philadelphia, Boston, Los Angeles and San Francisco—the principal gang cities of earlier decades. Evidence for this change is extensive, although we should recall that even in the 1960s there were major street gang problems in some smaller urban areas; San Antonio, Seattle, St. Louis, and San Bernardino are cases in point.

Miller's (1980) national census in the mid-1970s added Detroit, Miami, El Paso, and Buffalo to the list, for a total of 15. Other published reports yielded San Diego (with 35 gangs as well as 20 in surrounding suburban areas; Pennell and Curtis, 1982); a group of cities in the Chicago area such as Waukegan, Cicero, Harvey, and Maywood (Recktenwald and Sheppard, 1984), Evanston (Rosenbaum and Grant, 1983), Phoenix (Zatz, 1985), Milwaukee (Moore, 1985), and Sacramento (Brenneman, 1984). Others were included in a *U.S. News and World Report* story (1984) "announcing" the progression of gangs to the "suburbs," including Davenport, New Haven, Jackson, Portsmouth (Virginia), Peoria, and East St. Louis. Still other cities have been reported to us by enforcement officials and members of the press: Atlanta, Tallahassee, Baton Rouge, Jackson (Mississippi), and Jackson (Tennessee).

Southern Californians might be incredulous at Feinstein's report (1976) of 65 street gangs in the "inland empire" of the Riverside-Corona area, nine in the Hemet-San Jacinto area, and three in the Indio-Coachella area, the latter being generally known as desert resort areas. Feinstein may have been exaggerating the situation, but he noted quite correctly that the seriousness of the California situation led to the formation of a Southern California Gang Investigators' Association with periodic meetings to share intelligence among gang unit officers. A similar group was formed in Northern California.

In an attempt to determine how police were responding to gang developments, Stapleton and Needle (1982) surveyed a sample of jurisdictions nationally, reporting that six of 12 cities with populations between 250,000 and 500,000 were facing serious gang problems. Even in cities with populations between 100,000 and 250,000, the figure was 12 out of 31. Two-thirds of the surveyed police departments that reported gang problems were in cities with under 500,000 residents. In all, 30% of those reporting gangs were located in California, a state with only 10% of the national population. As for this latter point, we can confirm the ubiquitous nature of California gangs. Our own research on gang violence identified a pool of 24 jurisdictions outside Los Angeles in which gang problems had reached the point of justifying specialized units in local enforcement agencies. In five of these jurisdictions chosen for closer analysis, the police investigation files yielded sufficient levels of gang violence to carry out our research; that is, the gang activity was a measurable reality.

How has all this come about? Several patterns have been noted. Miller (1975) suggested that gangs have not moved out of the slums to the suburbs but that the slums have moved out. That is, population transitions from urban areas have carried gangs with them. Johnstone (1981) used self-report data from gang members that provided some confirmation, with gang membership reaching into transitional, lower-class suburban areas around Chicago in the late 1970s.

Moore et al. (1983) outlined at least five processes by which this suburban "invasion" may take place. Nonresident gang members—those not in the accepted gang territory—can be involved by kinship, by alliance, by the expansion of turf boundaries, or by the formation of "branches." Finally, gang members' families may move into new areas (ironically, sometimes as a way of escaping from the gang setting), yielding what Moore et al. labeled "ecological displacements."

Still, these transplanting and branching processes provide a better explanation for the expansion of gangs *from* urban centers *to* suburbs than they do for the appearance of gangs in separated cities. This second pattern has shown, in at least some jurisdictions, a somewhat predictable pattern.

(A) In Denver, a rather grisly homicide brought such a public outcry that the police department admitted what it had consistently denied—that the city had a growing gang problem. Indeed, the department had been denying the problem for several years even while gathering intelligence on five established gangs—names, addresses, offense records, and so on. In less than a week's time in the early 1980s, Denver was transformed from a gangless city to an acknowledged gang center.[7]

(B) In Minneapolis and St. Paul, in the fall of 1985, the death of a young woman in a reputed gang homicide led to a similar public outcry and a discussion of whether or not the Twin Cities were also gang cities. While some denied the existence of gangs and the police chief denied the validity of the issue, others reported their conversations with gang members and participated in a Twin Cities Task Force on Gangs headed by an ex-gang member from Chicago (Diaz, 1986).

(C) In 1984, various officials in Sacramento were quoted on both sides of the fence following one in a series of reportedly gang-related homicides of a particularly brutal nature. Disagreements surfaced between officials in the district attorney's office, the probation department, the Sacramento Police Department, and the county sheriff's department about not only the size of the problem but also its existence. One police executive was quoted as saying, "While there are gangs in Sacramento, it does not serve the interests of law enforcement to talk about them at this time." An involved church official noted, "I don't like the word gangs. I prefer to call them groups" (Brenneman, 1984).

Sacramento, Denver, and the Twin Cities are not suburbs of other gang cities. The expansion hypothesis does not apply well to them or to many of the other jurisdictions noted earlier. Rather, their agonizing confrontations with an emergent phenomenon suggest more likely explanations lie in the cities' increasing urbanization, racial in-migration and residential segregation, and perhaps the high youth unemployment rates of the late 1970s and early 1980s. By now, the question is not whether gangs exist in these localities but whether their form and the response to them will transform spontaneous gangs into traditional gangs.

A worst-case scenario is provided by the city of Evanston, outside Chicago, which exhibits both the expansion and independent emergence patterns. An interesting description of a city "going gang" was provided by Rosenbaum and Grant (1983) in one of the very few reports from these new gang cities.[8] The Evanston police went public about their gangs in 1981 following a series of gang incidents, including a homicide. Note the pattern seen in our earlier descriptions and also the fact that when public admission was made, the police—as in other cities—had already recorded details of gang existence and developed programmatic actions. By 1983 there were eight acknowledged street gangs. Five of these were described as serious offending groups, of which two were local (emergent) and three were "satellites" of Chicago gangs.

The average gang age was put between 17 and 18, although members of the Chicago satellites were more likely to be in their twenties. The police had a list of 300 suspected members, of whom only 55 were under age 17. An analysis of gang-related incidents reported to the police during a six-month period in 1983 showed the most frequent offense was firing gunshots (38.5%) followed by assault and then battery—a three-offense total of 64% of offenses listed as gang-related. Significantly, the study found the emergent gangs to be the more violent, while the "satellites" were more property-oriented. If Evanston represents the wave of the future, the renewed support of gang research will be needed along with careful attention to control programs that can deal with the problem without inadvertently acting to solidify it.

Violence

To be concerned with violence is to be concerned with a relatively rare event in the cafeteria of offenses committed by juveniles and adults alike. Property crimes predominate. Crimes against persons are, more often than not, minor in their physical consequences. Yet the violent act can be so devastating that changes in the incidence of violence garner our attention well out of proportion to changes in nonviolent events.

In the 1950s and 1960s, gang members talked much about their fighting episodes, but data from several projects revealed their bark to be worse than their bite. Miller's (1980) Roxbury Project yielded no homicides. Four years of the Group Guidance Project in Los Angeles yielded one homicide, and the Ladino Hills Project, three (Klein, 1971). Cities like Philadelphia and Los Angeles, toward the close of the period, reported gang-related killings numbering close to 30 or 40 per annum. These are not inconsequential numbers, nor are the deaths inconsequential. But the Chicago figures for gang-related homicides peaked at 84 cases in 1981. Los Angeles County, in 1980, peaked at a staggering 351 gang-related deaths and still reports between 200 and 250 per annum.

Homicide rates vary widely over several years (Block, 1985a); five-year cycles are not uncommon. But the cycles of gang homicide now seem to end with higher rates and retreat to higher plateaus before surging forward again. If homicide is any indication, gang violence has become a far more serious problem during the most recent decade.

Although we will document some of the violence patterns later in this chapter, it is well to remember that, notwithstanding definitional or recording differences that threaten any comparison, patterns in one city may not reflect those in another (Miller, 1980); patterns in one time period may not repeat those of another (Block, 1985a); patterns in one ethnic group may not resemble those in another (Spergel, 1983, 1985a); and, most clearly of all, patterns in one gang may differ totally from those in another (Spergel, 1984). And of course, gang patterns may not reflect nongang patterns (Maxson et al., 1985; Spergel, 1983). Further, it remains unclear whether the observed violence increase reflects greater levels of violence among and between gangs, whether it is the result of a growth in the number of gangs or of gang members, or whether it reflects an increasingly violent society. Finally, increasingly sophisticated gang intelligence gathering and recording by growing numbers of police gang experts could result in increases in the gang violence statistics offered as evidence for increases in violence.

Weapons

Closely associated with this last question is the weapons issue. Specifically, firearms are now said to be more readily available to gang members. No observer close to gangs questions this (CCCJ, 1986; Miller, 1975; Recktenwald and Sheppard, 1984; Quicker titles Chapter 5 of his 1983 review "From Switchblades to Smith and Wessons").

Does the ready access to guns explain much of the increase in violence? The notion here is that more weapons yield more shootings; these, in turn, lead to more "hits"; and these, in turn, lead to more retaliations in a series of reciprocal actions defending honor and territory. This escalation hypothesis, difficult to test empirically, nonetheless has high conceptual validity among those who find street gangs to be more than mere "law-violating groups," to be qualitatively different precisely because of their involvement in a confrontational world of crime and violence. The theory is that firearms have been the teeth that transform bark into bite.

Horowitz (1983: 84-86) spoke effectively of gang members' ambivalence around the use of easily available guns. Nonetheless, guns are used and used often by gang members now. Spergel (1983) reported the use of firearms in 86.7% of Chicago gang killings. Our own Los Angeles police and sheriff's data show gun presence in 80% and 82% of gang-related killings, respectively, figures 15% to 20% higher than those for nongang killings.

Of other weapons used, surprisingly little is known. Recent victimization data compiled by the Bureau of Justice Statistics (U.S. Department of Justice, 1986) are compressed into three nonfirearm categories: knife or other cutting edge, other dangerous weapon, and personal weapon (fist, feet, and so on). Other categorizations have similarly lacked detail, defeating any attempt to make conceptual sense of weapon type (Curtis, 1974; McClintock, 1963; Mulvihill and Tumin, 1969; Newton and Zimring, 1969; Shields, 1981; Wikström, 1985).

Attempts to relate weapon use to conceptual issues have been fewer yet. Examples include gun use and companionship patterns (Zimring, 1984), weapons and the offender/victim relationship (Wolfgang and Zahn, 1983), weapons and the "culture of violence" (Wolfgang and Ferracuti, 1982), and weapons' choice as a function of intent, availability, and victim resistance (Cook, 1982). Most of this research has pertained to firearms, but the concern for other weapons in violent incidents needs expansion as well. McClintock (1963) found that only 30% of the weapons carried in the incidents he analyzed were designed specifically as aggressive weapons. Similarly, Mulvihill and Tumin (1969: 234) concluded, "The world abounds in available weapons—they are usually commonplace, quick, brutal, and direct."

Our Los Angeles data provide an opportunity to look at the "other weapons" issue. We combine here both gang and nongang violent incidents in order to provide some stability in the numbers. Over a total of 1,232 violent incidents, guns and knives obviously predominated, but an examination of the other weapons category concerns us here because this is where the data are most skimpy in the existing literature.

Table 5.1 reports the presence of weapons, excluding firearms and knives, in eight categories (the last of which, predictably, is still an "other" category). The numbers for each category signify the numbers of incidents with the *presence* of the weapons—a given incident might well include more than one type of weapon or more than one mention of that type (for example, one victim and two assailants threw beer bottles at each other). And each incident may also include guns or knives. We are concerned here only with the nature of the other weapons.

As noted earlier in the comments of McClintock (1963) and of Mulvihill and Tumin (1969), potential weapons are available in almost any setting and are typically not instruments designed for felonious damage. Our favorite incident included a pepper shaker, a parfait glass, and a ceramic flower pot. By citing this example and listing others in Table 5.1, we do not mean to trivialize assaultive and homicidal occurrences; after all, we are reporting data on 1,232 cases of serious criminal activity, including the unnatural, premature deaths of more than 700 individuals. The parfait glass ceases to be a joke when it strikes the victim.

The main point of Table 5.1, rather, is to illustrate some commonsense patterns in the enormous variety of instruments that can be employed in violent events. There is, literally, no physical context, be it the home or the playing field, that is without a potential weapon. One can argue the merits of gun control on value, logical, or empirical grounds: Our homicide data certainly imply that fatal incidents will result from the presence of guns. But a residue of available weaponry will remain in almost any setting.

It seems plausible to suggest that the use of weapons other than guns and knives is principally a direct function of the setting—home, work, bar, recreational arena—in which incidents take place. Guns and knives are commonly brought to the incident by the participants, often, one assumes, in the expectation of their utility (see Wolfgang and Ferracuti,

TABLE 5.1
Number of Incidents with Presence of Other Weapons,
All Samples Combined

Category	Incidents	Examples
Tools	95	hammers, pipes, wrenches, screwdrivers
Body parts and clothing	94	fists, feet; combs, neckties, shoes, belts
Alcohol-related	89	bottles (usually beer), mugs, glasses, bar stools
Auto-related	84	tire irons, bumper jacks, car as battering ram, hit-and-run cases
Neighborhood items	58	bricks, boards, branches, asphalt chunks
Home items	55	vases, vacuum hose, forks, brooms, patio chair, flower pot
Sports-related	51	baseball bats, pool cues, barbell weight, golf club, ping pong paddle
Traditional and other	46	blackjack, fire bomb, mace; milk crate, cane, handcuffs, laundry cart, cash register

1982). But other weaponry will reflect the *settings* in which the interpersonal confrontations then take place more than they will reflect the intents and preparations of the participants. The suggestions implicit in the earlier citations on weapon availability by McClintock (1963) and by Mulvihill and Tumin (1969) seem confirmed; what has been added in the present analyses is a more detailed description and categorization of alternative weaponry.

Gang Violence Versus Other Violence

Very little research has been undertaken to compare gang crime with that of comparable-age peers. Early work by Cohen (1969) suggested a number of salient issues such as differences in age, prior record, weapon lethality, SES, ethnic and demographic heterogeneity, proportion of gang victims, and relationship to victims. Using data on Philadelphia youths who were gang-affiliated in the mid-1960s, Tracy (1979) demonstrated the greater volume of offenses among gang members, using both police records and self-reports of offending as the sources of data. Philadelphia gang members were far more criminal than others, even more so at the adult level. Quite independently, Friedman et al. (1975) used youth interviews and questionnaires in the same city and validated the greater involvement among gangs in specifically violent behavior. Prior to these studies, little verification existed of the common assumption about gang offense levels.

What we have found in Los Angeles seems to confirm some unhappy suspicions about the character of gang killings. For the county as a whole, as noted earlier, gang-related homicides, as reported by all police jurisdictions, reached an all-time high of 351 in 1980, a number constituting roughly one-fifth of all homicides reported for the county in that year. The reasons for such an increase are altogether unclear; and reasons for the subsequent decline to the current figure of about 220 per year are very much in dispute. Several agencies take credit, none with supportive research to back their claims.

There is greater clarity about the differences between gang and nongang homicides. These can be characterized under two headings: features of the homicide setting and descriptors of the participants. Tables 5.2 and 5.3 report the gang/nongang differences for setting and participant variables, including only those differences achieving statistical significance, generally at the .05 level. The sheriff's department's data (Table 5.2) were based on 226 gang and 220 nongang cases. The police department's data (Table 5.3) were based on 135 gang and 148 nongang cases. All of the cases occurred in Los Angeles between 1978 and 1982 (see Klein et al., 1984, for full details).

While one jurisdiction yielded larger differences than the other, and a larger number of differences as well, the pattern was obviously similar. The data from Chicago were also similar. The gang homicide is the outcome of a more visible, violent, even chaotic event. These data on gang homicides were not peculiar to homicide alone. A further analysis of other violent incidents in Los Angeles—assaults, attempted murders, robberies, shooting into inhabited dwellings, rapes and related sexual assaults, and felony child endangerment—have revealed similar though lesser differences between gang and nongang incidents. While parallel comparisons for prior decades do not exist, Tracy (1979) provided some corroboration with members of the 1945 birth cohort who would have been similar in age to our assailants in the mid-1960s.

Thus ethnographies of violent gang incidents would reveal events often of a very different character than the more common domestic incidents, commercial robberies, or drunken brawls. For gang violence, police investigative procedures often must differ from the usual procedures if they are to be successful. Special intelligence on gang

TABLE 5.2
In the Jurisdiction of the Los Angeles Sheriff's Department

	Gang (N = 226)	Nongang (N = 220)
Setting		
gang homicides more often occur in the street:	48%	14%
less often at residence:	24%	53%
gang homicides more often involve autos:	66%	56%
gang homicides more often involve guns:	80%	60%
more often involve other weapons:	31%	22%
more often involve a higher average number of weapons:	2.23	1.68
gang homicides more often involve additional offenses:	72%	52%
gang homicides with additional offenses are of a more violent character such as other homicide charges:	45%	22%
more often involve assault with a deadly weapon:	57%	39%
less often include robbery:	20%	34%
gang homicides more often involve injuries to other persons:	30%	10%
gang homicides more often include unidentified assailants:	19%	7%
gang homicides more often involve fear of retaliation:	33%	10%
Participants		
gang homicides involve a higher average number of participants:	8.96	3.59
gang homicides more often involve victims with no prior contact with their assailants:	54%	24%
gang homicides are more likely to include clearly gang victims:	47%	4%
gang homicide suspects on the average are younger:	19.16	24.02
victims on the average are younger:	23.50	29.00
gang homicide suspects are more likely to be all male:	97%	87%
victims are more likely to be all male:	92%	82%
gang homicide suspects are more often Hispanic:	74%	30%
victims are more often Hispanic:	83%	39%

members and structures is beneficial. Special search warrant procedures are helpful, as are attempts to protect witnesses from gang intimidation. The use of informants pays special dividends. Familiarity with special cultural accoutrements of gang activity is particularly useful.

There is, in other words, a special "flavor" to the gang incident that makes it more recognizable to the trained investigator and more

TABLE 5.3
In the Jurisdiction of the Los Angeles Police Department

	Gang (N = 135)	Nongang (N = 148)
Setting		
gang homicides more often occur in the street:	49%	34%
gang homicides more often involve autos:	64%	49%
gang homicides more often involve guns:	83%	68%
gang homicides less often involve knives:	24%	37%
gang homicides more often include unidentified assailants:	23%	10%
gang homicides more often involve fear of retaliation:	33%	9%
gang homicides more often involve injuries to other persons:	23%	14%
Participants		
gang homicides involve a higher average number of participants:	6.96	3.77
gang homicides more often involve victims with no prior contact with their assailants:	49%	27%
gang homicides are more likely to involve clearly gang victims:	40%	2%
gang homicide suspects on the average are younger:	19.40	23.68
victims on the average are younger:	23.67	31.06
gang homicide suspects are more likely to be all male:	94%	84%
victims are more likely to be all male:	95%	89%
gang homicide victims are more often Hispanic:	53%	39%

interesting to the researcher. Above and beyond the demonstration that gang violence is more complex, more violent, and more visible than otherwise comparable nongang violence, the issues of motive, territory, argot, and the like more quickly capture the imagination of practitioners and researchers alike and whet the appetite of both for continued attention to gang issues.

New Theories

A discussion of new theoretical approaches to the formation, character, or control of street gangs must, of necessity, be short. Little new has been offered, and reviews of past theorizing (Klein, 1971;

Stafford, 1984) suggest little continuity with developments in the 1980s.

Most of the very meager theoretical thrust in current gang literature stresses subculture or culture conflict factors (Erlanger, 1979; Horowitz, 1983; Vigil, 1983, 1985). Not coincidentally, most of this material concerns itself with Hispanic gangs. The basic themes are that gang violence is best understood as a response to culturally legitimated investments in group identity and autonomy, honor, and response to insult (machismo). Erlanger added to this the suggestion of a culture of violence, with the hypothesis that the violent response is the result of estrangement from society. He noted lower levels of gang violence during times of involvement in political movements.

Two interesting exceptions to this general approach seem more in line with dominant modes of criminological thought that flourished in the 1970s. In describing the emergence of a gang in an affluent suburban community, Muehlbauer and Dodder (1983) employed a labeling theory perspective. During the post-Vietnam era, when generational clashes were still common occurrences, they observed a group of marginally alienated youth become further alienated by the uncompromising community response to their disruptive behavior. The result was a disaster for both the youth and the community, creating a local counterculture by the rigidity of the stigmatizing adult reaction.

A contrasting suggestion was offered by Stumphauzer et al. (1981) who adopted a distinctly behavioral approach. They viewed gang violence as self-reinforcing, bringing to gang members rewards that are not otherwise available. The notion of violence begetting more violence is not dissimilar to the suggestion offered earlier that the dramatic increase in available firearms initiates a reciprocal cycle of violence. Both the self-reinforcement and reciprocality hypotheses reflect the recent concern for gang control rather than rehabilitation and the emergence of deterrence as a dominant perspective in the handling of street gangs.

With the exception of the few writings in the subcultural tradition, what we have seen in recent times is a relative abandonment of theoretical interest in the *etiology* of the street gang phenomenon (despite the plethora of smaller cities with emergent gang problems). Etiological interests tend to relate to programmatic interests in prevention and rehabilitation (or, in the gang arena, what we will refer to as the "value transformation" approach to gang intervention). Research in the 1950s and 1960s was closely related to etiological theory and sociopolitically liberal intervention programs.

But the 1980s are better characterized as a deterrence era. Political, economic, and social conservatism and increased violence levels have combined to bring about an emphasis on gang *control*. Theory has lagged behind. Deterrence theory is not yet well-developed; its manifestations in social policy tend more toward simplistic remedies and rhetoric. These, in turn, affect definitions of gangs and gang-related crime and dictate the direction of intervention. Finally, these trends affect the opportunities for research and the kind of research that is done. Current research, perforce, emphasizes violence and enforcement responses, as in much of the Chicago and Los Angeles research reported in this chapter. Hence, theoretical advancement and explanation have been eclipsed by the resulting focus on description.

Gang Intervention Programs

Experience with gang intervention practices in the past was mixed at best and realistically quite discouraging. The popular programs of the 1950s and 1960s stressed "value transformation" models in which gang workers attempted to turn individual members and their gangs from delinquent activities to more prosocial endeavors—recreation, schooling, work experience, community service, and so on. Evaluation of such programs either demonstrated no significant progress or actually provided evidence that such programs inadvertently increased gang problems. In these latter instances, gangs became more cohesive and more delinquent; added stature increased the recruitment of younger members, thus leading to gang perpetuation; and members receiving the most programmatic attention proved most likely to recidivate (Klein, 1971; Quicker, 1983).

These rehabilitation-oriented programs in our major cities reflected the best sociological and criminological thinking of the time and took place in an era of less violent gang activity. The causes of gang delinquency were located in the social structure and in the failure to provide adequate means for these youngsters to fit into that structure successfully. Thus efforts were concentrated on the integration of gang members into the school, work, and recreational institutions that would resocialize those who had slipped through the socialization sieve. A remarkable feature of the era was the sense of optimism underlying such programs. It was truly believed that society's workers had the conceptual and practical leverage to bring about such a change.

But changing times and values are reflected now in altered views. Data have not provided good support for the value transformation model. Quicker (1983b) argued that the individual transformation treatment focus inappropriately eclipsed the institutional implications of opportunity theory.

> In summary, the 1960's taught us many things about gang delinquency and the attempts to control it. It taught us that gang boys are not psychological misfits and that gangs do not form in social vacuums, but that their causes are intimately related to the social, economic and political structure. . . . Yet in spite of this knowledge, we find gang reduction programs that make only a partial attempt to deal with what is, at minimum, a complex two-sided problem: the individual and the system. They try to change the individual and neglect the system [pp. 80-81].

Thus the theoretical focus of the 1960s was invalidated not by programmatic failures but by the translation of the theory into an individual change treatment modality that did not fulfill its promise.

Current societal and political value systems are not supportive of "mucking about" with family, school, and other social institutions. Frustrations with rehabilitative failures have turned us to more control-oriented attitudes and systems of criminal justice: The gang arena is now dominated by efforts that stress deterrence and control through surveillance, incapacitation, and retribution. Several examples can be offered.

In the mid-1970s Philadelphia pioneered a new effort that generated claims of phenomenal success and has now been exported to other cities despite the absence of any reasonable demonstration of the program's impact. Known as the Crisis Intervention Network (CIN), the Philadelphia program put its workers in radio-dispatched cars to respond to hot spots, assigning teams to broad areas rather than to specific gangs. Dispute resolution and rumor control between gangs replaced resocialization within gangs. Heavy reliance on workers' street visibility and surveillance of gangs replaced individual worker/member rapport. Response to violence replaced general prevention. Claims of success for the CIN have never been documented adequately by independent research, while skepticism about the claims may well reflect upon the critics as much as upon the claimants. The dramatic reduction in Philadelphia's gang homicides, proffered as evidence for the value of the CIN's approach, generated questions regarding the credibility of law enforcement's labeling of homicides as gang-related (see Savitz et al., 1977, on Philadelphia's official reports of gang activity, and Klein et al., 1986, on the stability of designation practices in Los Angeles).

When the CIN was transported to Los Angeles (locally titled Community Youth Gang Services [CYGS]), independent research was discussed but was soon given such low priority that another opportunity for assessment was lost. Three major arguments against its success as a useful intervention model would have had to be countered. First, the program was implemented well after the major decline in gang violence had already been established, as was also the case in Philadelphia. Second, CYGS increasingly succumbed to internal and external pressure to alter its program from the CIN deterrence model back to the earlier, discredited value transformation model (Maxson and Klein, 1983). Third, the absence of Philadelphia's community organization tradition was given little weight in the CYGS adaptation. Thus two opportunities to assess the effectiveness of a gang intervention model in tune with its times have been lost. Could it be that independent evaluation, as a social phenomenon, is not in tune with the times?

Another approach to gang programming parallels and further illustrates the shift from rehabilitation to surveillance and deterrence. In past decades, probation officers with gang members in their caseloads attempted (a) to diminish the members' dependency on criminally oriented gang associates and (b) to provide precisely the same counseling services to gang members as were offered to other probationers. Sometimes this was done in collaboration with local gang workers as an extension of the value transformation model. In at least one major program the gang workers were, in fact, probation officers who left regular caseloads to become gang workers in a program administered by the probation department (Klein, 1971).

By way of contrast, some probation departments now have special units in which the officers have exclusively gang member caseloads. The officers' explicit goals are to apply intensive surveillance to their gang probationers and to "violate" them—return them to incarceration for technical or legal violations—whenever feasible. Violations used to be considered evidence of failure in an officer's program for his probationers. Thus the current procedure represents close to a 180-degree shift in attitude for many probation officers, but a shift widely applauded in the current atmosphere. At a recent major crime conference, significantly, an old-time, highly experienced probation officer complained bitterly that researchers didn't give credit to her and her probation colleagues for their successes in violating their charges:

"We've caught them," she said, "so why do they get counted against us as probation failures?"

A third, and perhaps most visible, manifestation of the deterrence orientation is to be found in Operation Hardcore and its near relatives in many district attorneys' offices. Operation Hardcore involves "vertical prosecution" (one deputy D.A. carries the case from start to finish) of carefully targeted gang leaders or major offenders. Hardcore deputies work closely with police officers in "making" their cases, often contributing to planning the investigation, gathering evidence, and developing and executing special search warrants. The close working relationships, the special expertise developed, and the concentration of specifically trained deputies on selected serious cases is said to have increased conviction rates quite substantially. Serious attempts to evaluate Operation Hardcore empirically have been undertaken but, for a variety of reasons, have not yielded adequate research (Dahmann, 1982). We are left with the promising but scientifically inadequate evidence of conviction rate increases and no research on the claims for general deterrence of gang member crime and violence owing to these rate increases.

Finally, we should note that in some cities—Chicago, Los Angeles, and San Diego—combinations of Operation Hardcore, probation gang caseloads, police crackdowns, and CIN street worker projects have been attempted. Since they have not been accompanied by adequate research, their effects are unknown.

In sum, two readily distinguishable approaches to gang intervention have been described. One, the value transformation model suited to the dominant prevention and rehabilitation values of the 1950s and 1960s, was accompanied by a significant level of research evaluation that seriously questioned that model's appropriateness. The other, the surveillance/deterrence model well-suited to the greater control and punitively oriented values of the late 1970s and the 1980s, has produced programs with equally satisfying logics but decidedly less satisfying attempts to assess effectiveness. These programs continue on the basis of faith and conviction, as did the value transformation programs prior to their research assessment.

Conclusion: Knowledge and Intervention

Gang programs, if they are rationally devised, must take into account the group nature of the phenomenon to be changed. What is known of gang recruitment and selection, ethnicity, age distributions, clique structure, leadership, cohesiveness, and criminal patterns should form the basis for enlightened programmatic actions. The programs devised under both the value transformation model and the surveillance/deterrence model have been based only vaguely on the accumulated knowledge of gang structure and functions. Indeed, in some instances program developers have badly misread the literature or misguidedly substituted experience for demonstrated patterns.

Logically, value transformation models, like most prevention programs, must find ways to overcome inefficient or even destructive targeting of clients. Young gang members and potential recruits, because they have not yet justified serious intervention by virtue of their own behavior, may inadvertently be engulfed in gang crime via workers' attempts to reach them. Net widening and group solidification are the dangers here.

Equally logically, surveillance/deterrence models, like many prosecution and corrections programs, must overcome the difficulties of arriving too late. Success with hardened offenders is difficult to achieve and more difficult to demonstrate. Natural maturation and attrition processes among offenders may be mistaken as proof of success, while seeming failure to achieve deterrence may merely reflect inefficient targeting and narrow programming.

More than anything, research on these two models has taught us what *not* to do: Do not undertake program activities that are likely to build gang cohesiveness, attract new (especially younger) members, bring special attention to the gang as an entity, or increase alienation between gang and community. Do not concentrate prevention or rehabilitation efforts on the hardcore members, where we lack leverage, but rather reduce attractiveness for younger members and reinforce alternative activities for older members (jobs, schooling, girlfriends, and so on).

Area-based programming is probably more useful than gang-based programming; empowerment of local community prevention is more efficient than mobile crisis response techniques (for example, Fattah, 1984). Gang members are limit testers, all the more so because camaraderie and clique structures reinforce such behaviors; responses that clarify behavior limits and react quickly to the tests must be built into gang programming. Acts of omission can be as reinforcing as those of commission.

But above all, gang programs must take advantage of the massive research that has been completed. Despite some gaps in the accumulated knowledge about gangs, the 170 reports cited by Quicker (1983b) and works published even more recently provide ample guidelines and implications for designing, mounting, and evaluating gang programs, whether of the value transformation or of the deterrence model—or another, for that matter. Programs that assign greater validity to personal experience and values than to available basic and applied research almost guarantee a waste of public money or increased gang offending and probably both.

NOTES

1. Many researchers have posited people with violent personalities or at least a characterological propensity for violent behavior. While there are undoubtedly a few such persons, their numbers are unlikely to account for most reported violence. For example, Piper (1985) compared violent to nonviolent members of a birth cohort (violent being defined as having one recorded violent offense) and reported that violent offenders exhibit more criminal acts of greater variety and are more likely to be "chronics." It is far more parsimonious to reverse the logic: More chronic offenders are more likely to exhibit a range of offenses including one or more violent offenses. Violence is as likely the result of a high offending pattern as the cause of it.

2. We exclude here, because they raise very difficult and different issues, youthful car clubs, motorcycle gangs, prison gangs, "stoners," and satanic cult groups.

3. Nonhomicide violent offenses and specified nonviolent offenses are tallied and maintained in aggregate form only. This procedure is necessitated by the sheer volume of gang crimes. As an illustration, the two jurisdictions' statistics for nine violent felonies totaled over 7,800 in 1984.

4. In the same paper, Spergel cited the Philadelphia inclusion of offenses as being even more restrictive.

5. Much of the description of gangs in earlier decades is taken from Klein (1971).

6. Consider the following two quotations. According to the head of a police gang unit: "The emphasis has shifted away from one gang fighting another to a gang versus some innocent citizen who just happens to be in the wrong place at the wrong time. There's been a lot more shooting and innocent people are being killed." And from the head of a prosecution gang unit: "It used to be gang on gang. Now anyone can be fair game for gang violence" (WGBH Educational Foundation, 1984: 3-4). Our data, gathered from the jurisdictions to which these statements refer, revealed that only 2% to 5% of gang homicide victims were innocent, nongang-affiliated bystanders. Miller's (1975) citation of an increase in nongang victims, coming from interviews with officials, must remain suspect.

7. This description was provided to the authors by a senior police official during a symposium on gangs held in Colorado Springs, a suburban sprawl anticipating its turn with gang violence.

8. The interested reader might want to consult Muehlbauer and Dodder (1983) for an extensive contrasting account of a spontaneous gang emerging in an even more affluent Chicago suburb. Here gang cohesiveness fed off the negative responses of the community with no need of "help" from rival gangs.

REFERENCES

Block, C. R. (1985a) Lethal Violence in Chicago Over Seventeen Years: Homicides Known to the Police, 1965-1981. Chicago: Illinois Criminal Justice Information Authority.

Block, C. R. (1985b) Specification of Patterns Over Time in Chicago Homicides: Increases and Decreases, 1965-1981. Chicago: Illinois Criminal Justice Information Authority.

Bookin-Weiner, H. and R. Horowitz (1983) "The end of the youth gang: fad or fact?" Criminology 21: 585-602.

Bowker, L. H., H. S. Gross, and M. W. Klein (1980) "Female participation in delinquent gang activities." Adolescence 14: 509-519.

Brenneman, R. J. (1984) "Gang problem looms" and "Escalating violence boosts fear of gangs" (two-article series). Sacramento Bee, October 14-15.

California Council on Criminal Justice (1986) State Task Force on Youth Gang Violence. Sacramento: Author.

Campbell, A. (1981) Girl Delinquents. Oxford: Basil Blackwell.

Cohen, B. (1969) "The delinquency of gangs and spontaneous groups," pp. 61-111 in T. Sellin and M. E. Wolfgang (eds.) Delinquency: Selected Studies. New York: John Wiley.

Cook, P. J. (1982) "The role of firearms in violent crime: an interpretive review of the literature," pp. 236-291 in M. E. Wolfgang and N. A. Weiner (eds.) Criminal Violence. Beverly Hills, CA: Sage.

Curtis, L. A. (1974) Criminal Violence. Lexington, MA: Lexington.

Dahmann, J. S. (1982) An Evaluation of Operation Hardcore: A Prosecutorial Response to Violent Gang Criminality. Washington, DC: MITRE Corp.

Diaz, K. (1986) "City's 'gang problem' seen as a youth problem." Minneapolis Star and Tribune, March 22.

Erickson, M. L. and G. F. Jensen (1977) "Delinquency is still group behavior: toward revitalizing the group premise in the sociology of deviance." Journal of Criminal Law and Criminology 68: 262-273.

Erlanger, H. S. (1979) "Estrangement, machismo and gang violence." Social Science Quarterly 60: 235-248.

Fattah, F. (1984) "Call and catalytic response: the House of Umoja," pp. 231-242 in R. A. Mathias, P. DeMunro, and R. S. Allinson (eds.) Violent Juvenile Offenders: An Anthology. San Francisco: National Council on Crime and Delinquency.

Feinstein, Mervin D. (1976) "Youth gangs: the problem and the approach." Crime Prevention Review 4: 21-25.

Friedman, C. J., F. Mann, and A. S. Friedman (1975) "A profile of juvenile street gang members." Adolescence 10: 563-607.

Galea, J. (1982) "Youth gangs of New York," pp. 215-228 in P. Marsh and A. Campbell (eds.) Aggression and Violence. Oxford: Basil Blackwell.

Gottfredson, G. D. and D. C. Daiger (1979) Disruption in Six Hundred Schools. Baltimore: Johns Hopkins University Press.

Horowitz, R. (1983) Honor and the American Dream: Culture and Identity in a Chicago Community. New Brunswick, NJ: Rutgers University Press.

Johnstone, J.W.C. (1981) "Youth gangs and black suburbs." Pacific Sociological Quarterly 24: 355-375.

Klein, M. W. (1969) "On the group context of delinquency." Sociology and Social Research 54: 63-71.

Klein, M. W. (1971) Street Gangs and Street Workers. Englewood Cliffs, NJ: Prentice-Hall.

Klein, M. W. (1984) "Offence specialization and versatility among juveniles." British Journal of Criminology 24: 185-194.

Klein, M. W., C. L. Maxson, and M. A. Gordon (1984) Evaluation in an Imported Gang Violence Deterrence Program; Final Report. Los Angeles: University of Southern California, Social Science Research Institute.

McClintock, F. H. (1963) Crimes of Violence. London: Macmillan.

Miller, W. B. (1973) "The molls." Society 11 (November/December): 32-35.

Miller, W. B. (1975) Violence by Youth Gangs and Youth Groups as a Crime Problem in Major American Cities. Washington, DC: U.S. Department of Justice, National Institute of Juvenile Justice and Delinquency Prevention.

Miller, W. B. (1980) "Gangs, groups, and serious youth crime," pp. 115-138 in D. Shichor and D. Kelly (eds.) Critical Issues in Juvenile Delinquency. Lexington, MA: Lexington.

Moore, J. W. (1985) "Isolation and stigmatization in the development of an underclass: the case of Chicago gangs in East Los Angeles." Social Problems 33: 1-12.

Moore, J. W., D. Vigil, and R. Garcia (1983) "Residence and territoriality in Chicano gangs." Social Problems 31: 182-194.

Morash, M. (1983) "Gangs, groups, and delinquency." British Journal of Criminology 23: 309-331.

Muehlbauer, G. and L. Dodder (1983) The Losers: Gang Delinquency in an American Suburb. New York: Praeger.

Mulvihill, D. J. and M. M. Tumin (1969) Crimes of Violence, Vols. 11-13, Staff Report to the National Commission on the Causes and Prevention of Violence. Washington, DC: Government Printing Office.

Newton, G. D. and F. E. Zimring (1969) Firearms and Violence in American Life, Vol. 7, Staff Report to the National Commission on the Causes and Prevention of Violence. Washington, DC: Government Printing Office.

Pennell, S. and C. Curtis (1982) Juvenile Violence and Gang-Related Crime. San Diego, CA: San Diego Association of Government.

Piper, E. S. (1985) "Violent recidivism and chronicity in the 1958 Philadelphia cohort." Journal of Quantitative Criminology 1: 319-344.

Quicker, J. C. (1983a) Homegirls: Characterizing Chicana Gangs. San Pedro, CA: International University Press.

Quicker, J. C. (1983b) Seven Decades of Gangs: What Has Been Learned, What Has Been Done, and What Should Be Done. Sacramento: California Commission on Crime Control and Violence Prevention.

Recktenwald, W. and N. Sheppard, Jr. (1984) "Gangs." Newspaper series published separately by the Chicago Tribune.

Reiss, A. J., Jr. (1985) "Co-offending influences on criminal careers," in A. Blumstein, J. Cohen, J. Roth and C. Visher (eds.) Criminal Careers and "Career Criminals." Washington, DC: National Academy Press.

Rice, B. (1977) "The new gangs of Chinatown." Psychology Today (May): 1-69.

Rosenbaum, D. P. and J. A. Grant (1983) Gangs and Youth Problems in Evanston: Research Findings and Policy Options. Evanston, IL: Northwestern University, Center for Urban Affairs and Policy Research.

Savitz, L. D., M. Lalli, and L. Rosen (1977) City Life and Delinquency—Victimization,

Fear of Crime, and Gang Membership. Washington, DC: U.S. Department of Justice, National Institute for Juvenile Justice and Delinquency Prevention.

Shields, P. (1981) Guns Don't Die—People Do. New York: Arbor House.

Short, J. F., Jr. and F. L. Strodtbeck (1965) Group Process and Gang Delinquency. Chicago: University of Chicago Press.

Spergel, I. A. (1983) "Violent gangs in Chicago: segmentation and integration" (draft of report). Chicago: University of Chicago, School of Social Service Administration. (cited with permission)

Spergel, I. A. (1984) "Violent gangs in Chicago: in search of social policy." Social Service Review 58: 199-226.

Spergel, I. A. (1985a) "Chicago's gang and response problem." Presented at the annual meeting of the American Society of Criminology, San Diego.

Spergel, I. A. (1985b) Youth Gang Activity and the Chicago Public Schools. Chicago: University of Chicago, School of Social Service Administration.

Stafford, M. (1984) "Gang delinquency," pp. 167-189 in R. F. Meier (ed.) Major Forms of Crime. Beverly Hills, CA: Sage.

Stapleton, W. V. and J. A. Needle (1982) Response Strategies to Youth Gang Activity. Sacramento, CA: American Justice Institute.

Stumphauzer, J. S., E. V. Veloz, and T. W. Aiken (1981) "Violence by street gangs: East Side story?" pp. 68-82 in R. B. Stuart (ed.) Violent Behavior: Social Learning Approaches to Prediction, Management, and Treatment. New York: Brunner/Mazel.

Tracy, P. E. (1979) Subcultural Delinquency: A Comparison of the Incidence and Seriousness of Gang and Nongang Member Offensivity. Philadelphia: University of Pennsylvania, Center for Studies in Criminology and Criminal Law.

U.S. Department of Justice, Bureau of Justice Statistics (1986) The Use of Weapons in Committing Crimes. Washington, DC: Government Printing Office.

U.S. News and World Report (1984) "Street gangs no longer just a big-city problem." July 16: 108-119.

Vigil, J. D. (1983) "Chicano gangs: one response to Mexican urban adaptation in the Los Angeles area." Urban Anthropology 12: 45-68.

Vigil, J. D. (1985) "The gang subculture and locura: variations in acts and actors." Presented at the annual meeting of the American Society of Criminology, San Diego.

WGBH Educational Foundation (1984) "Frontline: warning from gangland." Transcript of PBS broadcast, May 21, 1984, Boston.

Wikström, P.O.H. (1985) Everyday Violence in Contemporary Sweden. Stockholm: The National Council for Crime Prevention.

Wolfgang, M. E. and F. Ferracuti (1982) The Subculture of Violence: Towards an Integrated Theory in Criminology. Beverly Hills, CA: Sage.

Wolfgang, M. E. and M. A. Zahn (1983) "Homicide: behavioral aspects," pp. 849-855 in S. H. Kadish (ed.) Encyclopedia of Crime and Justice. New York: Free Press.

Yablonsky, L. (1963) The Violent Gang. New York: Macmillan.

Zatz, M. S. (1985) "Los Cholos: legal processing of Chicano gang members." Social Problems 33: 13-30.

Zimring, F. E. (1984) "Youth homicide in New York: a preliminary analysis." Journal of Legal Studies 13: 81-99.

About the Contributors

Sandra Baxter, a sociologist, is a Senior Study Director at Westat, Inc., in Rockville, MD. She is a coauthor of *Women and Politics* and has written several articles on women's status and cross-national research.

George S. Bridges is Assistant Professor of Sociology at the University of Washington. His chapter with Joseph G. Weis was prepared as part of an ongoing study of violence and its measurement funded by the National Institute of Mental Health. His research interests include issues in the measurement of crime and violence and the sociology of law and social control. He has recently completed a major study (with Robert Crutchfield) of racial inequality in the administration of criminal justice.

Lynn A. Curtis is President of the Milton S. Eisenhower Foundation in Washington, DC. In the late 1970s, he was Urban Policy Advisor to the U.S. Secretary of Housing and Urban Development and Executive Director of the President's Urban and Regional Policy Group. On President Johnson's National Commission on the Causes and Prevention of Violence, he was Codirector of the Crimes of Violence Task Force. He holds an A.B. from Harvard University, an M.Sc. from the University of London, and a Ph.D. from the University of Pennsylvania.

Malcolm W. Klein is Professor of Sociology at the University of Southern California and Director of the Center for Research on Crime and Social Control in the Social Science Research Institute. From 1962 to 1968, he directed evaluation and basic research projects dealing with juvenile gangs. Since 1969, his research has centered on comprehensive criminal justice planning, evaluation of deinstitutionalization programs, and assessment of legislative effects. His current research involves police handling of juvenile offenders and police investigation of gang-related homicides.

Cheryl L. Maxson is Research Assistant Professor of Sociology and a Research Associate at the Social Science Research Institute, University of Southern California. Her current research and publication activities concern the nature of gang violence and police identification and response to gang-related crime and drug distribution. Previous research topics have included predicting legislative change and evaluation of legislative implementation and impact.

Rita J. Simon, a sociologist, is Dean of the School of Justice at The American University in Washington, DC. She is the author of *Women and Crime* and coeditor of *The Criminology of Deviant Women.* Her recent publications include *Transracial Adoptees and Their Families: A Study of Their Identity and Commitment* and the forthcoming *The Insanity Defense on Trial: A Critical Assessment of Law and Policy in the Post-Hinckley Era.*

Neil Alan Weiner is Senior Research Associate at the Sellin Center for Studies in Criminology and Criminal Law at the Wharton School of the University of Pennsylvania and is Project Director of the Center for the Interdisciplinary Study of Criminal Violence at the Sellin Center. He received his M.A. and Ph.D. in sociology from the University of Pennsylvania and was a postdoctoral fellow at the Urban Systems Institute at Carnegie-Mellon University. His major and ongoing research interests are in the areas of individual violent criminal careers, situational analyses of violence escalation, historical patterns in violent crime, violent recidivism prediction, the administration of serious and violent juvenile offender programs, integrating criminological theory, and disparities in the imposition of the death penalty.

Joseph G. Weis is Professor of Sociology at the University of Washington. His research interests include issues in the measurement of crime and criminal careers and the correlates of juvenile delinquency. He also has a longstanding interest in delinquency prevention. He recently served as Editor of *Criminology.*

Marvin E. Wolfgang, Professor of Sociology and of Law and Director of the Sellin Center for Studies in Criminology and Criminal Law at the University of Pennsylvania, is also President of the American Academy of Political and Social Science and a member of the American Philosophical Society and the American Academy of Arts and Sciences.

He has served on numerous boards and commissions, including the Panel on Social Indicators, the National Commission on the Causes and Prevention of Violence, and the National Commission on Obscenity and Pornography. His publications include *Patterns in Criminal Homicide; The Measurement of Delinquency; The Subculture of Violence; Crime and Race; Delinquency in a Birth Cohort; Criminology Index; Evaluating Criminology; The National Survey of Crime Severity,* and *From Boy to Man, From Delinquency to Crime.* His current projects include a follow-up study of *Delinquency in a Birth Cohort* and a longitudinal study of biosocial factors related to delinquency and crime.

NOTES